Closing Arguments

WITHDRAWN

CLOSING ARGUMENTS

CLARENCE DARROW
on Religion, Law, and Society

Clarence Darrow

Edited by S. T. Joshi

Ohio University Press
Athens

Ohio University Press, Athens, Ohio 45701
www.ohio.edu/oupress
© 2005 by Ohio University Press

Printed in the United States of America
All rights reserved

Ohio University Press books are printed on acid-free paper ⊗ ™

12 11 10 09 08 07 06 05   5 4 3 2 1

Library of Congress Cataloging-in-Publication Data

Darrow, Clarence, 1857–1938.
  Closing arguments : Clarence Darrow on religion, law, and society /
Clarence Darrow ; edited by S.T. Joshi.
     p. cm.
  Includes bibliographical references and index.
  ISBN 0-8214-1632-4 (cloth : alk. paper)
  1. Darrow, Clarence, 1857–1938. 2. Law—Social aspects—United
States. 3. Religion and law—United States. 4. United States—
Politics and government. 5. Lawyers—United States—Biography.
I. Joshi, S. T., 1958– II. Title.
  KF213.D3J67 2005
  340'.115—dc22
                                                        2005010294

Contents

Introduction

CLARENCE DARROW (1857–1938), whose decades-long championing of the despised and powerless earned him the sobriquet of "The Great Defender," was born four years before the beginning of the Civil War and died a year before the beginning of World War II. These eighty years could well be considered the most *transformative* in United States history—years that saw America expand from a fledgling and sparsely populated nation of farmers and small businessmen to an emerging superpower. Darrow witnessed and, in no insignificant way, participated in the multifaceted growing pains incident to this transformation: on such issues as the relations between capital and labor, the role of women in society, the place of religion in a diverse population, and, particularly, the theoretical and practical status of crime and punishment, Darrow made signal contributions that endured far beyond the span of his own life. A lawyer first and a writer second, he nonetheless left behind a succession of treatises whose provocative content still challenges us. Darrow, a self-proclaimed rebel who sided, both intellectually and emotionally, with the minority, remains a figure to contend with.

Throughout his writings, whether they be on crime, religion, or morals, Darrow expressed the conviction that our views of life are fundamentally and unalterably shaped by childhood experience. In this assertion he may well have been considering his own upbringing, for the kernels of many facets of his thought can be found in the events of his youth and adolescence. He was born on April 18, 1857, in the village of

Kinsman, in northeast Ohio, the fifth of eight children born to Amirus and Emily (Eddy) Darrow. Amirus had studied theology in his youth, but in the very process of doing so he lost his faith; his son Clarence inherited that religious unorthodoxy despite receiving a conventionally Presbyterian upbringing, with regular church attendance and Sunday school. Clarence's mother was an ardent advocate of women's rights, and he no doubt absorbed these views as well in spite of her early death in 1872.

Darrow's schooling was spotty. He had an undistinguished record at the local district school; in 1873 he was sent to the preparatory department of Allegheny College in Meadville, Pennsylvania, but the depression of that year dried up the family funds and forced him to leave after a year. While employed as a schoolteacher at Vernon, seven miles south of Kinsman, Darrow began studying law on the side. He entered the University of Michigan law school in 1877 but again left after a year, instead joining a law office in Youngstown and studying for the bar exam. After a few months he took the bar exam—and passed. Darrow was fortunate that the standards for entering the legal profession were at that time quite low: almost any bright and motivated young man could become a lawyer with minimal study. He married a young woman from Kinsman, Jessie Ohl, on April 15, 1880.

Finding no work in his tiny hometown, Darrow set up a law office in nearby Andover. But law as such appears to have interested him less than politics, and he began both a career in public speaking and an affiliation with the local Democratic Party. His only son, Paul, was born on December 10, 1883. The election of 1884, which saw Grover Cleveland elected as the first Democratic president since before the Civil War, raised Darrow's fortunes, and he moved to the larger city of Ashtabula, on Lake Erie, where he was elected city solicitor in 1885.

By this time Darrow had developed greater political ambitions. He felt he needed to test his skills on a national level, and the place to go was Chicago, an immensely vital city that many contemporaries predicted would become the prototypical American metropolis and eventually eclipse New York as the nation's cultural center. Darrow's move there in 1887 proved permanent, and transformed him both as a man and as a lawyer.

Coming under the influence of John Peter Altgeld, whose successful campaign for governor in 1892 he managed, Darrow plunged into the convoluted thickets of the Democratic Party machine. He was first made special assessment attorney to the city of Chicago, then its chief corporation counsel. Through Altgeld, he secured a job in the legal department of the Chicago & Northwestern Railway, an immensely powerful company that largely controlled freight and trolley traffic in and around Chicago.

Darrow's decision not to follow Altgeld to Springfield, while it lessened his direct influence on state government, proved to be a blessing in disguise: Altgeld's political career was destroyed in 1893 when he issued pardons for the Haymarket anarchists, who in 1887 had been convicted (on flimsy evidence) of setting off a bomb that had killed several spectators and policemen. By this time Darrow had thrust himself deeply into the central economic conflict of the time—the struggles between capital and labor. Many fledgling labor unions, in the face of vicious and illegal reprisals by capitalists, felt they had no choice but to resort to violence themselves. Darrow took their side in several notable legal cases. The first was the trial of socialist and labor leader Eugene V. Debs, which grew out of the American Railway Union's strike against the Pullman Palace Car Company in 1893. Darrow, in taking up the case, resigned his position with the Chicago & Northwestern Railway as an obvious conflict of interest. Debs had been accused of conspiracy in violating an injunction against the strikers issued (unprecedentedly) by the federal government, and Darrow was withering in his arguments against the legality of the proceedings. The case against Debs was quickly dropped so as to avoid the embarrassment of having George M. Pullman, president of the Pullman company, face Darrow's tongue-lashing in cross-examination; but Darrow was disappointed that the injunction itself was upheld by the Supreme Court in spite of his eloquent argument against it. It was one of several occasions when Darrow faced the nation's highest court.

The Debs case augmented Darrow's standing as a radical firebrand and ardent friend of labor. Several sensational cases in the coming years— his successful defense of Thomas I. Kidd of the Woodworkers' Union in

1898 in a strike in Oshkosh, Wisconsin; his involvement in the anthracite arbitration case of 1902 between the United Mine Workers and coal mine owners in Pennsylvania; and, most spectacularly, his successful defense of "Big Bill" Haywood of the Western Federation of Miners in a murder trial in Idaho in 1907—cemented that reputation. The stress of all this work proved too much for his marriage, however, and Darrow and Jessie divorced in 1897. Darrow also lost a bid for national office in 1896 when he failed to campaign vigorously for a supposedly "safe" Democratic Congressional district in Chicago and lost narrowly to a Republican. In 1902 he was elected to the Illinois House of Representatives, the only elected office he ever held. To many people's surprise, he made a second venture into matrimony in 1903, marrying Ruby Hamerstrom, a journalist he had met four years before. They remained married for the duration of Darrow's life.

It was also in 1903 that Darrow set up a private law practice in Chicago with lawyer-poet Edgar Lee Masters and Francis Wilson. The eight-year partnership was under continual stress, with Darrow and Masters both feeling that the other was not pulling his weight. Darrow, indeed, was unwittingly setting himself up for a fall by his vigorous defense of labor cases. He was persuaded to take on the case of James B. and John J. McNamara, two brothers who were accused of murder in the bombing of the *Los Angeles Times* building on October 1, 1910. The case against the McNamaras—one of whom was a union official then engaged in fierce disputes with *Times* owner Harrison Gray Otis—was virtually airtight, and Darrow reluctantly concluded that the only way for his clients to escape the death penalty was for them to plead guilty. The result was an uproar in the labor community, which had in defiance of all the evidence believed the McNamaras to be innocent and also believed Darrow to be a miracle worker who could have gotten them off. Worse was to follow: the prosecution, perhaps out of anger of being robbed of the death penalty, indicted Darrow himself of jury bribery. The two cases that followed took up the bulk of the years 1912 and 1913; although the first trial ended in an acquittal and the second in a hung jury, Darrow's standing as a lawyer was seriously compromised. Darrow fell into a deep depression, believing that, at the age of fifty-five, his career was over and his usefulness at an end. He could scarcely have realized that his greatest triumphs were still to come.

For the next decade Darrow attempted to pick up the pieces of his life and career. To raise money, he began lecturing more and more widely, engaging in a series of public debates on issues ranging from religion to Prohibition. Forming a new law firm, he sought to handle more criminal cases, doing much work for no charge for impoverished clients whose cases he believed worthy. At a very early stage of his career he had determined never to work for the prosecution, and all his work was as a defense attorney. He shocked his socialist colleagues by strongly advocating the Allied cause at the outbreak of World War I and urging American entry into the war from the beginning. It was, ironically, this seeming betrayal of his radical roots that caused Darrow's reputation to be resurrected among the public at large.

That reputation would, however, be put to a severe test by two notorious cases, occurring within a year of each other in 1924 and 1925, that permanently sealed Darrow's reputation as "America's greatest lawyer." The murder of little Robert Franks by two wealthy youths, Nathan Leopold and Richard Loeb (the latter the son of a vice president of Sears, Roebuck & Co.), shocked the nation with its brutality and seeming lack of motivation: was it possible that two such privileged youths could kill merely for sport? As in the McNamara case, there was no likelihood that the defendants were innocent; accordingly, Darrow—by this time a relentless opponent of the death penalty—concluded that the only way for his clients to escape the hangman was through a legal sleight-of-hand whereby a guilty plea was entered, thereby thrusting the case immediately into the sentencing phase. Darrow relied on the judge's leniency in sentencing, and in the event his reasoning proved correct: Judge John Caverly brought opprobrium upon himself by sentencing Leopold and Loeb to life imprisonment for murder and a concurrent sentence of ninety-nine years for kidnapping.

The circumstances surrounding Darrow's other noteworthy case of this period—the Scopes trial of 1925—were very different: instead of a matter of life and death he confronted a scenario that came close to buffoonery.[1] The serious issue of the trial—the extent to which the Christian religion would be allowed to dictate the laws of a state or of the nation—was almost submerged in the atmosphere of personal rivalry between Darrow, the leading agnostic of his age, and William Jennings Bryan, the long-serving Democratic statesman (whose presidential campaign in 1896 Darrow had reluctantly supported, although he did little for Bryan's campaigns of 1900 and 1908) who now came to represent the forces of small-town conservatism and religious orthodoxy. Bryan's catastrophic decision to undergo merciless cross-examination by Darrow was the fitting capstone to a trial that riveted the nation. It is frequently overlooked that the defense—Darrow, Arthur Garfield Hays, and Dudley Field Malone, with journalist H. L. Mencken lending loud support in his pungently satirical reporting—deliberately sought a guilty verdict for the hapless teacher John Thomas Scopes, for it was only in this way that the anti-evolution statute passed by the Tennessee legislature could be challenged in federal court. But the Tennessee Supreme Court, keenly aware that the state was becoming the laughingstock of the nation, quietly overturned the conviction, and the statute was equally quietly rescinded a few years later.

It would have been difficult for any lawyer to have followed up the Leopold and Loeb and the Scopes trials with cases still more spectacular, and Darrow felt no inclination to do so. In 1925–26 he successfully defended two African Americans, Ossian Sweet and his brother Henry, on murder charges stemming from violence that arose after their move into a largely white neighborhood in Detroit. In 1932 he took up the case of Thomas Massie, a naval officer in Hawaii who was accused of kidnapping and killing a Hawaiian man whom he suspected (erroneously, it appears) of raping his wife. At the age of seventy-five, Darrow's powers were finally on the wane, and even he could not secure Massie's acquittal. The leftist firebrand made his final public appearance as the chairman of the National Recovery Review Board, which was to investigate the workings of one of the pillars of the New Deal, the National Recovery Administration. Darrow's harshly critical assessments of the NRA in 1934–36 were not well received in government circles, although they contributed to the Supreme Court's decision to decree the NRA unconstitutional.

Darrow's final years were plagued by illness, and, given his views on immortality, he probably welcomed death when it came to him on March 13, 1938. Thousands came to pay their respects to a man who had rarely compromised his principles, however unpopular they may have been, over his half-century of public life.

Darrow longed for literary success, but he was continually disappointed in his quest for renown. Although, during the first two decades of the twentieth century, he could well have been considered the most popular and controversial public speaker in the United States (taking up the role of another great agnostic, Robert G. Ingersoll, who died in 1899), Darrow felt that his writings were not receiving the critical acclaim they deserved. Perhaps Darrow had an exaggerated belief in his literary powers, but, while he may have left no single monument like his erstwhile colleague Edgar Lee Masters's *Spoon River Anthology*, the totality of his literary work is far from insignificant. And what is more, it is motivated by a carefully conceived philosophy that, although rarely articulated in full, unites his writings on philosophy, religion, law, society, and politics.

The religious skepticism that Darrow initially derived from his father's influence was central to his outlook. It is a bit puzzling why he continually referred to himself merely as an agnostic: there seems little doubt that he was an atheist. A member of the audience at one of Darrow's religious debates stated clearly that he "denie[d] the existence of the Deity."[2] Surely he of all people would not have worried about the general public's fear of and prejudice against the very word atheist. In a 1928 debate on whether there is a purpose in the universe, Darrow argued that the notion of a purpose necessarily implies a "purposer": is there such an entity? "On this question of a purposer, or a purpose, especially a purposer, I am simply an agnostic. I haven't yet had time or opportunity to explore the universe, and I don't know what I might run on to in some nook or corner. I simply say there is not a syllable of evidence in the world to sustain any such proposition, not a syllable." It is important to emphasize this point because it might otherwise seem that

Darrow's screeds against religion were merely attacking the social and political failings of religion or of religious fundamentalism. Those failings are, indeed, extensive, but Darrow would not have been so vigorous in exposing them if he had not felt that the religious point of view—as regards the existence of a deity, the existence and immortality of the soul, and the place of human beings in a boundless and impersonal cosmos—was in itself erroneous.

The chief harm that religion causes, in Darrow's judgment, is in its restriction of civil liberties by infringements of the separation of church and state. This is the thrust of two essays—a review of Maynard Shipley's *The War on Modern Science* (1927) and "The Lord's Day Alliance" (1928)—written shortly after the Scopes trial. Incredibly, the latter was deemed so intemperate by H. L. Mencken that he rejected it for the *American Mercury*. The actions of present-day fundamentalists who continue to rail against the teaching of evolution or protest against the "desecration" of the Sabbath may suggest that Darrow was, here as elsewhere, uncannily prescient. Darrow knew that fundamentalists would press their case as far as it could be pressed, and that the only defense was an equally vigorous counterattack by scientists: "They should . . . organize to meet the campaign [of the fundamentalists]. They should do this, not only in defense of themselves, but in defense of learning; and, still more important, in defense of religious freedom. This fight must be made by the scientists and the teachers. It is, above all others, their job."

There is a currently fashionable view that the "conflict" of religion and science was merely a tendentious fantasy of certain nineteenth-century secularists; but the Scopes trial—and the actions of contemporary fundamentalists in attempting to prevent or limit the teaching of evolution or in promoting creationism or its spruced-up counterpart, "intelligent design"—embarrassingly and overwhelmingly refutes this naive view. It may well have been the case that the medieval church was one of the leading advocates of scientific inquiry—how could it not have been, since it was the sole haven of learning in European society for centuries?—but the parameters of that learning were strictly circumscribed: any advance of science that threatened religious orthodoxy was mercilessly condemned. Both Darrow and Mencken were well aware that the reconcilers of science and religion—notably the Nobel Prize–winning physicist Robert A. Millikan—were in large part attempting to cling to an increasingly attenuated and dogma-free religiosity in the wake of scientific advances that systematically cast doubt upon the fundamental tenets of religion. For Darrow, such pussyfooting was impossible: religion may have its comforts for the weak and feeble-minded, but it was only an intellectual obstacle to the person of education.

Darrow's metaphysical views are again of central importance in the subject he made his own: the punishment of criminals. Initially influenced by such treatises as John Peter Altgeld's *Our Penal Machinery and Its Victims* (1887), which proposed that the sources of criminal behavior be more carefully examined, Darrow eventually founded his views on his conceptions of the metaphysical and moral status of crime. In such debates as "Can the Individual Control His Conduct?" and other writings, Darrow made clear his disbelief in free will as ordinarily conceived. But his determinism is not (as his philosophically untutored biographer Kevin Tierney appears to believe) equivalent to fatalism. Darrow merely believed that every human action, like every other action by any entity throughout the universe, was strictly a result of cause and effect. Human beings did not stand outside the chain of causation. The effect of this theory on the treatment of crime is evident: it is not that criminals are somehow "blameless," but that an effort must be made to understand the nature and sources of their behavior. What Darrow was combating here was the naive and vindictive view that crime must be punished severely because the criminal was somehow different in kind from law-abiding human beings—a view not far different, as Darrow pointed out in the lecture "What to Do about Crime" (1927), from the medieval view that mental illness was caused by demonic possession.

Darrow's writings on crime and criminals may appear to suggest an excessive sympathy for the criminal and an insufficient awareness of the plight of the victim, but Darrow felt that the treatment of crime in his day was so counterproductive that radical steps must be taken to remedy it. Darrow's first full-length treatise, *Resist Not Evil* (1902), addresses this matter forthrightly. It is a pungent irony that the agnostic Darrow unwaveringly repudiates the vengeance of the Christian or Islamic god in preference for the mercy and kindness of the god of Jesus. Is Darrow's concluding recommendation—"Hatred, bitterness, violence and force can bring only bad results—they leave an evil stain on everyone they touch. No human soul can be rightly reached except through charity, humanity and love"—merely the hopelessly naive pipe dream of a sentimentalist? A careful reading of this and other Darrow writings on crime—particularly *Crime: Its Cause and Treatment* (1922), his most exhaustive discussion of the subject—suggests that he is seeking to prevent crime at the source rather than merely treat its symptoms after it has already occurred. His emphasis is on the proper upbringing of children so that they do not enter a life of crime; once a crime has occurred, punishing the criminal vindictively accomplishes nothing except to ingrain that behavior in the criminal.

Darrow's longtime opposition to the death penalty was based on the belief that killing the perpetrator accomplishes nothing save to exacerbate vengeance. He states bluntly in the essay "Capital Punishment" (1928): "The real reason why so many people tenaciously cling to the idea of capital punishment is because they take pleasure in inflicting pain upon those they hate." Darrow relentlessly destroys the argument that the death penalty is in any way a deterrent to crime, specifically the crime of murder. Although he did not have access to statistics suggesting either that the death penalty has been inflicted erroneously upon the innocent or that race is a critical factor in capital cases—two of the chief reasons that many thoughtful persons today denounce the death penalty—Darrow knew that "[o]nly the poor are put to death." The wealthy, like Leopold and Loeb, can afford the best legal defense possible so as to escape the noose.

In his social and political theory, the notion of freedom is central. Whether Darrow was concerned about any possible conflict between his determinism in regard to criminal (or, in fact, all human) conduct and his advocacy of civil liberties is not apparent. It was, as we have already seen, his devotion to freedom that impelled his most vigorous attacks on the encroachment of religion or religious-based statutes upon civil society. One of his earliest essays, "Woman Suffrage" (1893), emphasizes the role of freedom in advocating the extension of voting rights to women: "More and more as the spirit of liberty has penetrated the darkness of the world, have rulers of high degree and low, surrendered power and place and privilege at the demand of the common people of the earth, until to-day, in the constitutions of states and nations, full political privileges are guaranteed to those who once were chattel slaves." It was to be expected that Darrow would join his colleague H. L. Mencken in relentlessly opposing Prohibition as an unconscionable intrusion upon civil liberties, and it is no accident that his fiery screed "The Ordeal of Prohibition" appeared in Mencken's *American Mercury*. He makes an analogous argument in another *American Mercury* essay, "The Eugenics Cult," in which he tackles the increasing tendency of anthropologists and geneticists to suggest making improvements to society by banning a nebulously defined group of the "unfit" from procreating. Here it is not science but pseudoscience that Darrow is criticizing, and his arguments dissect the fallacies of the eugenicist creed while simultaneously protesting the curtailment of freedom that any legislation based on eugenic principles would entail. (It is unfortunate, however, that Darrow feels obliged to add a religious argument—"haven't the eugenists . . . forgotten that man, as he stands, is created in the image of God?"—in which he manifestly did not believe.)

Darrow's essays, written over the better part of four decades, reveal an interesting stylistic progression. His earliest writings, such as his essay on woman suffrage, use a florid and sentimental diction typical of the public speakers of the time; his own addresses of the day (such as that on woman suffrage) followed this orotund manner. By the early twentieth century, however, Darrow had come to realize that a plain style was more effective in conveying his message than any amount of flamboyant extravagance could be. In *The Story of My Life* (1932) he consciously enunciated this principle:

> For years, before juries, on the platform, in conversation, I have first of all tried to know what I was talking about, and then to

make my statements clear and simple, and the sentences short. I am not at all sure that this is the best method for writing and speaking. The reader has time to consider, and go over the pages if he will; if he misses a word or does not understand one, or even an idea, he can look things up in the dictionary or encyclopædia. But the listener has but one chance, and that is as the information or opinion hastens along; so the words must not be too long, or too unfamiliar, nor spoken too rapidly for assimilation. Some grasp spoken matter quickly, and some need time to catch what they are not accustomed to hear. The speaker must aim to reach practically every person in his audience; therefore he must not speak too fast or use too many uncommon words.[3]

It is, moreover, abundantly clear that Darrow is at his best in those papers that are, in essence, the arguments of a defense attorney, whether they discuss religion or politics or law or society. The public debates in which Darrow engaged over a lifetime were the ideal venues for his chosen manner—a manner resting more upon the destruction of an opponent's arguments than the advocacy of his own, thereby allowing such weapons as sarcasm, repartee, and *reductio ad absurdum* to come into play. The wry, cynical, even misanthropic humor that suddenly and unexpectedly appears in Darrow's writings—in the sober lecture "What to Do about Crime," delivered before a society of lawyers, he can write blandly: "People are born without any ideas. Generally they die without any, too"—is not the least engaging feature of his style.

But if Darrow was only intermittently effective as an essayist or a philosopher, he was unfailingly on the mark when dealing with one vital subject—himself. Whether Darrow wrote one autobiography or two may be a vexed and unanswerable question: his bibliographer, Willard D. Hunsberger, refers to *Farmington* (1904) as a novel, but it is manifestly an unaffected and emotionally accurate account of Darrow's childhood and upbringing, for all that it is set in a fictitious town in western Pennsylvania and its first-person narrator disguises himself as John Smith.

The Story of My Life is a more straightforward autobiography, although it may perhaps have more to say on Darrow's beliefs and outlook than on either the outward facts of his crowded career or the intimate details of his private life.

But when we turn to such pieces as "Why I Have Found Life Worth Living" (1928) or "At Seventy-two" (1929), we see the real Darrow stripped of the pyrotechnics of the defense attorney or the self-conscious literariness of the essayist in search of fame. We see the quiet dignity of the man who can gain a kind of contentment even in the gaping absence of a loving God or the hope of life after death; who is temperamentally inclined to go against the opinions of the crowd; who finds that both the pleasures and the disappointments of life are less keen in old age than in youth. The real Clarence Darrow may not have been quite like the conflicted Spencer Tracy in *Inherit the Wind* or the unprincipled, radical, atheist bugaboo that the friends of capitalism and labor made him out to be; but he was, as the essays in this book reveal, far more interesting and engaging—as a man, as a writer, and as a thinker. He was a man who, while retaining his core beliefs over a lifetime, learned from his mistakes and gained an insight both into himself and into his society that only age, experience, and struggle can bring. And at the end, he could rightly say that he had made a difference, and a difference for the better.

A Note on This Edition

The great majority of the essays in this book have not been previously reprinted from their original appearances in books or magazines; none appear in the two previous major compilations of Darrow's work, *Attorney for the Damned* (1957) or *Verdicts out of Court* (1963). As they are derived from such a wide array of sources, and as manuscripts for most of them do not survive, the essays are understandably not entirely consistent in matters of style, punctuation, and the like; several are transcripts of oral lectures or debates given by Darrow, and it is not clear that Darrow had a chance to examine them prior to publication. I have, accordingly, not seen the need to impose uniformity in usage. The essays range over a forty-year period, and some of the earlier items contain usages (e.g., "base-ball") that Darrow abandoned in his later writings.

Most of Darrow's essays do not require extensive commentary, but I have added some explanatory notes in cases where Darrow refers to now obscure historical or literary figures or events, and I have also sought to supply exact citations for Darrow's quotations of the writings of others. Darrow was a bit cavalier in the accuracy of his quotations, and in one instance (see "Does Man Live Again?" note 3) the quotation is either apocryphal or misattributed.

ONE

On Philosophy and Religion

Is Life Worth Living?

PROFESSOR STARR HAS TOLD us what we cannot consider in this question, and what we can consider. Taking what we cannot consider and what we must consider, of course, it leaves nothing excepting his view of this question. Now, I think I will prove to him, from biology—and he certainly would not be mean enough to dispute me on biology—that we have a right to consider the future, and that we are bound to consider the past in giving an opinion as to whether life is worth while. It is not a question as to whether I enjoy life or not. I do the very best I can at it, anyhow, and as life goes, I think I do pretty well. But, I am willing to take the professor at his word and say that if I don't think life is worth while with what I get out of it, how is it possible that it could be worth while to anybody that cannot take dope? I will show you before I am done, I think, that a very large part of the professor's rules for living are dope, nothing else. Really, we all enjoy hearing him talk, and we are all very fond of him, but he didn't discuss this question. He really gave us some

---

Is Life Worth Living? (Chicago: J. F. Higgins, 1917) is a debate between Darrow and George Burman Foster, moderated by Frederick Starr (see "Is the Human Race Getting Anywhere?"). Foster (1858–1918) was ordained a Baptist minister in 1879 and taught philosophy and theology at various colleges, including the University of Chicago (1905–18). He also participated with Darrow in a debate on free will (*Resolved: That the Human Will Is Free* [1918]). He was the author of *The Function of Religion in Man's Struggle for Existence* (1909), *Friedrich Nietzsche* (1931), and other works. See Darrow's memorial tribute, "George Burman Foster" (1919), in *Realism in Literature and Art* (rev. ed. Girard, KS: Haldeman-Julius, 1925?).

excellent receipts as to the way to live our lives. He told us what we should do and what we should not do in order to make life happy. Now, that is not even logical, because when he tells me what to do to make life happy he simply tells me what he does or tries to do, to make life happy, and it is not at all certain that I could get happiness that way; and it is still less certain that I could do it if I wished to. His rules for the way to live may be good. They may be worth practicing, so far as we can practice them. But man does not live by rules. If he did, he would not live. He lives by his emotions, his instincts, his feelings; he lives as he goes along. Man does not make rules of life and then live according to those rules; he lives and then he makes rules of life. And, it is really an idle thing for anybody to tell anybody else how to live. Nobody is influenced by other peoples' opinions. Each must learn for himself, and find out where he makes his mistakes, and, perhaps the things he thinks are mistakes are not mistakes after all. No one can figure this out. But, telling you the way to live is not discussing the question of whether life is worth while.

In spite of the rules, is life worth while? Let me take the simplest one he gives. Thus in spite of the professor being a very able man and a very scientific man, the rule is as old as the first dope fiend. He says "work." Be busy. That is the first rule of living—get busy. Everybody who ever wanted to get rich, especially out of somebody else, has taught this to the people. Benjamin Franklin was one of the main exponents of this idea. Work is the great thing in life. I am inclined to think this is true. Now, let us find the reason for it. The reason is perfectly evident. Why should we work? Why, the professor says, it gets our mind off ourselves. That is true, too. That is the reason for it. If a man works hard, especially at something he is interested in, it takes his mind from himself. That is the only philosophical reason for hard work. There are reasons in the way of getting money which are poor reasons. But, to work hard, especially at what you are interested in, takes your mind from yourself. You may get up early in the morning at ten o'clock and try to enjoy yourself for two hours doing nothing. And, you think you have lived a whole lifetime, trying to enjoy yourself. But, if you have worked hard, the first time you may think of it, you think it has been fifteen minutes, when it has been half a day. What does that mean? It means just this: That work is good because it brings non-existence, and that non-existence is the most tolerable of all the forms of matter in life. There is no other answer to hard work. And I know of almost no one who has studied the philosophy of life but does not finally come up with the proposition that the only thing that makes life tolerable, is hard work, so you don't know you are living. So, I characterize hard work as dope for life.

There is one thing in life which is perhaps equal to it, and that is sleep. And, I never saw anyone, weary with the labor of life, or weary with the thought of life, that did not come home to his couch with pleasure in the thought that he would be lost to life for a time, at least. Now, I will admit, that this question is not a very satisfactory one for discussion. Perhaps the question cannot be settled by the professor bringing out all the good things in life and on the other hand by my stringing out all the evil things in life. Somehow or other, this must be settled, if settled, upon a much broader basis than that; upon some question of science or some question of philosophy. And, perhaps, it is not capable of being settled. I will say, with Professor Starr, as I said with Professor Foster, I would like to discuss this with a man who believed in it. I would like to discuss the question of whether life is worth living with one who believed that life was of value. I would like to discuss optimism and pessimism with an optimist. And, in the end, I presume this question gets down to optimism and pessimism. And the professor is too wise to be an optimist and too wise to be deluded with the beauty and pleasure of living, and too honest to say that he is.

But, let me make a few observations that it seems to me puts this question on somewhat broader lines. First, Professor Starr has said that whether there is a future life or not, has nothing to do with the question of whether this life is worth living; whether we come from anywhere has nothing to do with it, or whether we are going anywhere has nothing to do with it. All life and all experience contradicts him. If man was not cursed with consciousness, he would be right. If man was not cursed with memory he could forget the past. And, if he was not cursed with imagination, he would think nothing about the future. But there is no fairly intelligent man or woman who is not bound to think every day in his life of the question of whether life ends all and when that end will come. And with the great mass of men who live upon the earth, the question of the end of life affects their present feeling more than anything else affects it. If anybody says it does not affect it, he is simply bluffing. You may take one of the most eminent scientists of the world, Sir Oliver Lodge, and yet because he has the feeling that I have and the feeling that goes with living, that the fate of annihilation is abhorrent to the human mind—because of that, he almost consciously deludes himself with the silliest twaddle that has ever moved the minds of men.[1] Do you suppose Sir Oliver Lodge would be a spiritualist if the fear of death or the hope of immortality did not make him one? Why, there is not a single fact that he reports that could stand for a minute in the light of the scientific analysis that he gives to every question of physical science, and he must know it.

What does the great mass of the human race think about this question as to whether life is worth living, and whether this is in any way affected by the question of the destiny of Man? Why, since man began to dream dreams and see visions; since he evolved consciousness; since he looked around and asked the meaning of life and death, he has sought by every means to prove that death is not death. He has braced up his love of life by making for himself a dream that there was something more to life than is shown by science or philosophy, or the facts that are apparent to everyone who thinks. And, take that feeling from the human mind today, and take it suddenly, and it would be paralyzed, and men would not live their lives. There are a few who might live it out. But, to say that the question of the destiny of man does not affect his present happiness is to say that man has neither memory, nor imagination, nor consciousness, nor thought.

Men suffer from evils that never come, and they experience joys that never come. A very large part of our conscious life is dreaming. We believe in happiness that will come tomorrow, and in misery that passed yesterday. We are terrified sometimes by disasters that will come tomorrow, more than we are by those that we lived through yesterday. Man's brain is such that his mind will reach into the future and into the past and all about him, and the future and the past, whether it exists or no, does exist for the present, and is the largest part of the things which affect the happiness or the misery of the man. It is idle to say man must not take into account the question of his origin or the question of his destiny, when he considers whether life is worth living. Is it?

Now, I didn't know that I grumbled so much. I don't know why I should. I have got about through with the blooming game. I am about ready to retire. That does not mean I have money, but I study the actuary tables; I know I am about ready to retire. When I retire—well, while I will not be happy, I will not be miserable, and, as life goes, I believe I have as little cause for complaint as almost any person I know. And, I trust that I complain very little. At least I don't mean to. I have lived a life which is, approximately, as good as nothing. Not quite, but somewhere near it. And I will not be very much better off when I am dead; but somewhat.

Does Professor Starr prove that life is worth living, because man is here? If so, that is a simple question. By what process can you prove that everything that is here is worth while? Or, what do we mean by worth while? Of course you can ask a lot of questions in discussing this. Of course, if life is worth living to man because man is here, it is likewise worth living to every animal because it is here. It is worth living to the dog and the mouse and the cat that eats it. Of course, you might say that the life of the mouse is worth living to the cat that eats it. It is worth living to the ant and the grasshopper, and to those tiny insects who live only a fraction of an hour. And, in the sight of eternity, the longest human life is just as short. Even if the emotions, in the fraction of an hour, were all pleasant ones, it was not worth while to begin it when it was to end so quickly. The fact that life is here, to my mind, proves nothing, excepting that if you got a certain amount of earth and heat and water—if they were resolved into the simple elements—given these elements in certain proportions under certain conditions, life will develop, just as maggots will in a cheese. Does that prove it is worth while? I cannot see it. It does not prove it in any meaning of the words worth while. If it does prove it, then everything is equally worth while, and the living man is no more a part of nature than the corpse. And the well man is no more a part of nature than the sick man. The pleasurable emotion is no more a part of nature than the painful emotion. The fact that it is here simply proves it is here, that is all. The only way that this question can be discussed, it seems to me, is as an intellectual or philosophical question: Are the pleasurable emotions of life more than the painful ones? Is there a greater balance of pleasure than pain? And this cannot be discussed without taking into consideration every feeling and imagination that influences man, and influences the feelings of man. You cannot settle it by saying life is a question of health, wealth, happiness and wisdom. The second time he said wealth, health and happiness, he cut out the wisdom. Happiness surely is not a question of wisdom. It is a question of happiness, and happiness is a very complex thing. If life is a question of happiness, then it gets back to you, looking it over, with what has passed and what is still to come, has it more pleasure or more unhappiness? I believe almost every person who lives gets his pleasure in anticipation. All of the adages and teachings of life are built upon that idea. The young person should store up wisdom so that he may use it in old age—when he does not need it. He needs teeth more than he does wisdom. By the way, Professor, my digestion is bully. I can eat anything that tastes good and nothing that does not. A person should hoard up money so that he can spend it, and have a good time with it in the future—when he will most likely be dead. We should work today, so that we can have a vacation tomorrow. Better take it today, for tomorrow you may be dead and you will get out of working. I ought not to be personal, as the professor was, but I ought to be a very wise man for I have listened to him for two winters with the greatest of profit. I remember once last winter—you will excuse me, Professor, for quoting you here? He gave us a wondrous picture of Japan; its beauties, and its glories, and the emotions that he felt in visiting Japan. And, he told us he was going again the following summer, which was last summer. And, there was a very joyful expression on his face in the anticipation of all the fun he would have in Japan. When he got back this fall, he told us that he had been much disappointed when he went to Japan; things didn't turn out the way he thought they were going to. And when I heard him say that he had been disappointed the last time he went to Japan, I was quite sure, that when he remembered his trip to Japan, he had a better time remembering it than when he took it. And, I fancy that, if it is not good biology, it is good psychology. If I could ever have as good a time when I went on a vacation as I anticipated before I went, I would hope to die while I was gone.

So, the past does get into it, and the future gets into it. And, if you work hard there is no present. Let us see what the experience of man says—and really I don't preted there is any way to absolutely settle this question—but let us see what all human experience says about it.

Everybody, after they begin to think a little, and before they can think much, makes a heaven for themselves. There, the streets will be paved with gold. Christian heaven. Of course, I could picture something that looked better to me. In heaven, there will be no weeping or wailing or gnashing of teeth. They will not even have teeth. The streets will be paved with gold. That makes it alluring to a Christian banker. You can play on a harp forever. Your friends will not die. I don't know about your enemies, but your friends will not die. There will be no marrying or giving in marriage; nothing but one long dream of joy! You won't even have to work to forget yourself—you will not want to forget yourself; you will want to walk on the gold pavement. And, the poor old grandmother sits by the fireside mumbling, dreaming, happy, because she is going to heaven. And, the human race forgets its miseries and its sorrows because it is going to heaven. And man is happy in spite of himself because it is living on this pipe dream—I was going to say dope.

Now, isn't that just exactly what man does? From the Methodists up to Sir Oliver Lodge? All of them? From the highest to the lowest, they consciously use every effort in their power to delude themselves with this myth of happiness; this will-o'-the-wisp is right in front of them. And, I suppose when they close their eyes for the last time they see before them this illusion of the golden gates, and all the rest of the business opening before them.

Now, my friend quoted Epictetus, the stoic. Well, he was somewhat like my friend, quite a bluffer. He said, "What is the difference whether I am loaded with chains, my mind is free?" Well, that is a sort of self-hypnotism, if it is true. "What is the difference whether I am hungry or cold; my mind is free? You can do nothing to my mind, anyhow."[2] Well, I wish they could do something to the mind. That is the trouble with people. Before a piece of clay awoke to consciousness, it was getting along all right, but when it awoke, then came the trouble. Now is there any philosophy in Epictetus? Why, it is a great, big bluff. I think one ought not to complain of his troubles. Nobody is interested in them. I would rather hear other people's troubles than to talk about mine. Then I can forget mine. One of the prime receipts for being happy, which I will suggest to the professor, is hard work. I used to be taught that when I was a boy and wanted the moon—I haven't wanted it very lately—I don't know what in the dickens I would do with it if I had it and then I know I can't get it—one way not to worry about what you cannot get is not to want it; one of the prime ways. They used to tell us when we felt bad, to think how much worse somebody else was. You have heard that, haven't you? That proves that life is worth living, doesn't it? If I go out on the street, and get run over, taken to the hospital and lose a leg, I can be happy by thinking of some poor fellow in France that lost both of his! If I get one eye knocked out, I can get joy thinking of the blind! Now, that is a receipt for happiness. And, it is a good receipt; it is given out by everybody. Well, you are not happy today. All right. Think how much better off you are than some people. That proves that life is worth living. That is, it proves that it is not quite so bad as it might be.

Of course, emotionally, one may stick around, because while we live, we want to live. But, I think I am going to be happier next year than I was last year. Of course I know I will not be, but I think I shall. I think next week will be a good week. Last week was not so good. Next week will be fine. And next summer vacation will be good. Of course, as I said before, I might run into some mosquitoes, or some people, but I am not thinking about them now, because it is next year. That is what I ran into last year. Pretty much all of it is in the imagination. And I don't condemn the dope fiend. I think he is—I was going to say wise, but I will do better than that by him—I think he is foolish, and, blessed be foolishness!

When you leave the cruder religions of the world, and men begin to get up where they cannot believe quite all that has been said, then they turn to Epictetus, and he was one of these self-deluding mortals who could sit on a pin and say, "Why, my mind is free." Of course, that is not even scientific. For a man's mind, whatever it is, depends upon his brain, whatever it is, and that is a part of his body, whatever it is. So that he is not free; it depends entirely upon his body. It is just a bit of bluffing. Epictetus and a few other stoics bluffed their way through the world until their philosophy played out and now it has been taken up by the Christian Scientists, who say: "Oh, no, there is no such thing as corns, they are in the head, not on the toes." "There is no such thing as death. The friend you loved that made up a large part of the pleasures of life, is not dead. He has just passed on." Just passed on! Things are not what they seem to be. God is love and love is God. There is no sin; there is no pain—only a condition of mind. Well, with the most of them there is no mind; so there is nothing!

Does all of that prove that life is worth living? It proves that it is not worth living. I will tell you why it proves it. It proves that there is no-body on earth who can stand the realities of life. That is what it proves. It proves that when the consciousness of life comes to one who is intelligent, that he straightway uses every effort in his power to prove that life is not life; pain is not pain and death is not death; that he takes every dope that is given him by someone else to make him dream, and if he cannot find anything given him by someone else that will put him to sleep, he makes one for himself that puts him to sleep. And, if perchance he is too intelligent, even to manufacture a dope that will put him to sleep, and if he cannot find one that will put him to sleep, then he resorts to hard work, so he cannot think of himself. Looking life over I have nothing to complain of—I am a real optimist; it might have been worse. There is optimism for you. It might have been worse. And, in spite of the pleasures that I have experienced in studying biology and listening to lectures on anthropology, and in spite of the companionship of my friends, and in spite of good food and vacations, in spite of all of these—and I have had my full share of them—and a good digestion with it—and before I finish that sentence I want to call attention to one thing my friend suggested, then I will go back where I left off. He said digestion is good. Eating tastes good, but if you eat too much it hurts you. Well, now why should it? You like to eat, but if you eat too much it makes you miserable. What a glorious thought that is, isn't it?

Well, in spite of my pleasures, and all of my friends—I am glad I have so many; if they knew me better, I would have more—in spite of all of these, when I look back over life, with the many pains I have suffered that happened, and the many more I have suffered that did not happen, the greatest satisfaction that I find in any of it is when I am asleep. And, intellectually, I feel it will be the best thing that can happen to me—to go to sleep again. Still emotionally and physically, I draw back from it, just like everyone else who ever lived. All this enters into my personal feeling of whether life is worth while. But as an intellectual question, I insist that practically everything that my friend has said and practically everything that everyone says in favor of optimism and the worth-whileness of life—pretty near all of it—proves that life is not worth while; that it is an unpleasant interruption of nothing, and the best thing you can say of it is that it does not last long.

Is the Human Race Getting Anywhere?

PROFESSOR STARR IS SO MUCH like my old time friend and antagonist whom I am still mourning, Professor Foster, that it makes my side easier. He is not a lawyer; he is a college professor, and is honest. It is impossible for him to put his side of the question without pretty well putting my side too. Of course, I have an advantage. I can put my side without putting his. I am aware, though, that this advantage is more than overcome by his superior learning in those things that are important in a discussion of this kind.

I am not here to discuss whether man is better and higher than the Ameba. I could not discuss that for I really do not know. Of course, man has more legs to—get the gout in and he has a bigger stomach—to be diseased, and he has a bigger brain—for the home of more false theories. Most of these questions get us back to another question, "What is it all about anyhow, and what do we mean by getting anywhere?" The Ameba has one advantage over us, if it is an advantage, the Ameba is endowed

---

Darrow-Starr Debate: Is the Human Race Getting Anywhere? (Chicago: J. F. Higgins, 1920) is a debate between Darrow and Frederick Starr (1858–1933), who had been in charge of ethnology at the American Museum of Natural History in New York (1889–91) and was professor of anthropology at Chautauqua University (1892–1923). Starr had gone to Japan in 1904 on behalf of the St. Louis Exposition, and led expeditions to the Congo (1905–6), Japan (1909–10, 1917), Korea (1911, 1913, 1915–16), Liberia (1912), and elsewhere. He was the author of many books on Japan, the Philippines, Korea, and the Indians of Mexico.

with immortal life. I am not saying that this is an advantage; neither does the Ameba have to work so hard. Whether his simple organism is better than the complex organism that is given to man, I don't know. I have to ask myself, "better for what?" Then, I am lost, as I fancy anybody else is lost. The Ameba can't construct words as man can, and he does not need them. Probably man does not either, but that is not the question. The question is, "Is the Human Race Getting Anywhere?" not whether the Ameba is not.

If the human race is higher, which we will assume, to save trouble—then is this higher race getting anywhere, and if so, where?

I did not know that I had such an antipathy towards art. In fact, I thought I was some artist myself. I am rather fond of art; the world has lost a large part of what art it once had. We have abandoned art to make money, which to me is not a sign of progress. If I did not believe in art, I might think that steam engines were better than pictures or sculpture, but I don't think so. I suppose there is a certain value in measuring the seconds and the hours and the weeks and the years. It gives us a chance to know about when you are going to die.

Really, I am unable to say what are the valuable things in life. I used to think the main thing was to have property evenly divided. I am now uncertain about that. I used to think if we could get property evenly divided, we could get brains evenly divided. I am sure now we could not, and if we could nobody would have very much to boast of. The trouble with all these questions is to get a starting point. What is life for?

No one can answer that question. I am sure of it, because I cannot answer it myself. If we can not answer that we may then ask the question: What are we to do with life now that we have it thrust upon us? In this case we are not very much better off. My own idea is that on the whole, the life is the most tolerable which has the greatest measure of pleasurable emotions against painful ones. Some people might say that life is to gather wisdom. But, I don't know what we are going to do with our wisdom. I have been gathering it all my life, and I don't know what to do with it now that I have it. Or, is it to build steam engines? What for? Suppose these produced painful emotions instead of pleasant ones?

Or, to make flying machines, so we can use them in war? There is no starting point. But, that never discourages me. I see in life, just what the Professor showed us in the end, a continual coming and going. One civilization or one set of ideas taking the place of another. Nations growing civilized, as he calls it, so they can get along with each other, and then killing each other.

I see it in the Persians, creating what was a great civilization, and then in that civilization being destroyed. I see it in the Greeks, and the Romans, creating what in many ways was a great civilization, and then going to pieces, utterly destroyed. And, generally, by what and by whom? Generally by some primitive people who are living close to the foundation of nature, close to the earth and air, and the sunlight, who have not the seeds of disease and disintegration, which a civilization plants in all human kind.

I see no beneficent power in evolution. I see no beneficent power in the universe which says that of necessity man shall get better or higher, or what to me is more important, happier. I see with human life what I see with the ocean, an everlasting ebb and flow, the flow pretty clearly marked and the ebb pretty clearly marked; marked by an inexorable nature. Nothing that man can change, and the more he tries to change it, the sooner he dies.

We all protest the cruelty of nature. And, yet, if we live, we must live the abject slave of this unfeeling monster which we call nature; she, to my mind, has fixed the limits of man and fixed them absolutely.

Civilization, as the Professor says, is the faculty of living together, and he likewise says that the world is getting more crowded every day. So, sooner or later we will have to turn to and cut each other's throats, because there won't be room for us, and ever since the world began we have been doing this, so the more you are civilized, the more the necessity of cutting your neighbor's throat.

Assume we have reached man in animal life, and that man is the highest organism that that the earth has ever known. Perhaps he is. Then, what about this "human race"? Is it getting anywhere, and if so, where? If I were to ask you the question as to whether the ants and the bees are getting anywhere, you would probably say no. The ant and the bee take just as good care to see that its species is perpetuated as man does; and nature seems to be interested in one thing, and that is the preservation of life.

At a certain stage the ant and the bee were evolved and the types became fixed. I fancy there will be no dispute about that. The ant and the bee today can do nothing that their ancestors could not do, when the first ant and the first bee no doubt proclaimed to each other the wonders of the ant and bee creation. They cannot get beyond their structure. It is fixed. The same thing, I take it, is true of all other animal structures. You can develop nothing from a cow but a cow. You may put more fat on it so it will be more desirable to eat, but you can make nothing out of it but a cow: any amount of fat that you put on is limited, because too much fat will kill it, just as it kills civilization. The species is fixed.

Nature, we will say, by some mutation produces the ape and the monkey, and when these were produced it got through with that job. There are some monkeys that weigh more than others, and some that can chatter louder, just the same as there are some of us debaters that can talk louder and longer than others. But, the ape and monkey business is finished. I suppose that even a socialist would not care to go to the apes to teach socialism. He would think he was wasting time. The ape hasn't the stuff in him. He is finished. Assume that by a twist of evolution, man came into being.

Is man different from the ant and bee and the cow and the ape? Of course the theologian says he is different, because the Almighty made his body and then planted in him a soul; but the scientist cannot find the soul. The doctors have dissected men, and they cannot find it; and the grocers have weighed the dead and the living, and they cannot find it; and the evolutionist and the scientist have pretty much come to the conclusion that he was made just as the ape was made and the ant was made and is purely a natural product, in fact, a machine. Man, as I take it, is finished.

I am not saying that some day on account of a change of climate or some mysterious turn of nature, some higher species might not appear upon the earth. I can not tell and I never will know. Perhaps some day the superman will be born, but if he is, he will be like the ape and the monkey and the ant and the bee,—he will be fixed. When the superman comes, if he does, what about the "human race"? Why, the superman will treat the human race as horses, to be slaves, or as hogs, to be eaten, to feed the superman. Man's stature is fixed, according to all the laws of biology you spoke of. According to all we know of life, according to all we know of nature which is heartless and cruel, and has no interest in anything—except to fix the contrivance up so that she will persist. Although you are not sure of that. In two or three different periods in the last two hundred thousand years, the ice age has swept down upon the earth and destroyed any amount of living species, men with the rest; not entirely, but in many localities.

Now, what is man? He has a clear history. You can tell what man came from and how much he will come to, just as much as you can tell what will happen to an egg if a hen sits on it. Some hens may be bigger than others, and noisier, and some foolisher, but they won't be much bigger, or much noisier or more foolisher; could not be. And it has been true since the first hen, or the first egg, whichever came first—and we will not settle that, either.

Man has a plain history. A germ is fertilized and he is built cell on cell, and you know how big he will be and what size his brain will be, and about when he will die. Of course, he may be a little bigger or a little smaller, but not very much bigger or very much smaller. The biggest brain that any intelligent person ever had, as I recall it, and I asked the Professor here, before he came on the stand, to make sure of it—the biggest brain was sixty-four ounces. If you get up to sixty-six it makes an idiot. So you can't get it any bigger, so far as experience shows, and sixty-four was a mighty close shave. Of course, you can make an idiot with a great deal smaller brain; I have known lots of them. But, when you get above that it is sure to be one. So, what are you going to do?

To hear some people talk who believe in eternal progress—that is the eternal progress of the "human race," you would think that some time a man was to have a brain as high as the Masonic Temple; but he is not, and if he did, he must have legs, and a stomach to match, and all the rest of the machinery to go with it, or he would be lost. He is fixed. And he has probably been fixed for tens of thousands of years. Not only is it impossible to change his brain but his brain and its action depends on his stomach and lungs and his legs, and he must keep up the balance. A man buys an automobile and stops running and cannot digest his food, so he dies. Of course, the surgeons work on him awhile, but they cannot keep him alive forever, because he is out of balance, any more than you can keep an ape living in a cage. He is a part of nature, and he must live with her, or he dies. His brain is fixed; his whole structure is fixed, and if we can learn anything from other animal life and from life, it is impossible to change it.

Of course, he may turn his brain in one direction or another. He may go a certain distance in one direction or another, but if he goes east, he cannot go west; and if he goes north, he cannot go south; and if he takes up mechanics, he will probably lose art and the things that are the most worth while for man.

Now, I fancy that Professor Starr would have an easy time to prove that we have more railroads and taller buildings and larger cities now than there were a hundred thousand years ago, or even six thousand years ago, when perhaps the written history of the human race began. He would have an easy time to prove that so-called civilized people have more thickly inhabited cities or more mechanical devices or more money than the savages in Africa. That is easy. But he might have a very much harder time to prove that man is intrinsically stronger, and a still harder time to prove that he is happier, which to my mind, is the best measure of whether we are getting anywhere or not. Of course, the Professor is more familiar with the savage than I am. I don't say this because he has lived so long with the College Professors down at the University, but because he has traveled in Mexico and Africa and countries outside of America. Of course anybody outside of America is a savage! At least he can not be a hundred per cent American! But I could not prove that a savage in Africa was not as happy as a civilized banker in Chicago, if you can put those two words together. The savage does not have to watch the ticker to see whether stocks are going up or down; and he does not need to worry because he can't get all the money there is in the world, and he does not have to be operated on for appendicitis or anything like that, and he knows nothing about germs.

On the question of happiness, I doubt whether civilization gets you anywhere. Of course, the African lives a sort of life close to nature, and I presume he does pretty well. I could picture the African sitting on the banks of the Congo. That isn't so bad—sitting in the shade, playing with the alligators, his children around him, and his wives out gathering bread, fruit and cocoanuts for him. What's the matter with that? I fancy you couldn't improve his condition by putting up a silk mill for his children to work in or a steel mill for him to work in!

I think it is impossible to say that civilization has done anything to make life happier, or more tolerable for the everlasting stream of men and women that come and go. Is there any sense in saying that the world is getting anywhere; and if so, where? Is this generation happier than the last? A great many things have come into being in my lifetime. Of course, I am not much older than the Professor, but still I can remember when the telephones came. Now, I get sore every day by being called up every three or four minutes on the telephone. Has the telephone added to the pleasures of life?

I can't see that life is any happier now than it was when I was a youngster. I fancy the people when I was a youngster were just as happy as they are now, and perhaps happier. They were all sure they were going to heaven after they died, and most of us are not so sure now. Really, one must find a starting point, and I can't find one. Wherever you place your feet, is quick-sand. Is it intellect that makes you happier? Why, of course, I know better than that! Because I am not happy. Is it money that makes you happy? I know better than that, too. Is it tall buildings? No, my office is on the thirteenth floor. What has that got to do with it? Is it railroads? I hate to ride on the cars.

What makes happiness? Well, I fancy it is largely a state of mind and I know nothing between savagery and Christian Science that can change the state of mind. Of course, socialism may to a degree, but it is only to a degree, because the Socialists expect something here, and the others don't so even they can be disappointed. But take any basis that we can think of. The intellect is a poor one. Can you prove that the intellect of man is better than it was, or that it is going to be? I don't know about the Neanderthal man, who lived sixty thousand years ago; a little of his skull was found in a cave in western Europe. We haven't got enough to judge. But I know something about man as far back as the history of the human race goes, and our men are certainly no more intelligent today than they were then. We haven't got beyond Plato, and Aristotle and Socrates, although we have Mary Baker Eddy and Dowie and Billy Sunday and Bryan![1]

When I was making a memorandum coming down about what I should say, the only thing I put down was "Bryan, to prove that the world did not move." It is perfectly clear that man has not improved in twenty-five hundred years. It is true that there have been more books written lately, but very few of them are worth reading. Anybody can write books if he has learned how to write. Everybody can speak because they have learned how to talk, but it does not show that they are saying anything, so we still go back to Plato and Aristotle and Socrates and that brilliant galaxy of philosophers and thinkers who have made up a large share of all the geniuses of the world.

Intellectually man has got nowhere. If he has, I don't know where. What has he done? Intellectually he has done nothing. He has turned his mind to this thing and that, and he has preserved some of the things that other generations knew of, but as an intellectual machine, as a human being, he is no better. Swept onto the earth with the rest of life, born, lives his time and passes away.

Have we learned anything about war? Why everything that was said against war was said twenty-five hundred years ago, at least. The world has been educated about its cruelty for hundreds of years, and yet in the midst of our wondrous civilization, we have seen the greatest war of history, and every bit of science that we knew has been called into play for the purpose of killing men. I wrote a book on non-resistance fifteen years ago and we have had a war since that! And I believed in it myself. The primitive man, with all of his old primitive instincts, is here just the same as the first man, and these instincts rule his life.

When we come down to modern life, what have we learned? One hundred and fifty years ago we formed a nation, dedicated to freedom of speech and freedom of action, and what has become of it? Look at the great galaxy of scientific men who have taught the world for the last two hundred years at least. Yet, the world has gone crazy over tipping tables and hearing raps on the ceiling to prove immortal life. Think of the more or less philosophical ideas of life, and the future, and religion. And you can plant in a civilization like the United States the doctrines of Dowie and Mary Baker Eddy. Think what has been done and said by all the wise of all the ages, about philosophy, and along comes a cheap evangelist like Billy Sunday and a cheap politician like Billy Bryan, and they make the people declare by law what you and I shall drink and not drink! Have we got anywhere? If we have, I wish we could go back!

America entered into a war, partly to make democracy safe in the world; we founded a nation with a constitution, which was meant to preserve liberty and a declaration of independence which came from the wisest and the freest men of their age, declaring the mind to be free and that men should be free; and we finished with the war and then a few vote-mongering politicians moved by the people who love wealth and power have turned a great, free country into a mad-house! A mad-house where the human mind is paralyzed and the human lips are dumb for fear of the wrath of the money changer! We have destroyed as far as a few years can destroy, the free institutions that it took centuries to rear; we have made a psychology that causes us to look at Herod and the Duke of Alva[2] and the Witch-burners and admit that they were pikers compared to us!

"The War on Modern Science"

Maynard Shipley: "The War on Modern Science"
(Knopf, $8.00).

THIS BOOK WILL BE a revelation to most readers. Mr. Shipley has taken the trouble to go over the whole story of the recent campaign of the Fundamentalists, not only to bar the teaching of science from the public schools, but to make education and life correspond to the weird fables found in Genesis and other parts of the Bible.

No more brazen and dangerous attempt to control thought can be found anywhere in history. The campaign is simply an effort by organized ignorance and bigotry to destroy the learning of the modern world. Under the leadership of the late William Jennings Bryan, the forces of ignorance and intolerance were marshalled from Maine to California, and from Canada to Mexico. These forces laid siege to state legislatures and school boards throughout the whole land. Their efforts were not confined to the solid south, but the campaign touched every part of the United States.

Even states like New York and California, together with most of the other northern states, have modified education to conform to the campaign of ignorance that has overspread the land.

This review was published in *Modern World* 1 (July 1927): 301–3. The author of the book, [Howard] Maynard Shipley (1872–1934), was founder of the Seattle Academy of Science (1898) and the Science League of America (1924), the latter an organization devoted to protecting freedom of teaching and to resisting attempts to unite church and state. Shipley also wrote *The Key to Evolution* (1929) and many "little blue books" on various scientific subjects for the Haldeman-Julius Company.

Mr. Shipley has marshalled the facts, and the story he tells should awaken the intelligent people of America, if the emotion for liberty is not already dead.

This campaign of the Fundamentalists began by presenting bills in many of the states making it unlawful to teach any theory of the origin of man which was contrary to the "divine" account as contained in the Bible. This, of course, provided that by legislation the stories of Genesis should be made the standard of truth, and that no teaching should be permitted which in any way conflicted with these fables. Every discovery of science, accepted as true by practically all students, is denominated by these fanatics as "science, so-called."

Not content to proceed with legislation, they have attacked school boards in almost every state in the union, and in this way have made much more progress than in legislation. Few, if any, states have escaped this campaign. The Fundamentalists have sent their committees to the boards of almost every state and county throughout the land. They have made, and are now making, publishers withdraw and modify their text books. They are making scientific teaching conform to Genesis. Not only are they fixing the text books of the schools to suit their purpose, but are reaching out to dismiss every teacher who dares to allow intelligence and learning to have anything to do with his mental processes.

Mr. Shipley tells this story in this most important book. It is an amazing revelation. That such an onslaught against science could make headway in the twentieth century shows how completely an active, aggressive and ignorant body, when organized and moved by fanaticism, can influence the world.

Not only is this movement striking at evolution, but, in states like New York, it is compelling religious teaching in the public schools. In California, which is one of the progressive states, while they have failed to pass a law prohibiting the teaching of evolution, they have not stopped here. School boards have deliberately deleted well-known text books of scientific teaching; and, without law, but simply by terrorizing school teachers, have placed Genesis over science.

After the success of the Fundamentalist, the Christian Scientist has demanded that the school books shall say nothing about anti-toxin, but shall leave pupils to believe that a cancer is not the destruction of tissue, but is simply "error." Every denomination, sect, and bunch, however weird and grotesque, will make the public schools their bone of contention, and with force and energy, born of ignorance and bigotry, bulldoze and terrorize Congress, legislatures, school boards, and teachers.

This is the "Pandora's Box" that Mr. Bryan opened for the destruction of culture and intelligence. This is the legacy that he has left to America.

Mr. Shipley makes it perfectly clear that what the Fundamentalists desire is not so much that evolution shall not be taught, but that it shall be made clear, once for all, that in science and every branch of knowledge everything is to be tested by the Bible. It must be assumed that this book is the word of God, and is so complete and plain that nothing can be taught that can be construed as contrary to "Holy Writ." Upon this point the ubiquitous Mr. Bryan enlarged in a speech before a Southern legislature, in support of a bill drafted to meet his ideas, if his vagaries can be so designated. Mr. Shipley tells the story in his book.

The half-educated persons behind the measure, Mr. Shipley relates, engaged the services of the eloquent, if not learned, Mr. Bryan to help in "putting the law over." Appearing on the floor of the House, the aggrieved Commoner told the legislature that it was his purpose:—

"To show how religious faith and Christian ideals are being undermined by teachers who believe that man is a descendant from the brutes, and who, in our public schools and colleges, are substituting the Darwinian hypothesis for the Bible account of man's creation.

"The scientist must not be elevated above the minister," continued the celebrated anti-evolutionist. "The minister learns and teaches from the Book of Books, the scientist from nature." The Book and Nature are both sources of truth, and since "all truth is of God," religion has no quarrel with "true science." But if the scientist derives from the Book of Nature conclusions antagonistic to the revelations of the Book of Books, then the scientist is wrong.

Mr. Shipley's book is bristling with quotations from Mr. Bryan and other Fundamentalists which show plainly that their purpose is to create a state religion—this religion to control all teaching and place under the ban of the law all men and ideas in conflict with what they conceive to be the direct revelation of God to man. To them nothing has much importance except religion.

Mr. Bryan puts it, "The age of the rocks is not so important as the rock of ages."[1] Meaningless phrases like this are once more to establish the inquisition which has already been set to work on many teachers throughout the length and breadth of the land. Mr. Shipley has had the industry to find any number of these incidents, which are constantly increasing. All of this is the work of an ignorant minority, supported by a strong organization and financed by unlimited contributions of cash.

The facts revealed in Mr. Shipley's book should be amply sufficient to put scientists and teachers on their guard. They should do more than this; they should organize to meet the campaign. They should do this, not only in defense of themselves, but in defense of learning; and, still more important, in defense of religious freedom. This fight must be made by the scientists and the teachers. It is, above all others, their job. How has the issue been met up to the present time? That practically every scientist in the world has accepted evolution as a fact is beyond dispute. Even Fundamentalists accept it in the inorganic world, and in the organic world up to man. The scientist is permitted to teach evolution in every field except in the development of *Homo Sapiens.* Man must be exempt from the general working out of nature; this in spite of the fact that the evidences of evolution are seen clearer in the structure and work of man than in any other field.

In the face of the onslaught of the Fundamentalists, some scientists are content to repeat over and over that they believe in evolution, but that there is no conflict between science and religion. They only obscure the real issue. The statement may be true, but it depends entirely upon the definition of "religion." If "religion" means the emotions of sympathy, charity and humanity, which to some extent are a part of every human structure, then this statement is no doubt true. If it means that great seers and prophets of the world, from the earliest times, have almost without exception emphasized these emotions, then the statement is true. The scientists who repeat that there is no conflict evidently define "religion" in some such way. If "religion" means that the earth and man were created in six days measured by the morning and evening; that the sun was made on the fourth day; that the first woman was made from Adam's rib; that the sun stood still for Joshua; that the earth was completely drowned out by a flood; that the ark saved two of every kind of organic life, gathered from all over the globe to start a new world; that all present life comes from the animals that were saved in the ark; that each species is the result of separate creation; that the human race was doomed to eternal torture because Eve was tempted by the serpent and man tempted by Eve; that two or three thousand years later man was offered a chance for redemption by believing in an immaculate conception, and a physical resurrection; if all this is a part of "religion"—and it must be believed if one is religious—then the chances are that there are no scientists who will say that religion and science are in harmony. Why should not these scientists, who sat that science and religion do not conflict, define in plain terms what they mean by "religion"?

The time is past due for the scientist to speak in no uncertain terms. The Fundamentalist does not quibble or dodge. He is honest if not intelligent. He is using every means in his power to place the Bible and his interpretation of religion in the field of learning. The battle has been fought many times in the history of the world. Once more the combat is upon us. It cannot be won by quibbling and dodging. Science must openly and fairly meet the issue. The question to be determined is whether learning should be hampered and measured by dogmas and creeds. Mr. Shipley has done a great work in making the issue clear. "The War on Modern Science" is the most important book published on this subject since Andrew D. White's "Conflict Between Science and Theology."[2]

Can the Individual Control His Conduct?

I AM SURE THAT this audience will thank me for helping to present the scholarly and lovable man who has recently come to Chicago and has taken part in this debate. I never heard him speak before, but I have heard of him, and he has fulfilled all my expectations; not to my regret, because I am very glad that I have had the chance to hear him and that you have had the chance to hear him. I fancy he is like myself about this question; he does not take it as a matter of life or death with himself or with anybody else.

I am thoroughly open minded myself. I am willing to be convinced, but not likely to be. I have really greatly enjoyed his talk. If I had time to think it over I might be able to figure out exactly wherein we disagree. So, I will proceed to talk about free will and determinism and mechanism just as if I had not heard him. Then, after we get through we can decide whether we agree or disagree. I am sure that very few of you have listened to a teacher of philosophy with as much interest as you have listened to Dr. Smith. I scarcely knew the time was passing and I think

"Can the Individual Control His Conduct?" is a debate between Darrow and Thomas V. Smith published in the *Haldeman-Julius Quarterly* 2 (October-November 1927): 15–28. Smith (1890–1964) was professor of philosophy at the University of Chicago (1926–48) and associate editor (1924–31) and editor (1931f.) of the *International Journal of Ethics* (later retitled *Ethics*). He was the author of *The Democratic Way of Life* (1926), *Beyond Conscience* (1934), *Constructive Ethics* (1948), and many other books on philosophy and politics.

I understood some of it, which is saying a good deal for philosophy and for me.

As nearly as I can follow the drift of the argument of Dr. Smith he believes that a man can choose to do what he wants to do when he wants to do the thing he chooses; at least, it comes pretty near to that. I am inclined to think he is right. I very seldom do anything that I do not want to, because I have found out pretty well that there are a lot of things I can not do and so I do not want to do them. If one gets that mental attitude he is not apt to be disappointed by wanting the moon, or even wanting to be president, or some other useless thing. The one way I have found effective in this world in having my way is not to want a whole lot of things. That seems to me to be my friend's idea.

Dr. Smith says we have no will for a thing unless we desire that thing, or practically that. The desire comes first before the will to do it. I think he is right.

Then the question is, where does the desire come from? How much has a man to do with his own desire? I would assume he had nothing to do with it. Dr. Smith gave us a few illustrations about how men act and he spoke of me as winning cases with juries, which I sometimes do, and sometimes do not. There are always stupid juries. He says I talk to them. I do. I can lose a good many cases that way. But, he says, I convince and reason that my side is right. No, Dr. Smith is not a good psychologist. I never try to convince anybody of anything by reason; I know that nobody acts in any important thing through his reason. I know that the decisions that make for life or death in this world are not arrived at by reason.

Dr. Smith has said there may be something due to the selection of jurors. There is a lot. Does any lawyer select a man because he is intelligent? No intelligent lawyer does. Does he select a juror because he is unintelligent? No. No intelligent lawyer does that. And, I most always find that, if I am on one side selecting a jury, the fellow on the other side wants the jurors that I excuse. He wants one kind and I want another; and intelligence has little if anything to do with it. If I am an attorney for the defendant—which I am if I am in a criminal case—I do not inquire whether a juror is intelligent. I want to know what kind of a machine he has. I want to know whether he is imaginative, whether he is idealistic, whether he is so made originally or so shaped by experience that he can put himself in another man's place. If he is intelligent, so much the better. There are emotional men and there are unemotional men who are intelligent. There are ignorant men who are sympathetic and kindly, and there are ignorant men who are stolid and cold. Why should I want that sort of a juror? Because I know that when you get down to the final conduct of men they act from feeling; they find reasons for doing the thing they want to do; and that applies just the same to intelligence as to ignorance and a little more so, because, as a rule, the intelligent man has the most sensitive nervous system. The imaginative man puts himself in the other fellow's place. Unless you can get him to do that he does nothing for you. I think my friend would agree with me that the conduct of individuals in most of the important things of life is not directed by reason and judgment but is controlled by the emotional part of life. I think everybody agrees with that nowadays.

Dr. Smith says that he has run across the statement somewhere from something I have said or done—you can run across all kinds of "fool" statements if you read all my stuff, and, I hope, some intelligent ones; this was an intelligent one—that, while a man could not influence himself, he could influence someone else. Is that true or is it not? What have any of us to do with the making of our views of life? Something I may say might influence you people. It might not. It might influence a number of you and not the rest of you. It might influence some of you to accept the views I hold. It might influence some of you to accept the views Dr. Smith holds if you can tell what they are. You might have come in here believing you had free will and go out believing you had not.

Now, why? In case the debate changes you, then if you had not met either of us your present opinions on that subject would have remained entirely different. If you had gone away from this meeting, they would have been different. If I believe, as John Calvin believed, that up there somewhere is a Being that figured out each one of our lives, then I would say: "The Lord knew you were going to attend this meeting." He looked down through the ages and foresaw that you would be here, and that being here would affect your opinion and send you to heaven or hell, as the case might be, and that is the reason that God could make so close a guess as to where you are to go. You may have come here just because some fellow on the street asked you to, or because you had no other place to go, which is a very good reason, or because you read Dr. Smith's name or mine casually somewhere. But, the whole thing was the result of endless sequences—and a being that could foresee it all and arrange it all knew it would happen?

Now, of course, as Dr. Smith has said, my view on this subject is not the Calvinistic one. My friend falls into a slight error. I do not disbelieve in a first cause. I don't know anything about it. I have got one of those limited minds, if any, that cannot get so far back. So, whether there is a first cause or whether there is any such thing as a first cause, I have no opinion. I know there are circumstances and facts and events that operate as causes for each individual's conduct.

As we understand cause and effect, the first thing we need to take account of is what is a man anyhow. He is an organism with a plain origin. We know when he was born and when his life started and how long before his birth. We know what has entered into it. We know he has a certain strength and a certain weakness of the physical body. We know that he has a certain nervous system and that no two men are exactly alike. We know he has a certain size and sort of brain and no two brains are alike. We know that he had nothing whatever to do with this to start with.

There are very few advocates of the doctrine of free will who think a man is responsible for what happened before he was born. Dr. Smith is not one of them; neither is he an advocate of free will, as I am very glad to learn. But, what is going to happen to an individual at least is partly due to the kind of machine he has. If his nervous system is not too sensitive and he is not too imaginative and sympathetic, he is liable to have some money left when he dies; if he is stolid, he has good judgment; so I am informed by the people who have money. If he has no imagination that puts himself in the place of other people, then he will not worry much about the world. It is unfortunate for the world—because it does it a lot of good to worry over it!

All of this, so far, is the result of the human machine, and there are no two alike, and up to that point certainly nobody is responsible; that is, the individual machine is not responsible. Other things happen after that. For the first part of his life he gets ideas and views of conduct from those about him; these enter into his machine and affect his machine, and how he develops these views is due to the machine's construction. Some are affected more and some less. Before the child has any chance to choose his teachers he has a mind pretty well set on all the ideas that he calls right and wrong. Sometimes he is shaken out of what he has his mind set upon and comes to a point where he feels called upon to judge questions; where he feels the necessity of action, and where he must do one thing or another. We will say he comes to a cross-roads in life. The question may come about in this way: on Sunday, which is the Sabbath day, here is a movie picture on this side of the street, and here is a church on the other. Which shall he go into? I do not imagine that Dr. Smith would go into either; he might take to the woods! I do not know which any one of you would go into. I do know this: That in deciding that problem, each individual decides it according to the equipment he has when he makes the decision. He cannot decide it any other way. He decides it according to his machine. He may have a sensitive nervous system that would lend itself to pleasure; he may not. He decides according to his machine and according to what he has gathered in life, as he came along. If he believes in hell he would probably stay out of the movie because if he stayed out he could go to heaven and see better movies for less money. If he were doubtful about that, he would be the more apt to go. If he has a structure that calls for certain kinds of entertainment, and has enjoyed experiences that added to it, he would probably go to the theater. Two people might come along together; as they often do. One of them will go to church and the other will go to a theater. I have seen those things happen myself. I have seen people on their way to church when there was a theater nearby. What is the reason for the different action? It is a matter of judgment. How many infinite things determine what place you will go? Can any human being figure them out?

Suppose you stop at the outset to determine, then, what do you do? You bring up in your mind the reasons for going to church, if any. You marshall on the other side the reasons for going to the theater, and whichever are the stronger you follow. You do not go according to the weaker. You can not do it. And which are the strongest reasons to one person are not the strongest to another person. That all depends, first, upon the kind of equipment one has and, secondly, upon the experience one has had in life.

I have said in picking a jury that the lawyer who is liable to take the side I take wants an imaginative person. From where does he get that idea? First, from his structure. But, that is not the only place. He can get it from the experiences he has had in life. Everything one meets and everything one feels enter into one's being, and whenever one makes a judgment one makes it in view of everything that has gone before. I have seen many a hard, unimaginative, cruel person, who when caught in what I will call the web of fate, has gotten into trouble. Almost universally, it has made him more kindly and sympathetic to others in trouble. He finds out how easy it is to get into trouble. Nobody is able to untangle all the threads with all their ramifications which ultimately lead or pull one here and there.

Nobody is the same at twenty as at ten. He may be worse; he may be better; he may be more emotional or less emotional. One is not the same at thirty as at twenty. One is not the same at fifty or sixty as at thirty. What difference is there? There are two kinds of differences or two that I can think of. First, the physical structure is not the same. The things that would attract one, the strong emotions that would lead one to love or to hate or to fear, may be deadened and modified. And, next, one's experiences in life have affected his outlook on life. When one has run against a lot of things he looks out for them again. When he approaches that same kind of a thing again he approaches it not only with the machine but with the experiences that have gone into the machine. Life has made us what we were as we started; it has constantly shaped and re-shaped us over and over again, and when we approach a certain thing and seek a conclusion we approach it with our full equipment, whether it was with us at birth or has come to us through the countless experiences that most of us have met. I cannot see how it is possible for most of us to make conclusions without throwing into the scales the things that weigh for one side against the things that weigh for the other and then determine which side is heavier. I cannot see how it is possible to do anything else. And, one must determine it with the machine that Nature gave him, and with such experiences as life has thrust upon him. I can see no chance for him to do any other way.

Let me see how much chance we have. Now, my friend says that my doctrine is inconsistent with much of my life. Well, probably that is true, or apparently true. I probably do have a sensitive "fool" nervous system that makes me laugh and cry. I cannot help putting myself in the place of other people, if they get close enough to me so I listen to their troubles. Of course, I try to keep them away for the most part, because I know myself fairly well. Why do I do it? Isn't it plain? How much free will is there in any of us?

I know I have undertaken many things that I did not want to do; many things that gave no pleasure. In that instance, I would weigh up the pain I would get in doing them against the pain I would suffer by not doing them. For instance, I am getting along in years, and, naturally, I have had a good deal of experience with dentists. Now, I never went to a dentist's office for pleasure. I know I am going to get a pain that begins sometime before and lasts for a while after I go. Why then do I go? I measure up the pain and discomfort the dentist will give me with the pain and discomfort I will have to endure if I stay away, and I choose the lesser evil, or at least I think I do. I may be mistaken, at that.

Is it an exercise of free will? With me, it is a necessity. So, I fancy it is with everybody. That is one reason why I never mean to judge people. Perhaps I do. If I do, I do not stand by my philosophy. Now, my friend says I am inconsistent in that I may take a person's case out of pure sympathy; true, I do, sometimes. But, is there anything inconsistent in it? Not at all. I do it because it hurts me if I do not. I do it, if not to get pleasure, to avoid pain, for myself.

Now, to get back to the jury, and I will follow it further: I try to convince a jury that they ought to do so and so. I say the jury has no more free will about it than I have. I could not help doing it. I cannot help giving them the reasons for doing what I think they ought to do. And, after they get the reasons sometimes they cannot help acting. I have seen them try awfully hard not to do it. There is no mystery about it at all.

Is there a single step anywhere in the process where there is any chance for what is generally called free will? Just try yourself once in a while. Watch people on the street. Stop a few minutes some day when there is a one-legged beggar taking up a collection. He appeals to the same emotional side of you as he does to everyone else. Everybody who passes sees the same thing. Some people give him something and some do not. What is the difference? Sometimes you give him something, and sometimes you do not. Why? Is there ever a time when there is not a reason? Sometimes you will pass him and come back. Why do you come back? Because you cannot get the fellow out of your mind; he bothers you. When you come back you can forget him. Is there anything else in it? Is there a chance for anything else being in it? You come back and give him a coin for exactly the same reason that I go to the dentist's; you get less pain by giving up the money than if you didn't do it, and had him on your mind all the the rest of the day. You do not give to relieve the beggar; you give to relieve yourself. If giving will not relieve you, then you will not give. That is the universal experience; everybody can see it every day on the streets. You may go by one day, and give another day. Why? Is there a reason for it? Well, one reason might be that you did not have the money. Another reason might be that you had seen the fellow before, and you thought it had come to be a habit with him. Another one might be, you had seen some others like him before; and another, that you were saving up your money to buy a Ford. There is a reason, anyway. Nobody can act without one. That does not mean that one acts through intellectual processes, but it means one balances up in one's mind the things that move one in one direction against the things that move the other way, and then acts according to the strongest urge.

I am glad to see in the talk of my able opponent here, that slowly the old idea of free will is getting out of the minds of the people who have minds. I am glad they are learning to see how far everybody is a creature of circumstances, and in the hands of what I might call "Fate." One need do nothing more than to examine oneself to know it: that is enough. Nobody can look over his own life and not understand why one wants this thing and that thing at the different cross-roads that mark one's path. All any one needs to do in judging others kindly is to use the same reasons in judging them as he uses in judging himself.

If man has anything that approaches free will then he stands alone in the universe. None would contend that the planets in their endless course go and come as they please. No one would contend that animal life below man has to any degree freedom of will or of choice. If man has anything else in him, he must be different from all the rest of the universe. Science and life, and what we know of things as they are, show that man is subject to all the laws and all the rules of control that govern everything else in the universe.

[Printed below are Darrow's comments in a discussion following his lecture.]

Mr. Smith said that I compared man with the Ford car. I did not mean to; I have nothing against the Ford car.

I happened to be in the country one summer where we had an electric pump. We had to use it to get dinner or a bath, if we wanted it, but every time we wanted to use it the thing would not work. When we did not, it would work all right. According to my light, that was the greatest example of free will I have ever seen. Somebody who understood electricity might have known why it would or would not run, and somebody who understands the principles of human conduct might know why man acts as he does.

What is this discussion about, anyway? My friend says we have a certain freedom to do what we want to do. This ought to be a discussion then as to whether a person has freedom to want to do something. Where does the desire come from? It comes from the constitution of the body and from the experiences in life, doesn't it? There is nowhere else to get it. It is wished on us. That goes to make up our desires. Now, that makes our desire, and then we have the freedom to do what we desire. I want to get my dinner when I am hungry. I have the freedom to get it because I want it, and I do get my dinner if I am where there is anything to eat. That is true. I am thirsty, and I want a drink. I have the freedom to get a drink if I can find anything. I have no control of my desire. That comes from something else. What you mean by freedom is the power to get it if you want it, and can get it. That is all it means. If I desire something and desire it strongly, I may try to get it. I may know how impossible it is and not waste energy on trying, but take some lesser desire that I might possibly be able to fulfil.

This is what Dr. Smith seems to mean; if I am in jail, and am weary, I may want to sleep. I find a cot and lie down and sleep. I do as I wish for there is nothing else to do. What I really wish is to get out of jail. Because we do as we wish it does not follow that we control ourselves. It needs no control to do as we wish. The act automatically follows the wish.

I wonder which one of us will win this debate? Have any of you got a clear idea of how much of conduct you can control? What is it that you can control? You can control yourself to do something that you want to do, if you can do it. Of course, an orthodox friend would say that was just the lack of controlling yourself because you never should do anything that you want to do because you could not go to heaven then. Dr. Smith found some fault with my statement of cause and effect, and perhaps he is right about it. We perhaps use those words rather carelessly. If there is a cause for what I do now, of course it follows logically that there was a cause for the cause, and a cause for that cause, and so on to the end—if there is an end—and there is no man who can follow it back to the end.

Is there any such thing as a cause? It seems to me perfectly plain that there is a sequence of events everywhere in life, and after one thing happens then another happens. It does not always follow that the events are in the direct relation of cause and effect, but usually they are so nearly so that we may call them cause and effect.

If I take hold of a wheelbarrow, which is standing perfectly still and behaving itself, and push it, it is perfectly plain that I am the immediate cause of the wheelbarrow moving. There are many things not so plain as that, but all of life and all of everything, so far as I know it, is a sequence of one thing following another thing in such a relation that it substantially amounts to cause and effect, if one can find the exact moving thing.

Suppose we had such a thing as free will? Suppose it was a universe of free will? Suppose there was no room for anything which—for lack of a better word—we call "law," then, what kind of a universe would we have? No one could be in the least sure of another's conduct.

My friend said that wisdom is an advantage, for it allows you to tell what you would do twenty years from now. How can you tell what you will do twenty years from now? No matter how much wisdom you might have, would it be possible to tell; except that you could foresee the events and sequences that would cause you to do special things?

If you believe in free will there is no chance to prophesy anything. If there was free will in the physical world and one sowed wheat it might take a notion to grow down to China instead of growing up! If there was free will, human beings would not know how one single motive would affect another. It would not be worth while to talk to them; they would not be influenced by talk. It would not be worth while to teach them; it would not change their conduct. After all, they would do as they pleased before they got through with it.

The whole world and all of life is built upon the theory of cause and effect, and ruled on the theory of mechanism, which only means this: That, so far as we can get at it, man is made of the same stuff as all of the rest of the universe. He has a somewhat different structure; but he acts and reacts according to stimuli; the stimuli outside of him, and the stimuli that become part of him from his experiences in life. There is nothing that exists without a cause, and there is nothing done without motive, and, therefore, you can, to a certain extent, bet on what will happen in the future, otherwise you could not even guess. Which is the most logical thing? And, after all, it is one of the subjects which, perhaps, is very difficult to prove. You may prove it in your own life as to why you did this and why you did that. Do any of you do anything without a cause? If you are a Christian would you be a Christian if you had been born in Turkey? If you are a Republican, would you have been that had you been born in Texas, or had intelligent parents, or anything like that? If you are a Methodist, how did that happen? If you are a Presbyterian, how did that happen? Did you do it yourself? No one in his own life ever explained himself in that way. Everyone gives a reason for his conduct. Everybody can show, probably, a number of things that caused them to do the things they have done. They may not show exactly, and they may not know exactly. But we know that there is no such thing as chance, unless it is the first great chance and of this we are too ignorant to know.

We never speak or think of freedom excepting as related to man, and, granting freedom, all animals and plants do as they wish and are the result of the wish.

I think that in the last analysis this question gets down to this proposition: Is it a monistic world? Is it one substance? Is it one force operating on all things? I fancy nobody would pretend that in the physical world, outside of man, there is any such thing as choice. The earth has gone around the sun, so far as I know, forever and ever, and keeps on acting without any reason, so far as I can discover. We are informed that man does something to control the environment, and we are told that the environment does much to control him; Man, like everything else, is born out of the environment and is a product of it, and until the time came that man could be born out of the environment there was no such thing as man. We are part of all of it. There is not a single thing in any part of the human being that we know anything about that you cannot buy at the drug-store. There is not a thing on the earth, so far as we know, that is not is found in the farthest planet that we can analyze. There is not a single thing in one form of animal life that is not in another. There is not a single thing in organic matter that is not in inorganic matter. So far as we can understand the universe, those various manifestations include human life; it is one thing and operates in the same way, in an endless succession of events under the relation of cause and effect, and if one believed in free will that belief would upset the scientific theory of the universe for him.

The Lord's Day Alliance

AMONG THE VARIOUS SOCIETIES that are engaged in the business of killing pleasure, the Lord's Day Alliance of New York deserves a place of honor. If any poor mortal is caught enjoying life on Sunday its agents gleefully hie themselves to the nearest legislature and urge a law to stop the fun. Their literature and periodicals tell very plainly the kind of business they are in. This association of crape-hangers seems to be especially interested in the State of New York, which contains about one-tenth of the population of the Union, and among them an unusually large number of foreigners and other heathen who have not been taught the proper regard for the sanctity of the Sabbath.

This essay appeared in *Plain Talk* 2 (March 1928): 257–70. It had been submitted to the *American Mercury*, but editor H. L. Mencken, although agreeing with most of its points, had reluctantly rejected it for being excessively harsh. It treats of the Lord's Day Alliance, a religious organization founded in 1888 as the American Sabbath Union in Washington, D.C., by delegates from Baptist, Methodist, Reformed Church, and United Presbyterian churches and devoted to lobbying for the passage of Sunday-rest laws. A parallel organization, the Lord's Day Alliance of Canada, was founded at the same time by the Reverend J. G. Shearer, who lobbied the Canadian government to pass the Lord's Day Act in Canada in 1906 (repealed 1985). Darrow uses the essay to condemn all Sunday laws as an unconstitutional violation of the First Amendment. It was an issue of long standing with him: one of his earliest published works was "Shall the World's Fair Be Open on Sunday?" (*Sunset Club Yearbook 1891–92* [Chicago: Sunset Club, 1893], p. 21). Darrow also exposes the harshness of his own Presbyterian upbringing, an issue he delicately avoids in *Farmington* (1904).

The activities of this Alliance in New York still leave them ample time to watch the sinners in the other states and bring to book the wicked who are bent on having pleasure on the holy Sabbath Day. In their own language, the work is "in the interests of the preservation and promotion of the Lord's Day as the American Christian Sabbath . . . to oppose all adverse measures seeking to weaken the law and to seek the passage of such measures as would tend to strengthen it." The Alliance informs us that "in the last four years it has furnished sixty-seven addresses per month, on an average. During this time over three hundred and twenty institute meetings have been held for the study of the Sabbath question. Several million pages of literature have been distributed." It "also furnishes press articles and syndicate matter for the newspapers." Imagine an institute spending so much time in the study of the Sabbath question! If they have learned anything on that subject it is not revealed in their tracts.

These Lord's Day folk seek to protect the day "in the interest of the home and the church," "to exalt Jesus Christ who is Lord of the Sabbath Day and to spread the knowledge of the will of God that His Kingdom may come and His will may be done." Though the organization is still young it points to a long list of glorious achievements. We are informed that "no adverse measure affecting the Sabbath has passed at Albany during this time, although forty-two such measures have been introduced in the legislature. . . . A representative of our organization has been present on each occasion to oppose any such adverse measures." It boasts that it "opposed the opening of the State Fair in 1925 on Sunday, by vigorous protest to the members of the Commission and the Attorney General." The result was a ruling from the Attorney General sustaining the law. Of course, so long as no one could go to the fair on Sunday the people were obliged to go to church. It "has defeated annually an average of forty commercial and anti-Sunday bills in our legislature and has brought about the closing of the First and Second-Class Post-Offices on Sunday. . . . As a result, thousands are in our churches each Sunday." It has been "thanked by President Coolidge for the services rendered hundreds of thousands of government employees in District of Columbia and elsewhere throughout the nation." What further honor could anybody get on earth? It has "accepted the challenge and in scores of places defeated . . . commercialized amusement forces which have declared a nation-wide fight to the finish for Sunday movies and are even proposing to enlist the aid of the churches in their unholy campaign." It succeeded in "changing the date of the gigantic air carnival to which admission was charged, from Sunday, August 2, to Saturday, August 1, 1925, held at Bolling Field, Washington." No one but a parson has the right to charge for his performance on Sunday. Through its request "the War Department issued orders on November 2, 1925, covering every military post in the United States, banning Sunday public air carnivals and maneuvers." It is "now leading a country-wide movement for the enactment of a Sunday rest law for the District of Columbia. Washington needs and must have a Sunday rest law." It informs us that the "day must be kept above the Dollar, Christ above Commercialism on the Lord's Day, the person must have the right of way over the Pocketbook on our American Sunday."

Surely this is a great work and deserves the active support and sympathy of all people who are really interested in driving pleasure-seekers from golf grounds, automobile trips, baseball parks, moving-picture houses and every other form of pleasure on Sunday. It is possible that for lack of any other place to go, some of them might be compelled to park themselves in church. If America does not succeed in bringing back the ancient Puritan Sabbath with its manifold blessings, it will not be the fault of the Lord's Day Alliance.

As a part of this noble work the organization publishes various pamphlets and leaflets and scatters them broadcast through the land. As a rule, these pamphlets are the effusions of more or less obscure parsons. These preachers have special knowledge of God's plans and God's will. Their sermonettes are conflicting in their statements and utterly senseless in their assertions. The sentries of the Alliance on guard at the state capitals and in the national Congress, while these wise bodies are in session, have no doubt succeeded in coercing spineless members of legislative bodies to yield to their will and their parade of votes; and thus spread considerable gloom over the United States on the Sabbath Day.

These Lord's Day Alliance gentlemen are not only religious but scientific. For instance, they publish a pamphlet written by one Dr. A. Haegler,[1] of Basle, Switzerland, in which he says that experiments have shown that during a day's work a laborer expends more oxygen than he can inhale. True, he catches up with a large part of this deficiency through the night time, but does not regain it all. It follows, of course, that if he keeps on working six days a week, for the same time each day, he will be out a considerable amount of oxygen, and the only way he can make it up is to take a day off on Sunday and go to church. This statement seems to be flawless to the powerful intellects who put out this literature. Any person who is in the habit of thinking might at once arrive at the conclusion that if the workman could not take in enough oxygen gas in the ordinary hours of work and sleep he might well cut down his day's work and lengthen his sleep and thus start even every morning. This ought to be better than running on a shortage of gas all through the week. Likewise, it must occur to most people that there are no two kinds of labor that consume the same amount of oxygen gas per day, and probably no two human systems that work exactly alike. Then, too, if the workman ran behind on his oxygen gas in the days when men worked from ten to sixteen hours a day he might break even at night, since working hours have been reduced to eight or less, with a Saturday half-holiday thrown in. It might even help the situation to raise the bedroom window at night. These matters, of course, do not occur to the eminent doctor who wrote the pamphlet and the scientific gentlemen who send it out. To them the silly statement proves that a man needs to take a day off on Sunday and attend church in order that he may catch up on his oxygen. To them it is perfectly plain that for catching up on oxygen the church has a great advantage over the golf links or the baseball park, or any other place where the wicked wish to go. This in spite of the fact that in crowded buildings the oxygen might be mixed with halitosis.

The exact proof that these parsons marshal for showing that the need of a Sunday rest is manifest in the nature of things is marvelous. If the need of Sunday rest was meant to be shown by natural law it seems as if this should have been clearly indicated, especially if the righteous God had determined to punish Sunday violations with death and hell. There was no reason why the Creator should have been content to leave the proof to a revelation said to have been made in a barbarous age to an unknown man, hidden in the clouds on the top of a high mountain peak. Humans would not have graven such an important message on a tablet of stone and then insisted that the tablet should be destroyed before any being except Moses had set eye upon it. Even God should not ask for faith that amounts to credulity and gross superstition.

A deity could have written the Sabbath requirements plain on the face of nature. For instance, he might have made the waves be still on the seventh day of the week; the grass might have taken a day off and rested from growing until Monday morning; the wild animals of the forest and glen might have refrained from fighting and eating and chasing and maiming and have been made to close their eyes on the Sabbath Day, and to have kept peace and tranquility. The earth might have paused in its course around the sun or stood still on its axis. It should have been as important to make this gesture in homage of the day as it was to help Joshua hold the sun in leash that a battle might be prolonged. If nature had made plain provision for the Sabbath Day it would be patent to others as well as to the medicine men who insist that the Sabbath Day was made for their profit alone.

BUT LET US PASS from the realm of science, where pastors never did especially shine, into a field where they are more likely to excel. Here it is fairly easy to see what it is all about. The Reverend McQuilkin,[2] Pastor at Orange, New Jersey, furnishes a pamphlet for The Lord's Day Alliance. Read what the Doctor says:

> God claims the Sabbath for himself in a very unique, distinctive way as a day of rest and worship. He again and again commands you to spend its hours in the conservation of our spiritual power in the exercise of public and private worship. To spend this holy day in pleasure or unnecessary secular labor

is to *rob God.* We have got to be careful how we take the hours of the Sabbath for secular study or work, for God will surely bring us to judgment concerning the matter. Church attendance is a definite obligation, a debt which we owe to God.

Here is where the Alliance seems to strike pay dirt! What reason has God to claim the Sabbath for Himself, and why is God robbed if a man should work on Sunday? It can hardly be possible that the puny insects that we call men could disturb God in His Sunday rest. Is it not a little presumptuous even to parsons, to say that a debt to the church is a debt to God?

To emphasize the importance of leaving the Sabbath to the preachers, we are warned of the fate of the sinner who profanes the Sabbath by work or play. The Lord's Day Alliance has issued a little folder on which there is the following heading in large letters: THE IMPORTANCE OF THE DEATH PENALTY. Under it is printed this timely caution: "Six days shall work be done, but on the seventh day is a Sabbath of solemn rest, holy to Jehovah; whosoever doeth any work on the Sabbath Day shall surely be put to death. Ex. 31–15." The pamphlet also states that a wealthy business man is furnishing the money for the distribution of this sheet. If this barbarous statement represents the views of the Lord's Day Alliance then what is the mental caliber of the Congressmen, members of the legislatures, judges, and the public that are influenced by their ravings? Can anyone but an idiot have any feeling but contempt for men who seek to scare children and old women with such infamous stuff?

Let us see what the Bible says on this important subject. In Exodus 19:8–12 we find not only the commandment which was delivered to Moses in reference to the Sabbath, but the reasons for such a commandment:

> Remember the Sabbath Day to keep it holy. Six days shalt thou labor and do all thy work; but the seventh day is the Sabbath of the Lord thy God. In it thou shalt do no work, thou, nor thy son, nor thy daughter, nor thy man servant nor thy maid ser-

vant nor thy cattle which is within thy gates; *for in six days the Lord made heaven and earth, the sea and all that is in them and rested the seventh day, wherefore the Lord blessed the Sabbath Day and hallowed it.*

It is plain from this commandment that the Sabbath was not instituted in obedience to any natural law or so that man might catch up on his supply of oxygen, but because the Lord in six days had performed the herculean task of creating the universe out of nothing, and took a day off to rest on the seventh. Therefore, every man must rest on the seventh, no matter whether he has been working and is tired or not. This is made even more binding in Exodus 35:2:

> Six days shall work be done; upon the seventh day there shall be to you a holy day, the Sabbath of the rest of the Lord. Whosoever doeth work therein shall be put to death.

In view of the commands of God, certainly his special agents on the earth cannot be blamed for cruelty, no matter what ferocious doctrine they may preach. In Numbers 28:9–10, in connection with various offerings that the Law required on the Sabbath, a provision is made for meat offerings and drink offerings. The meat offerings enjoin the sacrifice of lambs by fire as "a sweet savor unto the Lord," and then the Lord provides that the pastor shall further:

> Sacrifice on the Sabbath Day two lambs of first year without spot and two-tenths of a part of an ephah of fine flour for a meal-offering, mingled with oil and the drink offering thereof: this is the burnt-offering of every Sabbath, besides the continual burnt-offering and his drink offering.

It is evident that the lambs less than one year old, without spot, were to be burned because they were so young and innocent and would therefore make such a "sweet savor unto the Lord." Nothing is lacking in this smell but mint sauce. If Moses is to be obeyed on pain of hell in his command to abstain from work or play on the Sabbath why is the rest of the program any less sacred? How can the holy parsons release their congregations from the sacrifice of the two spotless lambs and the two-tenths of an ephah of fine flour mingled with oils?

IN THE FIFTEENTH CHAPTER of Numbers, it is related that while the children of Israel were in the wilderness they found a man gathering sticks on the Sabbath Day. The Hebrews were evidently at a loss to know what should be done with him for this most heinous offense, so they put him in "ward" to await the further orders of the Lord. It is then related, "and the Lord said unto Moses: The man shall surely be put to death; all the congregation shall stone him with stones without the camp. And all the congregation brought him without the camp and stoned him to death with stones: *as Jehovah commanded Moses.*"[3] In spite of manifold texts like this there are persons who protest that they love this bloody, barbarous, tribal God of the Jews. The literature of the Alliance clearly indicates that its sponsors would follow this command of Jehovah at the present time if they could only have their way.

Dr. McQuilkin further tells us that the defenders of the day have often been too superficial in their contentions on behalf of this holy Sabbath; that they should soft-pedal the "thou shalt nots" and "we should thunder our 'thou shalts' into the ears of the foolish, wicked men who for the sake of pleasure or financial profit would rob their fellow men or themselves of the precious rest God had given them for the cultivation and nurture of their immortal souls. Such men," he continues, "must be identified with murderers and suicides." The common punishment for murder is death, and suicide *is* death, therefore Dr. McQuilkin, with the rest of his associates and with his God, believes in the death penalty for working or playing on the Sabbath.

How one involuntarily loves this righteous Dr. McQuilkin of Orange, New Jersey. He must be a man whose love and understanding oozes from every pore of his body. No doubt the people of Orange who are burdened with sorrow or sin bring their sore troubles and lay them on his loving breast. I am sure that little children in their grief rush to his outstretched arms for solace and relief.

THE REVEREND DOCTOR MCQUILKIN makes short work of the idea that you cannot make people good by law. In fact, that seems to him to be the only way to make them good. Therefore people and enterprises that commercialize Sundays by baseball games and moving pictures, who "whine about the impossibility of making people good by law, ought to go either to school or to jail." Probably the pastor would be in favor of the jail. The Reverend Doctor is very much exercised about his idea that the Sabbath should be spent in cultivating our "spiritual nature." From the gentle and kindly character of the doctor's utterances, one judges that he must spend several days a week cultivating his "spiritual nature."

The godly doctor is indeed earnest about the church-going. He says, "God will surely bring us to judgment in the matter of staying away from church, for church attendance is a definite obligation, a debt which we owe to God." The doctor has a naïve way of mixing up himself and his private business affairs with the Lord.

Could it be possible that the Reverend Doctor McQuilkin's serious case of rabies might be due to vacant pews? Such cases are related in the following extract from a very disheartening paragraph put out by the Lord's Day Alliance in a folder entitled "Let's Save Our American Christian Sabbath."

> A significant part of this falling away from old American ideals has been the neglect of the churches—life among Christian people dropping to a lower plane on Sunday. The lure of pleasure and the drift to seven-day slavery within a few years have utterly changed the character of the day. The average attendance at Sunday morning services, taken for all the churches of New York State—counting large city churches as well as small country ones—has steadily dropped until it has now reached only *fifty-three* persons. This amounts to but little more than

one fourth of their total enrolled membership! The old days of tithes are gone! Lack of support is making the situation more and more critical and many churches have had to be abandoned. Is the church to survive? *Are we to remain a Christian nation?*

This is indeed distressing. I can well imagine the feeling of chagrin that steals over the parson when he talks to fifty persons on a Sunday morning. Here are the few parishioners, solemn-visaged and sitting impatiently in their pews while a joyous crowd rolls by in automobiles on their road to hell. I cannot help thinking of the parson on a Sunday morning, telling the same story over and over again to his half hundred listeners.

I have seen this pastor and this congregation in the country church and the city church. What have they in common with the world today? Who are these faithful fifty? One-third of them, at least, are little boys and girls, twisting and turning and yawning and fussing in their stiff, uncomfortable clothes, in the hard church pews. Then there are the usual fat old women, wearing their Sunday finery. Their faces are dull and heavy and altogether unlovely. They no longer think of the world; they are looking straight into space at the Promised Land. They hold a hymn book or a Bible in their time-worn hands. Perhaps there are ten full grown men in church; two or three of these look consumptive; one or two are merchants who think that being at church will help them sell prunes; the rest are old and tottering. It has been long years since a new thought or even an old one has found lodgment in their atrophied brains. They are decrepit and palsied and done; so far as life and the world are concerned, they are already dead. One feels sympathetic toward the old. But why should the aged, who have lived their lives, grumble and complain about youth with its glow and ambition and hope? Why should they sit in the fading light and watch the world go by and vainly reach out their bony hands to hold it back?

Aside from the Lord's Day Alliance's way of appealing to the law to make people go to church, I can think of only two plans to fill the pews.

First, to abandon a large number of the churches and give the parsons a chance to find some useful and paying job. Secondly, to get more up-to-date, human and intelligent preachers into the church pulpits.

THE LITERATURE ISSUED BY the Alliance shows great concern about Sunday newspapers. These papers consume a great deal of valuable time on the Sabbath Day. They are in no way the proper literature for Sunday reading. Automobile trips, too, are an abomination on the Sabbath. One pamphlet records approval of the conduct of the "venerable" John D. Paton who even refused to use street-cars on Sunday while visiting in America.[4] He kept his appointments by long walks, sometimes even having to run between engagements. This sounds to me strangely like work. Still it might have been necessary in order to get the proper amount of oxygen gas.

Playing golf on Sunday is a sacrilegious practice. A whole leaflet is prepared by Dr. Jefferson on golf.[5] "No one ought to play golf on Sunday. . . . The golf player may need oxygen but he should not forget his caddie." The doctor calls our attention to the fact that men in the days of Moses were mindful of even the least of these. How our parsons do love Moses and his murderous laws! We are told that a caddie works, that it is not play to trudge after a golf ball with a bag of clubs on his back. The leaflets say that the caddie does not work on Sunday for fun but for money, and it "isn't a manly thing for the golf player to hire him to work on Sunday." We are told that "there are now over one hundred thousand caddies on the golf links every Sunday. These caddies are making a living." Of course this picture is pathetic. It is too bad that the Lord's Day Alliance cannot get these hundred thousand caddies discharged. Then possibly some of them would go to church on Sunday. They might even drop a nickel in the contribution box.

Does anyone believe that if the caddies were offered the same money for going to church that they get for hunting golf balls they would choose the church? It takes a bright boy to be a caddie.

The caddies do not inspire all the tears; we are told that chauffeurs and railroad employees are necessary to take the players to and from the golf links. This no doubt true. Still, we have seen chauffeurs sitting in automobiles outside a church where they had driven their employers to get their souls saved. On our suburban railroads there are many trains put in service on Sunday to take people to and from church, but these have not come under the ban of the Lord's Day Alliance. Its complaint is that so few trains are needed for this blessed work.

There is some logic in this folder. We are told that "if golf is allowable on Sunday, then, so is tennis, baseball, basketball, football, bowling and all other games which our generation is fond of." "You can't forbid one without forbidding the others," says the Alliance. We heartily agree with the Reverend Doctor on this particular question.

No one needs to go to ball games or movies or play golf on Sunday unless he wants to spend his time that way. I have never seen anybody who objected to the members of the Lord's Day Alliance or any others from abstaining from all kinds of work and all sorts of play and every method of enjoyment on Sunday.

DR. ROBERT E. SPEER[6] of Englewood, New Jersey, is very definite and specific as to the proper way to spend Sunday and the sort of recreation man should naturally enjoy on this holy day. Dr. Speer says, "God wants the worship of the Lord's Day and he wants us to have the indispensable comforts and pleasure of it." One would think that Dr. Speer got daily messages from God. "We need the day for meditation and prayer and plans for better living." No one questions the good doctor's right to satisfy his needs in such way as seems necessary and pleasurable for him. All that I contend for is that I, too, shall decide these questions for myself.

Dr. Speer says:

> There are some things deadly in their power to spoil it (referring to the Sabbath). One is the Sunday newspapers. . . . I pass by all that may be denounced as defiling in it. . . . There is harm enough in its "wallow of secularity." . . . Look at the men who feed their minds and souls on Sunday with this food. They miss the calm and holy peace, the glowing divinity of the day.

It is just conceivable that one might read a Sunday newspaper and still have time for "the glowing divinity of the day," to glow long enough to satisfy every desire.

DR. SPEER CONDEMNS THOSE who berate the quality of the sermons preached on Sunday and informs us that the wisest man can learn something from the poorest preacher, although he neglects to say just what. He tells us that a country preacher's sermon is superior to the country editor's writings or the country lawyer's speeches. This may be true. It is, at all events, true to Dr. Speer, and there is no reason in the world why he should not hunt up the "poorest preacher" that he can find and listen to him on every Sunday. No doubt Dr. Speer might learn something from him.

Dr. Speer disapproves of riding on railroad trains on Sunday if it can be avoided. "Certainly no one should take long railroad journeys on Sunday." He tells us, "Sunday golf, newspapers, and all that sort of thing are bad and weakening in their influence. These are particular evidence of the trend of the man who thus abandons his birthright." The doctor is more definite in his beautiful picture of just what one ought to do on the Sabbath Day. On this subject he says:

> I do not believe that anyone who grew up in a truly Christian home in which the old ideas prevailed can have any sympathy with this modern abuse of the old-fashioned observance of Sunday. There, on Sunday, the demands of the week were laid aside. The family gathered over the Bible and the Catechism. There was a quiet calm through the house. Innumerable things rendered it a marked day, as distinct from other days, and probably it ended with a rare walk with the father at the son's side and some sober talk over what is abiding and what is of eternal worth.

We could hazard a guess that the reason that the mother was not present on this joyful occasion was because she was at home washing the dishes from a big Sunday dinner that she had prepared.

IT IS ENTIRELY POSSIBLE that Dr. Speer's picture of the ideal Sabbath is a good picture. Doubtless it is good to him. Still, hidden in my mind and recalled by Dr. Speer's alluring language, is the memory of his ideal Presbyterian Sunday. This was a day of unmitigated pain. No spirit of life or joy relieved the boredom and torture of the endless hours. The day meant misery to all the young. Even now I can feel the blank despair that overcame youth and hope as we children left our play on Saturday night and sadly watched the sun go down and the period of gloom steal across the world. Why should Dr. Speer and the other dead seek to force that sort of a Sabbath upon men and women who want to take in their oxygen gas in the baseball bleachers, or the golf links?

FROM DR. SPEER'S PICTURE of the ideal Sabbath I infer that he is a Presbyterian. This opinion has been confirmed by reference to *Who's Who*. I find that for long years he has been a Presbyterian preacher, not only in America, but he has carried the blessed gospel even into China that the heathen of that benighted land might not live and die without the consoling knowledge of eternal hell.

Dr. Speer's beautiful picture of the old-time Christian Sabbath describes "the family gathered over the Bible and the Catechism." I, too, sat under the ministrations of a Presbyterian preacher and was duly instructed in the Westminster Catechism.[7] In spite of the aversion and terror that its reference inspired, I took down the book to read once more the horrible creed of the twisted and deformed minds who produced this monstrosity which has neither sense, meaning, justice nor mercy, but only malignant depravity. A devilish creed which shocks every tender sentiment of the human mind. I am inclined to think from their internal evidence that most of the sermonettes circulated by the Lord's Day Alliance had their origin in the warped minds of the Presbyterian clergy. I would hazard a bet that the tender, gentle, loving Dr. McQuilkin is a Presbyterian. I sought to confirm this belief by consulting *Who's Who*, but found that the editors had stupidly left out his name. Still I am convinced that he is a Presbyterian.

IN THIS ANCIENT WESTMINSTER Catechism which few men read I quote question and answer number sixty:

> QUESTION: How is the Sabbath to be sanctified?
> ANSWER: The Sabbath is to be sanctified by a holy resting all that day, even from such worldly employments and recreations as are lawful on other days; and spending the whole time in public and private exercises of God's worship, except so much as is to be taken up in the works of necessity and mercy.

Small wonder that these croakers should seek to call children from joy and laughter to spend "the *whole time* in public and private exercises of God's worship." The wonder is not that these Divines should seek to place their palsied hands upon the youth but that an intelligent people, who really do not worship a God of malignancy and hate, would ever let these lovers of darkness invade a legislative body. They have no more place in the sunlight and pure air than croaking frogs and hooting owls. Here is the first question and answer in this wondrous catechism:

> QUESTION: What is the chief end of man?
> ANSWER: Man's chief end is to glorify God and to enjoy Him forever.

What sort of a God is this in which these parsons believe? A God who can find no other work for man and no other use for the emotions that nature placed in him, except to spend his life in glorifying His maker? Imagine taking a child from play and the life and activity that nature has made necessary for its being, and seeking to make him understand something that no preacher can possibly comprehend.

AGAIN, AS TO THE simple nature of the God-head, the catechism says: "There are three persons in the God-head; the Father, the Son and the Holy Ghost; and these three are one God, the same in substance, equal in power and glory." Imagine a family spending the whole Sabbath unravelling a mystery like this. It is evident that any child whose mind has been permanently twisted by this wondrous logic would later be found visiting legislative bodies and imploring them to pass laws to blot the sun from the sky on the Sabbath Day.

Here is Number 7:

> QUESTION: What are the decrees of God?
> ANSWER: The decrees of God are His eternal purpose according to the counsel of His will, whereby, for His own glory, He has fore-ordained whatsoever comes to pass.

After the child had been made to thoroughly understand how to harmonize freedom and the responsibility of man with the statement that God had foreordained whatever comes to pass, he might then on pain of hell tackle number 8:

> QUESTION: What is the work of creation?
> ANSWER: The work of the creation is God's making all things of nothing, by word of His power, in the space of six days, and all very good.

Any child could understand how God, as the catechism says, is a "spirit" and could make all things out of nothing, Himself included. God's justice to man is lucidly explained in the Westminister Catechism which tells the Sabbath Day student that "the sin whereby our first parents fell from the estate wherein they were created, was their eating the forbidden fruit."

Question 16 and answer make this a living issue:

> QUESTION: Did all mankind fall in Adam's first transgression?
> ANSWER: The covenant being made with Adam, not only for himself, but for his posterity, all mankind descending from him by ordinary generation, sinned in him, and fell with him, in his first transgression.

The answer to the seventeenth question says: "The fall brought mankind into an estate of sin and misery."

There are thousands of generations between the first man, if there ever was one, and the boy who likes activity and play on the Sabbath Day. Unless the boy is perverse and wicked he should understand the justice of being condemned to an estate of sin and misery because Adam made a covenant, not only for himself, but for all his posterity. It is not worth while to quote further from the Westminster Catechism. This brutal creed runs on for 107 questions and answers. And this is the *shorter* catechism!

It is amazing to think that any human being with ordinary intelligence would accept such doctrine now. It is still more amazing that in spite of the brazen effrontery of the Lord's Day Alliance, legislative bodies should help to enforce such teaching upon the young. But even this is not sufficiently terrible for a Sabbath Day diversion. In answer to Question 19 we are told, "All mankind by their fall lost communion with God, are under His wrath and curse, and so made liable to all the miseries in this life, to death itself, and to the pains of hell forever." Of course, no one would believe this today except on fear of eternal torture. Does the fear never enter the minds of these parsons that God might punish them eternally for believing that He is such a monster?

WHEN ONE THINKS OF this organization with its senseless leaflets, its stern endeavors, its blank despair, its half-shut eyes blinking at life, one is reminded of the frogs in the green scum-covered pond in the woods who sit on their haunches in the dark and croak all day. No doubt these frogs believe that the germ infested pond is a sacred pool. They are oblivious of the rolling, living ocean that lies just beyond.

Dr. Speer, like all the other members of the Lord's Day Alliance, is very sure that one of the chief occupations of Sunday should be attending church. But what church, pray? We are informed that any preacher is better to listen to and read from than any editor, lawyer or other person. Most of us have heard all sorts of preachers. We have listened to some whose churches could only be filled if the Lord's Day Alliance should succeed and make it an offense punishable by death not to go to church. We have heard preachers who had something to say and could say it well. There is as much difference in the views and ability of preachers as in other men. Would Dr. Speer think that we should go to hear the Fundamentalists or the Unitarians? Should we listen to the Holy Rollers or the Modernists?

There are few men outside of the Lord's Day Alliance who would care to listen to their favorite preacher for a *full day* and there are few preachers who would undertake to talk for a whole day. What, then, must one do for the rest of the time? One simply cannot sleep *all* day on Sunday.

IN ALL THIS LITERATURE we are constantly urged to preserve our "American Sabbath." Is there any special holiness that lurks around an "American Sabbath"? Are not European Christians as competent to determine the right way to employ their time on Sundays as American Christians? The Lord's Day folk say that reading the Sunday newspapers, playing golf, riding in automobiles, and witnessing baseball games and movies is "un-American." This compound word has been used to cover a multitude of sins. What it means nobody knows. It is bunkum meant to serve every cause, good and bad alike. By what license does the Lord's Day Alliance call its caricature of Sunday an "American Sabbath"? On what grounds does it urge it as against the European Sabbath? Is this nightmare which the Lord's Day Alliance is so anxious to force upon the United States a product of America? Everyone knows that Sunday, with the rest of the Christian religion, came to us from Europe. The weird ideas of the Lord's Day Alliance are European. When and how it came to us is worth finding out.

Jesus and His disciples did not believe in the Jewish Sabbath. They neither abstained from work nor play. St. Paul, specially, condemned the setting apart of days and said to his disciples, "Ye observe days and months and times and years. I am afraid of ye lest I have bestowed upon ye labor in vain."[8]

The early fathers did not approve of any such day as the Lord's Day Alliance insists shall be fastened upon America. St. Jerome and his group attended church services on Sunday, but otherwise pursued their usual occupations. St. Augustine calls Sunday a festal day and says that the Fourth Commandment is in no literal sense binding upon Christianity.[9] Even Luther and Calvin enjoined no such a day upon the Christians as these moderns wish to fasten upon America that the churches may be filled. The righteous John Knox "played bowls" on Sunday, and in his voluminous preaching used no effort to make Sunday a day of gloom wherein people should abstain from work and play. It was not until 1595 that an English preacher of Suffolk first insisted that the Jewish Sabbath should be maintained.[10] The controversy over this question lasted for a hundred years and resulted in a law proscribing every kind of Sunday recreation, even "vainly and profanely walking for pleasure."[11] England soon reacted against this blue Sabbath and permitted trading, open theatres and frivolity in the afternoon and evening. Under the leadership of the Church of England the Sabbath no longer was a day of gloom and despair.

THE REAL AMERICAN SABBATH was born in Scotland after the death of John Knox. It fits the stern hills, the bleak moors and the unfriendly climate of this northern land. It was born of fear and gloom and it lives by fear and gloom. Early in the Seventeenth Century, Scotland adopted this stern theory of the Jewish Sabbath and applied it ruthlessly. The Westminster Confession was adopted by the General Assembly of the Kirk of Scotland in 1647 and has remained the formal standard of faith to the present day. Ordinary recreations were disallowed. Books and music were forbidden except such as were recognized as religious in a narrow sense. No recreation but whiskey-drinking remained. This Presbyterian Sabbath of Scotland was brought to New England by the early settlers of America and is, in fact, a Scotch Sabbath—not an American Sabbath.

Even in spite of the natural gloom and cold of Scotland, Sunday strictness has been greatly modified there in the last fifty years. It is not the present Scotch Sabbath that these modern Puritans insist on forcing upon America. It is the old, ferocious, Scotch Sabbath of the Westminster Confession. It was brought from a land of gloom into a land of sunshine, and the Lord's Day Alliance prefers the gloom and hardness of this outworn, out-lived Scotch Sabbath to the sunshine and joy that comes with a fertile soil, a mild climate and natural human emotions.

IT IS ALMOST UNBELIEVABLE that a handful of men without reason or humanity should be able to force their cruel dogmas upon the people. Not one in twenty of the residents of the United States believes in the Sabbath of the Lord's Day Alliance. Our cities, villages, and even country districts, protest against the bigotry and intolerance of the Lord's Day Alliance and their kind. Still, in spite of this, by appeal to obsolete statutes, religious prejudice, crass ignorance and unfathomable fanaticism, they carry on their mighty campaign of gloom.

After long years of effort, with the lazy, cowardly public that does not want to be disturbed, the Legislature of New York, in the face of the opposition of the Lord's Day Alliance, managed to pass a law providing that incorporated cities and towns should have the right to legalize baseball games and moving picture shows on Sunday after two o'clock in the afternoon and charge an admission fee for seeing the entertainment. Why after two o'clock? The answer is perfectly plain: It is possible that someone might be forced into church in the morning if there was nowhere else to go. Were the hours after two o'clock any less sacred in the laws of Moses and the prophets than the hours before two o'clock? Or was the Legislature induced to pass this law simply to give the minister a privilege that it grants to no one else?

Ours is a cosmopolitan country, made up of all sorts of people with various creeds. There should be room enough to allow each person to spend Sunday and every other day according to his own pleasure and his own profit. In spite of the Lord's Day Alliance and all other alliances, it is too late in the history of the world to bring back the Mosaic Sabbath. Regardless of their best endeavors it will probably never again be a crime punishable by death to work or play on what they are pleased to call the Lord's Day. Those ministers who have something to say that appeals to men and women will be able to make themselves heard without a law compelling people to go to church. If the Lord's Day Alliance can provide something equally attractive to compete with the Sunday newspapers, golf, baseball games, movies and the open air, they will get the trade. If they cannot provide such entertainment, then in spite of all their endeavors the churches will be vacant. It is time that those who believe in tolerance, and in freedom, should make themselves heard in no uncertain way. It is time that men should determine to defend their right to attend to their own affairs and live their own lives, regardless of the bigots who in all ages have menaced the welfare of the world and the liberty of man.

Why I Have Found Life Worth Living

THE TOPIC ASSIGNED FOR discussion is not one which I would choose. I am by no means a professional optimist. The only proof that I can see for finding life worth living is that I have always tried to avoid dissolution. However, this is by no means a human quality. Every animal, plant and organism is imbued with "the will to live." This "will to live" is automatically a part of a going machine. The answer to the question on an intellectual plane is not necessarily the same as an answer that is founded on the emotion to live. Looking back over a long span of years, it is probably difficult for most men to say that their lives have been worth while. In spite of this the emotions that are part of the human organism are ever urging men to seek pleasure and avoid pain, which means to live.

In the ordinary meaning of the word, I am not an optimist. I have never listened with any great sympathy to the expression: "God is in His Heaven; and all is well with the world."[1] If there is such a condition in the universe as right and wrong, then all is not right with the world.

This essay appeared in the *Christian Century* 45 (April 19, 1928): 504–5. It addresses a topic that Darrow broached on a number of occasions: how to justify continued existence under a generally pessimistic view of life. See, e.g., *Pessimism: A Lecture* (1920; rpt. in *Verdicts out of Court*, pp. 280–94). The subject is also treated in Darrow's discussions of such writers as Omar Khayyam and A. E. Housman: see "A Persian Pearl" (on Khayyam), in *A Persian Pearl and Other Essays* (1899), and *Facing Life Fearlessly: The Pessimistic versus the Optimistic View of Life* (1929?), a lecture on Khayyam and Housman.

Right and wrong are simply human conceptions and as such both right and wrong are incident to life. It matters not what one's creed may be nor how loudly he proclaims his belief in ethical conduct, all men act from the same motives. Animal organisms are like seeds in the ground that instinctively turn toward the light and warmth. Probably man consciously and directly tries to make life worth living more obviously than other animal and vegetable life. What we are pleased to call the lower orders do not seem to be wasting their time asking perplexing questions and discussing right and wrong, but do their best to enjoy the present regardless of any fear of future pain or ultimate dissolution. Man's experience has taught him that no matter how much satisfaction he gets in life, "still the game is soon over and the puppet is laid away."[2] He has studied to protect himself against disquieting fears and obvious facts by believing that death is not death, and that, in some mysterious way which no one can possibly understand, he will live in some future form where joy will be more abundant and pain less common and severe.

No doubt this dream has done much to make life happier for human beings. It is a common precept and an everyday statement that if there is nothing in life except the manifestations which we see and know as we live in the body, then it is not worth while. This view seems to be generally accepted, for men have made heaven and hell from their hopes and fears. No one living can give any tangible reason for this belief which would even be considered in any affair of life. Still, it is probable that if man gave up this dream he might adjust himself to his brief period of activity, to be followed by an endless sleep.

I speak as one who has rather reluctantly let go of any hope of existence beyond death; as one who feels fully convinced that personal consciousness ends at the grave, and, strange as it might seem to some, this feeling which is as strong as any conviction that I hold, gives me no apprehension, terror nor despair. I find that at seventy I am scarcely conscious that the end grows near. I find that the things which I still desire and enjoy furnish me the same pleasure in their anticipation as they did when I was young.

Every person automatically forms some philosophy of life. He may not formulate this philosophy as an intellectual process, but he cannot live without carrying with his life a conscious or unconscious philosophy of living. I am convinced that the common statement is true; that to make life tolerable, one must work almost unceasingly. This does not necessarily mean manual toil, or even intellectual labor, but it means more or less conscious adaptation of means to an end. It means that one cannot walk nor run nor live without the feeling that he is going toward some goal. At the base of this commonly accepted idea there is to my mind the real philosophy of life.

The bald statement that life would be intolerable without work might seem like a confession that life was not worth living. I know of no religious conception of a future life which visualizes work as being the means of enjoyment in a celestial land. Why then is work, or rather, activity, after all, the true philosophy of life and the only thing that makes life worth living? The reason seems to be that in effect one loses his consciousness by his intense interest in some result to be achieved. It is true that the result hoped for or expected may be of little consequence. The possession may bring no satisfaction nor furnish any emotion. But this does not change the fact. The aim of the activity is only completely satisfactory when one, as it were, loses his identity through his interest in accomplishing a result. Hard work, which I interpret to mean an intense interest in some object to be accomplished, leads to an automatic life. And, after all, the automatic life is the fullest, the least painful and most enjoyable that human beings can comprehend.

Most people, who have grown weary with the burden and toil of the day, turn to sleep as the highest satisfaction that the human organism can achieve. It is the highest because in sleep the individual forgets himself. The man is unconscious of living. Existence under those circumstances is purely automatic and the subject has no opportunity for disturbing the workings of his organism by regrets and pains and fears. If intense work means practically loss of self-consciousness and if an automatic existence is good, then sleep is still better, and death is best of all. I am inclined to think that if a hundred people were to be asked the reason why they have found that life is worth living, ninety of them at least would use words that have no meaning, or that convey some fantastic dream, or they would give reasons which have no basis whatever in fact and human experience. Most of them would base their optimism upon some theory that is purely a figment of the mind.

If the question were asked, What makes life worth living, some would say it was the abiding hope of heaven; others that it was the thorough consciousness that the world is getting better; still others would base their conclusions on the belief in eternal progress. Some would almost religiously assert that their conviction that there was a soul in the universe was all-sufficient. No doubt a large number of the people who inhabit the earth would base the worthwhileness of existence on the belief that somewhere in the universe they would once more meet loved ones who had gone before. They would base their belief in life upon this theory quite regardless of the fact that they were building on a dream or guess and that the universe furnishes not a shred of evidence that their ideas or their dreams have the slightest foundation in fact.

It is plain that one's dreams alone might justify one's optimism. There are many people who are thoroughly happy in a padded cell. The ideas and conduct that impress everyone else with their insanity, are to them the greatest realities in life. Perhaps they are right. No one knows. Sane people, when they come to dealing in futures, believe practically everything that is common to the inmates of the padded cells. For me, I can only answer the question from my own standpoint. The path behind me is very much longer than the path before. Intellectually, I know this perfectly well. Emotionally, it seldom enters my head. I have unconsciously and perhaps even consciously tried to make life worth while by seeking to work out my strongest emotions. I have sought to make life worth while by following my abiding convictions, by the deep and compelling effort to use my energies to accomplish ends that emotionally, at least, seemed worth while to me.

In this way, seventy years have passed by with scarcely a consciousness of living. A deep interest, a strong emotion, an appealing cause, have made me forget the machinery of existence in view of the ends that I have always tried to reach. This, too, may be a dream. It really means living on futures. Intellectually, I am quite certain that the things I have desired the most and the dreams I have clung to with the greatest tenacity, will never come to pass. But, I have lived in these dreams and emotions. I have lived in them so strongly that I have been practically unconscious of life. And the fact that I have measurably succeeded by this means in negating life itself has made existence tolerable and on the whole worth while.

Is There a Purpose in the Universe?

I WANT TO FIRST compliment my friend for his scholarly and philosophical handling of this question. If he had known less about it, and had more faith, he would be easier to combat.

I don't really care much whether he is right or wrong. I sometimes do. But I must find a little fault: I have the negative of this question, he has the affirmative. He says there is a general purpose in the universe or we have reason to think so. I deny it. Now, while I am a lawyer, I am not a picayunish one, I don't care anything about technicalities.

However, if one says that there is a purpose in the universe, it seems to me that he ought to tell us what that purpose is, or give us some sort of an idea of it. I would terribly hate to tell an audience that there is a purpose in this universe, and not tell them what it is; and so far we have had no light on that subject. Of course, there is a reason for it: he cannot give it. There are other men much more ignorant than he is, however, who can tell what the purpose is.

Now, I would really be glad to know if there is a purpose in the universe, how do you know it, and what is it? We haven't heard. I will admit

This item is a debate published as *Wishart-Darrow Debate* (Grand Rapids, MI: Extension Club of Grand Rapids, 1928); the title has been supplied by the editor. Alfred Wesley Wishart (1865–1933) was a Baptist minister and pastor at the Central Church in Trenton, New Jersey (1895–1906) and the Fountain Street Church in Grand Rapids, Michigan (1906–33). He was the author of *Primary Facts in Religious Thought* (1905), *Evolution and Religion* (1923), and other works.

that there are men who claim to be scientists that are not mechanists; there are preachers that are not evolutionists, too; there are scientists who are not scientists, there are scientists who are side-steppers, just as a man may belong to church to sell prunes, and still not believe in them. There are scientists and scientists. I would like to have some of these eminent scientists say what they mean. What does Mr. Millikan say there is?[1] What does Mr. Conklin, whom I know very well, say there is in life, but mechanism?[2] What does he say the purpose is in the universe? He knows nothing whatever about any purpose in the universe, and I never found where he says so.

Of course, there are differences of opinion among scientists and all other people. If a list of names [were] counted, I would give him Darwin, I would give him Spencer, and Huxley, and Tyndall, and Loeb, and Crile,[3] and any amount of others whose names I could mention. This does not prove that my friend is wrong; this is not a question of authority, it is a question of what reasons can be found to support the different sides of this question.

The word "purpose" implies a purposer, doesn't it? There is no purpose without a purposer, and a purposer means a mind and intellect. Therefore it must follow, if there is a purpose in the universe and back of it all, and above it all, creating it all, there is some individual, or some power that has mind, intellect. And nobody ever had any experience of mind without body. Mind cannot exist, so far as anything that is known is concerned, mind cannot exist without a brain, a nervous organism, and these in turn cannot exist without a stomach and food and all the paraphernalia that goes with living.

On this question of a purposer, or a purpose, especially a purposer, I am simply an agnostic. I haven't yet had time or opportunity to explore the universe, and I don't know what I might run on to in some nook or corner. I simply say there is not a syllable of evidence in the world to sustain any such proposition, not a syllable.

If there is a purpose in the universe, where is it, and how is it shown, and what is it? I know what the religious man says. That the purpose back of it is a God, that you spell with a capital "G." We know his origin and his history, how he came into the universe, and when and where, and his various modifications, we know all that, and that the universe is created, and human beings are created for some general purpose. What? Some of them say "going to heaven, that ought to be enough," or "going to hell, that ought to be enough." It was all done for some general purpose.

I insist that there is not a scrap of evidence of purpose anywhere in the universe. There may be some, there may be a purposer, but he is hidden out of the universe, and he has made no manifestation whatever. I expected my friend to argue from design and various other outlined ideas that there must be somebody back of it all, or something back of it all. Now, mind, I don't say there isn't, I say there is no evidence of it, anywhere, no evidence.

Although my learned friend is a very good scientist, he has made at least one glaring mistake here. Probably I will make more, so I won't have anything on him. He separates man from the rest of the universe. There is only one difference that I know of between man and the other animals. We write books. If the flies could write books they would say to the housewife, "get dinner for us." If the crocodile wrote books there would be nothing so beautiful as crocodiles. If the birds wrote books, it would be perfectly clear that they are the most important things in the universe, because they can sail up in the air without a flying appliance. We are given to writing books and bragging, therefore we are different.

Now my friend says he is an evolutionist, and he is. I am glad to know it. Everybody is who thinks and studies. I doubt if there is a scientist in the world today who is not an evolutionist, not one. Then how does he get the idea that man is any different from the rest, excepting in degree? He says there is nature and there is man. Oh, no, there is not. You might as well say there is nature and there is wood-lice; or there is nature and there are stones, there is nature and there is grass; just exactly as well. Man is a part of nature, one of the products of nature, and he came here just like every other living organism, no different. So if there is any purpose in man, there must be a purpose in flies, too, and mosquitoes. I never found any purpose in mosquitoes, except to sting us.

I never found any general purpose in it, neither is there, as far as we can get any light on it.

We have to use such mind as we have and ask ourselves what the reasons are for believing this, that and the other. Man does nothing that is not done by other animals, so far as we can see, and so far as we can know. The higher apes plainly think and reason, not perhaps as much as this audience, not much more than fundamentalists perhaps, but they think, and they reason. If you read of the experiments with a chimpanzee—put him in a cage, and put some food where he cannot reach it, put two boxes in the cage, he will try by getting on top of one box to reach the food, and if he cannot do that, he will use the other until he reaches it. Or put it a little out of reach and put a stick in the cage, and after trying he will use the stick to drag it in.

I was down to the anthropological—no, I mean the zoo, I mean the zoo where they keep the lower animals, I have always been in the other— I was down in the zoo in New York, and there was one old, wise chimpanzee there that would rake in things with a pole, who had learned from necessity, exactly the way man learns, if at all, and he attracted the attention of the crowd. He would shake hands with everybody that came along, just like the rest of us, although we may not be quite so democratic. He received attention, and gave the plainest evidence of enjoyment of it. The crowd lingered with the chimpanzee for a little while. They recognized him as their cousin, if not a brother; the poor chimpanzee could not help it if we thought he was a relative of ours.

Then we passed on, and got on a little way, and then we heard a terrific din in that direction, a terrible hammering of metal on metal. The crowd all rushed back, and here was this chimpanzee, he had something like an iron crowbar in his cage, and he was pounding on the gas pipe to bring the crowd back to him, just like any of us ballyho artists do to attract attention. They came back and he laid down the bar, and began shaking hands with them all over again. Now, if any one of you want to see it, go down to the zoo in the Bronx. But there is not the slightest question of the intelligence and the reasoning power, not only of the ape, but of all sorts of animals, nobody can tell where they leave off, the dog, the horse, the whole animal creation. You may get down as low as the oyster and not discover it, but so far as we can go we find it.

Of course, mind has some relation probably to the brain, certainly has to the brain, as far as we know what certainty means. The chimpanzee about the size of a man has a brain about half as big as a man. Man's brain is twice as big, he doesn't act as if it was, but it is. Everything we can do he can do to a less extent. We have only just begun to get acquainted with him. I was talking with a very able man, who is in charge of the zoo; he says they can clearly distinguish many of the sounds, and he believes when we study them enough we can almost bring it down to words. But that is not strange. You can do it in with barnyard fowls, with dogs. You can tell the difference in the clucking of a hen when she finds some food for her brood and the screaming of a hen in the presence of a hawk.

Man is just a part of nature, a part of life; he is not the whole thing, and he is not separated from it.

Let us see from another standpoint. Has man been taken special care of? Oh, no. I don't know why my friend says there would not be any universe without man, I really cannot understand that, brother. [. . .]

There was a universe, this universe existed for millions of ages without man. Now, of course, I am guessing as to time, I was not here, I have been here quite a long time, but not that long—but the evidence is perfectly plain that this earth went on its fool way around the sun without any living substance of any sort in it, even vegetation, let alone human beings. Man is a late thing on this earth. I don't know how he may be in the infinite other worlds that fill the starry heavens, he may have reached some of those places before he did here. If he did, I don't know why he ever came here, they are so far ahead of us from all the observations we have made. But he is a latecomer, probably not over a million years, whereas the age of the universe runs into hundreds of millions, if it ever had a beginning, and nobody knows whether it ever had a beginning or not. Our imagination cannot go to it, there are some things that even intelligent people cannot explain, it takes foolish ones to do it, and whether we ever had a beginning or not, nobody knows, or when, or what, or why was that beginning, nobody knows. But so far as we do know, from every indication that we have, from all that science and experience can point out, the origin of man was just like the origin of everything else. There is no more mystery about the origin of a human being than there is about a chicken. Exactly the same process, the fertilization of a single cell, by heat. The cell, after being fertilized, develops into its kind. The human being is a product of a single cell on his mother's side, fertilized by spermatozoa on his father's side, just the same as any other single cell in the world. And all life came that way, practically all, perhaps not all, but practically all. Where is there anything different that got into man?

Well, let us see a minute. We know that each one of us originated in a single cell in the bodies of our mother. She had the capacity of some ten thousand children. Before a child could be born, that cell must be fertilized by the spermatozoa of the body of our father, he having a capacity of a billion children. What has become of all your brothers and sisters who were never born? Billions of them; because a cell did not happen to be fertilized, although any one of them was capable of fertilization, and you remember that each one of you is the product of one cell in ten thousand on your mother's side, and one spermatozoa in a billion on your farther's side. You know you had one chance in ten thousand, multiplied by one chance in a billion of being here. Why did they pick on you?

And there is not a single thing about it that cannot be explained upon the plain principles that govern every other life. They tell us we are higher; I don't know which way is higher and which way is lower. We are somewhat more complex than most of the other animals, although we have bone for bone and nerve for nerve and muscle for muscle of the higher apes, and although there is no test in the world that can determine the difference between the blood of a man and that of the higher apes, the one might be from the other. We are the last, so far, of another stem, that parted from the apes perhaps two or three or four or five million years ago, but we are very close kin, in every way that you can reckon kin. I wonder if anybody doubts this; I don't imagine how you can, but there are very unreasonable people in the world. If there is any difference in man, where did it come from? And when did it get into him? It was not in a cell, it was not in a sperm; where did you get it? If there is any purpose in it, where is the purpose, and what is the purpose? Beneficence? The sun and the earth, moving around in space for an infinite period of time, going over the same fool path year after year for ages and ages, and nothing to see. After a while some kind of life appeared on the earth, some sort of life, vegetable life. Finally great animals, the great lizards of the past, who could eat an acre of trees for lunch. He was adapted to that and therefore he lived. But at a later period the carnivorous beasts came upon the scene and ate him up. You might say there was a purpose in creating the dinosaur, so that the tiger could eat him, but what was the purpose on the dinosaur's part? I don't know. You might say that there was a purpose in creating the lamb so that man could eat it, but how about the lamb?

Where is all this scheme, and all this purpose? Take the earth itself. If there is any plan thought out, it was not very carefully done. We are always shaking up the earth. It comes by what seems to us chance. Ten thousand earthquakes every day in the year, somewhere in the earth. The crust in some places is too thin, in others too thick, because it was not put together right and a rock slipped. Ten thousand of them.

You may sail the sea, and all over the sea are islands that are thrown up by volcanic eruptions, and they sometimes disappear, with whole populations, in a day. What was the purpose?

When we talk of purpose, we talk of purpose as human beings consider purpose; that is the only way we can do it. Why has one form of life after another gone down in the infinite ages that are past? What purpose was there in what Fabre tells us of the infinite—the terrible carnage between all the animals of the earth, every life feeding on every other life, and man feeding on the rest and himself feeding the rest. Fabre says, "At the banquet of life every man is in turn a guest and a dish."[4] So he is! Purpose? If there is purpose it is malignant! Nobody can harmonize it with a fine purpose, or a great purpose or an important purpose, or *any* purpose!

What do we know about the earth and man, excepting that they are here. Where they came from I can tell as to each individual person. I can tell that, science has told us, and of that there is no dispute; but why? and how? and where are they going? Man, tickled into existence for a few brief days, living largely in trouble, disappointment, and misery, and going out into the great eternal mystery! Purpose! It does not correspond with anything that human beings ever dreamed of as purpose.

What is the purpose in a cyclone, excepting to blow something down? What is the purpose in an earthquake destroying a city? What is the purpose in the birth of an idiot, or the most of the rest of them? What is the purpose of the infinite slaughter that marks the pages of man's life? Nobody can harmonize it within the meaning of the word. We know we are here, we know what occurs, it is all night around us, and we pass into it very quickly, and there is not a scrap left behind of which there is the slightest evidence anywhere on earth. Not a scrap.

Where did this idea of purpose come from? I will tell you where it came from. I know. I was not there, but I know. The primitive man looked out at the earth; he thought it was flat. Why not? It looked flat. He considered himself the center of existence. He was, to himself. That is the trouble with all of us. We all have what Weber and Field used to call too much proud flesh.[5] We consider ourselves the center of the universe. He looked out on the earth and tried to explain it. He explained it easily. The earth was made for man, and he was placed in absolute control of the animals, to do what he willed with them. He was put in the garden of Eden. It must have been a beautiful spot. I have seen most of that Eastern country, but I never saw that. The sun was made to light his path by day, and they hauled out the sun in the morning and took it in at sundown, and then the moon was run out at night to light his way by night. What he did when the moon did not shine I am not informed. Man himself was made full-born from dust. Of course, God could not be busy making a human being every time he wanted a new one, so he had to make Eve. He made Eve out of a rib, spoiled a perfectly good rib for a woman. He looks up at the stars, and he says, "the stars He made also";[6] there was just "also," nothing but also. Now we have looked up in the heavens and we find stars so far away that light has to travel a million light years, as fast as light can travel at the rate of two hundred thousand miles a second for a million years, for the light to get to the earth. We have found stars so big—well, the sun itself is now a fly-speck to it. Who are we, anyway? Made for us?

The origin is plain, the origin of the idea is clearly seen, and is still more clear because so many people hang on to it today, and in spite of all the evidence in the world that it is not there. That is where it came from; it came from the ignorance and the conceit of man. It came from his hopes and his fears, and his longings and desires. It came from the infancy and the childhood of the human race. It is one of the old hangovers, and we are full of old hang-overs, both our bodies and our minds. Our bodies are made up of everything that goes into the making of almost every kind of an animal; muscles that are no longer of value anywhere, hang-overs from the long dark past, and our minds are made up of the same thing. And this idea that somewhere in the universe was a plan made for us, and a purpose plain, so that somewhere we would be happy and blissful and sit on the damp clouds and play on a harp through all eternity, that's where it came from. You remember the simple proof of it in Jacob's experience. Jacob went to sleep and he dreamed that he saw angels going up and coming down from the firmament above, where the stars were stuck in, just a little way up, about like the ceiling of this place, and they went up to heaven and down on a ladder.[7] It was the only means of locomotion they had at the time of Jacob's dream; if he dreamed it now, he would dream of a flying machine. The whole idea comes from the childhood of the earth, and of man, and we don't like to give it up. I don't blame people for not liking to give it up. We live largely on hopes and dreams, a desire to see forever those we love, but when you build something from a dream and a hope, it is a mighty poor scientific basis to rest upon.

Does Man Live Again?

I WANT TO THANK my brilliant friend over here [indicating Judge Musmanno] for his kind words about me. I guess they are all right. [Laughter.]

We have now had the oratorical argument. Let's see if we can get down to earth. First, I want to give a little attention to some of the things my friend has said with so much assurance. "Everybody knows that telepathy is true," he says, "Everybody knows it is true." It is not true. I say, "Go and try it." It is a plain, cheap humbug. Upton Sinclair's testimony is of no value.[1] I would have had some confidence in him if he had not so strongly recommended that fake doctor in California, who could tell all about your diseases by a lock of your hair.[2] He is too gullible for this word. He cannot prove anything by testimony of that sort. He said he thought the Creator made man to die. Well, there are two

---

Does Man Live Again? (Girard, KS: Haldeman-Julius Co., 1936) is a debate between Darrow and Michael Angelo Musmanno (1897–1968), a trial lawyer in Pennsylvania (1923–31) and later a judge of the County Court (1932–34), the Court of Common Pleas (1935–51), and the Pennsylvania Supreme Court (1952–68). He was a judge at the Nuremburg Trials. In the 1920s he attempted to assist Sacco and Vanzetti's lawyers, and made personal appeals on their behalf to the U.S. Supreme Court. He later wrote a book on the case, *After Twelve Years* (1939). Although a vigorous defender of the underdog, he was also not averse to censorship and was a rabid anti-Communist: see his treatise *Across the Street from the Courthouse* (1954).

Darrow had long argued against the immortality of the soul, and against the soul's very existence; see "The Myth of the Soul," *Forum* 80 (October 1928): 524–33 (rpt. in *Verdicts out of Court*, pp. 417–28).

difficulties to that. First, he has not proved any such thing as a Creator, and he cannot, if he lives a thousand years, and, secondly, if there was, it would be entirely impossible for him to make a man who would die.

Now, just think a minute. According to his logic, God made me, and I am to live here a while on this earth. Then I am going to die, and go somewhere else. Isn't that noble? Clear as mud. Why the dickens did he bring me here? So he could take me away and plant me somewhere else? It does not sound intelligent to me, and it is not intelligent.

He talks, too, about the spirit of man. He does not know what he is talking about. Can anybody tell me what he means by the spirit? That is something undiscovered, unknown and impossible.

Now, he tells you about all the people who believe in immortality. Nobody believes it. Nobody believes it. Some people hope about it, and some talk about it. I talk about it, but I don't hope for it, or fear it. When I get through with this job, I am through with this job. I have no fear about it; no worry about it, and no hope of another job that might be worse.

He said, "Look at man and look at an ape; man thinks; an ape does not." Now, where did he get that? There isn't a scientist in the world who does not know better than that. Why, even Bryan knew better than that. [Laughter and Applause.] An ape does think. I have seen human beings that thought less. Every animal thinks, just the same as to man; generally less, sometimes more. There is some difference between an ape and a man, of course. A few lessons in evolution would help him out on that.

In the development of life there come sports. Take fruit flies; they have a brood every 10 or 15 minutes; a brood of fruit flies are hatched, and some of them are different; what we call sports. Some of the sports are better; most of them worse; but it is the breeding of the sports that is better. That is the cause of evolution. Man is a sport, and a good one, instead of a bad one, from the monkeys, or the apes, or, still more correctly, the lemur. Most of the sports are far worse than the original ape. We may have human sports that develop something else; we might get a good one, and he would be so intelligent he would eat us, just as we are intelligent enough to eat the other animals, because we have the power to do it. That is all there is to it. Every scientist knows it. You cannot get it in poetry, theology, or grab it out of your head. That has been demonstrated over and over again by every man who has studied science and who is an investigator in that particular field.

Men will argue that they did not come from the ape. Well, if they didn't, a lot of them should. In every way, they look like an ape; they act like an ape; they hobble around like an ape; they chatter like an ape. It is perfectly obvious where they came from. Human man is little better than the ape. We might possibly get a good sport out of the human race, one that is worth while. It could certainly stand a good deal of improvement, a great deal.

Now, a little anecdote about John Quincy Adams. I happened to read not long ago, in one of our leading magazines, about another letter which they had found which had been written by John Quincy. He was always writing letters. He wrote them to himself when he could not think of anybody else, and in this letter, he said: "On this day (this day is Sunday), I am 82 years old; I have gone to church today. Barring a few times in France, when I was Minister to France, I have gone to church every Sunday. I feel it is necessary to go to church, in order to refresh and invigorate my religious ideas, but in spite of all that I have the deepest and profoundest doubt about the whole blooming scheme."[3] He did not use the word "blooming," otherwise it is his.

I say that nobody believes in a future life—nobody. Now let's see. You are going to be happy in heaven, are you not? How do you know? You don't believe any such stuff. You take a Christian with a cancer—and a Christian cancer is just the same to a Christian as it is to some other fellow. He will travel all over the world, and get cut to pieces by inches, so he can keep out of heaven a day longer. It is nonsense. Nobody believes it. They cannot believe it. They try to. You cannot believe a thing just because you want to. Did you ever see a Christian who wanted to die? I never did; I never saw any such thing, or heard him say so.

I used to sing when I was a little boy, "I want to be an angel and, with the angels stand." I didn't want any such thing and neither did anybody else. Every act of their lives is direct proof that they don't believe what they are talking about—every one of them. Nobody sticks any closer to the doctor than a Christian. [Laughter.] I will have a little confidence in somebody believing in it when they stop calling doctors. And, you know, they get tired of their doctors because they do not get well quick enough, and then they call on chiropractors, or Christian Scientists. Not only are Christian Scientists treating them, but treating their dogs.

Everybody wants to live. Now, don't be silly. You all know it. Your friends may be mostly on the other side. On the other side of what? I don't know. But they don't want to go and meet their friends. [Laughter.] They are going to stick on this side, and the more they pray, the stronger they stick. [Laughter.] No, no, their conduct belies their talk in every instance. A man's wife might be in heaven, or one of his friends. Does he want to go, too? Oh, no, he will stay here just as long as he can stay. He knows that life is full of pain; he has rheumatism, or gout, and, of course, his heart goes "fluey" on him, or he awakens during the night and can't go to sleep again, because there are not enough windows to raise. But still he wants to stick here instead of being happy.

I say again, there isn't a human being who ever lived that believes in a future life. They hope. Where is the evidence of it? If anybody will give me one fact, then it is worth while to talk about it—just one.

Let's take the life of man. You are born from the races of father and mother. Your mother had the capacity for 10,000 children, and your father had the capacity for billions. Then where are all the rest of them who didn't get born? There isn't room in heaven for them. [Laughter.] When did life begin? And in all animal life the process is just the same, the manifestation the same; they live the same, and die the same.

He talked about our having an intellect, while a cow does not. I never asked a cow what she thought. When there is a union of the father and mother, a child is born. We know when it began, absolutely when it began, and we know when it ends. Yes, man is immortal, with one end cut off. He had a beginning, but he did not have an end. All right, any of you people that want to believe it, and can believe it, go ahead and believe it, if it makes you happy. If this world has not been miserable enough, why, try another one. [Laughter and Applause.]

Let us look at it and see how silly all of it is, how absolutely silly. Man is born—before his birth he grows—he is born, he lives, he grows, and then he starts downhill. I will probably start downhill sometime myself. It does not worry me any. I have seen the show, and what is the use of getting worried? I could not help it, anyhow—impossible to help it.

Everything that is born, dies. Talk about a body and a soul. Let me tell you this. You can take a man, put him on the scales, and let him die, and the dead man weighs just as much, no more, no less, than he did when alive. What left him? There isn't a chance, let alone an argument. What left him, pray tell me, what left him? It had neither length, breadth nor thickness, that is true; it did not have any weight or substance. Where does it go to? I tell you, on any other subject, if a child three years old believed such nonsense, it would not be fit to raise, on any other subject excepting this. This has been the poaching ground for priests, men who threaten you with damnation, men who teach things that are impossible, to all kinds of people, from the beginning of the world.

Everything that lives, tries to keep on living. We are no different than a tree, in that a tree tries to keep on living; animal substance tries to keep on living. Throughout life, everything that lives tries to keep on living. Now, when you die, then what? What leaves you? Where does it go? A soul does not weigh anything. Where does it go? Roost in the trees? Where does it go on a nice winter evening, like this, without any clothes, without any body, without anything?

The trouble is, as I look over this audience—and I am not finding fault with it—I can see people here, there and everywhere, saying, "I am not going to take any stock in that; I am going to believe in a soul." Believe in a soul you haven't got. Do you suppose anybody would believe any such nonsense if it involved anything else? Why, it would be silly. But it is not silly as it is because they have heard it preached forever and ever, and hope for it forever and ever, and are going to hold onto it, anyway.

Now, what goes, and where does it go? Do you ever think about it, and, if you don't, why don't you? Just because you don't dare, that is all.

You don't have to think long about it—just a second—when the soul, which is nothing, passes away from the body, which is everything, where does it go to? This is not a very close estimate, but we will say 250 million miles away, or 10 billions of miles away. Do we go to any of those places, and if so, how do we get there? Do we take a balloon, or do we walk, or do we fly, or have we a wishing cap, or what is it? Do we eat? You don't want to be a soul if you cannot eat. You don't want to be a soul, of course, when you cannot drink—all the pleasure in life would be gone.

Nobody can imagine himself wanting to be anything except what he is. He says he wants to be an angel, but, no, he wants to be just what he is. When you die, are you going to see your grandmother? Now, how are you going to find her? You would not recognize her; she hasn't even got a false-face—just nothing. You go out into infinite space. Here is a man who leaves his wife; she sails away at midnight, and he sails away at noon. How soon will they find each other? How soon?

Now, I will tell you where all this nonsense came from. I know the idea of immortality had no connection with the soul. Jesus did not believe in a soul—and He is one of the High Priests we have heard mentioned. What did He believe in? He believed in the resurrection of the body. We lie in our graves, buried there perhaps a million years, and then we are going to get resurrected on Judgment Day, when they are going to divide the sheep from the goats, if there are any sheep. Then we are going to live again, with our old body, which has been decayed, passed into weeds, fruit and vegetables, and been eaten over and over again. Suppose a subject eats a missionary, which are they going to resurrect? [Laughter.] They don't have to resurrect either of them, as far as I am concerned—I wouldn't play any favorites between them—which is it going to be?

Everybody through the ages has been born, and died, and is mixed with all the elements of nature, mixed with snow and wind and sun and heat and cold, until all of us are part of everyone, and every one of us are part of all the rest. If you get eaten, or some of you get a potato planted above you, or an apple tree, and the roots reach down and live off you, then you are part of the apple tree, and if somebody else eats the apples, then what? You are eaten over and over again, and will be as long as life persists.

Now, just think of the nonsense of a person talking about heaven, when we do not know where it is; do not know how far away it is; do not know whether it is hot or cold; don't know how we will get there, or anything about it. Still we say we believe in it. Nonsense.

We have a literary club, to which I belong, in Chicago, which has as intelligent people as anywhere else. A man read a paper on immortality at that club, a while ago, stating that he did not believe in immortality, and they took a vote on it, in the club, and there was not 20 percent of them believed in a future life—not 20 percent. If anybody believed in it, they would not know what they believed in. How can you believe in something when you do not know what you believe in? You hang on, cut out the cancer, stay a little longer. Why? Because you cannot come back. Nobody ever did come back. Why hasn't somebody strayed back here once in a while? How many pairs of idiots have promised each other that the first one who dies will come back to see the other fellow? Did you ever hear of anybody coming back? There isn't anything to come back; they are all the time getting mixed up with something else.

It is a dream, a blind hope, that nobody dares to examine.

Priests will tell you, "Have faith." Noble thing that is. As if you could have faith without some proof. Nobody can believe a thing without some evidence. You have got to have evidence to have belief, and if anybody will show by any rational reasoning, or any rational argument, any evidence whatever, then I for one am willing to stop, and look, and examine it. But nobody ever showed me.

We have all kinds of religions; there were scores of them before Christianity was born, and there will be others after it dies. We have had all kinds of faith. We have spiritualists who talk with their friends who have gone. I have been at many meetings, and watched those tipping tables, when I did not know any better.

My friend talks about the instinct of immortality. There isn't any such thing. What is an instinct? An instinct is something that arises directly from the emotions of the body. Instinct of immortality? It is a dream, passed on from ignorance to ignorance, buoyed up by the will to believe. Take that away, and nobody believes.

Now, men have sought all kinds of ways to call back their beloved ones; they have tried all schemes that could be conceived by man; they have dreamed all dreams. But out of the darkness that overlooks the earth has come no word, or no look, or nothing. I might ask you, do you suppose if any of your friends who have died are still living, and could come back, or send you some word, they would not do it? They certainly would. They would give up their job of playing the harp a little while, and would come and tell you about it, but they don't do it.

It is a vague, impossible dream that is born of hope and fear, and, let me tell you this, it is passing away—people ought to think sometime— it is passing away, and one or two generations will end it, and when it is ended, we will be a sight better off. What the dream is gone, we will have more happiness, more of the pleasure of living, and we will live and meet death without regret and without fear. [Great Applause.]

TWO

On Law and Crime

The Right Treatment of Violence

SENTIMENTAL AND HUMANE THOUGHTS and purposes are often, perhaps generally, based on real life, and have a natural reason for their being. To "turn the other cheek" or to "resist not evil" may seem at first glance to have no support in the facts of life, but after all that which makes for a higher humanity, a longer life, and a more vigorous community, is the true philosophy. To use violence and force upon the vicious and the weak must produce the evil that it gives. Like produces like. Clubs, jails, harsh language, brutal force inevitably tend to reproduce the same state of mind in the victim of the assault. This is not merely a fact in human nature. It is a fact in all nature, plant and animal and man. So long as the gentle springtime rather than the cruel winter brings vegetable and animal life to an awakening earth, just so long will kindness and love triumph, produce joy and life, where force and violence bring only evil and death. Harsh treatment kills plant life, and kind treatment builds it up. Violence and brutality produce their like in animal life, and kindness tames and subdues. With gentleness and kindness

---

This is the sixteenth and last chapter of Darrow's early treatise, *Resist Not Evil* (Chicago: C. H. Kerr, 1902), pp. 165–79. The title of the treatise is taken from Jesus's Sermon on the Mount: "But I say unto you, that ye resist not evil: but whosoever shall smite thee on thy right cheek, turn to him the other also" (Matthew 5:39). The work is largely an elaboration of the theories of nonresistance propounded by Leo Tolstoi; see Darrow's early essay, "Tolstoi," *Rubric* 1 (January 1902): 21–38 (rpt. in *Verdicts out of Court*, pp. 186–200), and the debate *Marx vs. Tolstoy* (1911), with Arthur M. Lewis.

a swarm of wild bees may be handled and controlled, but approach them with violence and force and each bee is converted into a criminal whose only purpose is to destroy.

With all animal life the same rule exists; even those beasts whose nature calls for a diet of flesh and blood may be subdued in time by gentleness and love. Man with his higher intellect and better developed moral being is much more susceptible to kindness and love. Likewise he more easily learns to fear and hate. Man readily discerns the feelings and judgment of his fellows, and as readily renders judgment in return. The outcast and abandoned form not the slightest exception to the rule—they know and understand the ones who meet them with gentleness and love, for these they make sacrifices, to these they are faithful, to these they exhibit the higher qualities that show the possibilities of the soul. Cases where one convicted of crime comes from a place of safety and risks his liberty and life to help save his friend are not rare in the least. True comradeship and loyalty is met quite as often here as in the higher walks of life. Nothing is more common in ordinary selfish society than to see one man refuse all aid and help to another in financial need. Many convicts and outcasts could teach a much needed lesson of loyalty and generosity to the exemplary man.

No amount of treatment can reclaim an evil heart if the treatment is administered without love. As children at school we knew with our young natural instincts the teacher who loved us and the teacher who despised us—the one awoke feelings of love and kindness, the other hatred and revenge. No heart is so pure that it may not be defiled and hardened by cruelty, hatred and force, and none so defiled that it may not be touched and changed by gentleness and love. Unless this philosophy of life is true the whole teaching of the world has been a delusion and a snare. Unless love and kindness tends to love, then hatred and violence and force should be substituted and taught as the cardinal virtues of human life. The mistake and evil of society is in assuming that love is the rule of life, and at the same time that large classes of people are entirely outside its pale. No parent ever teaches his child any other philosophy than that of love. Even to quarrelsome playmates they are taught not to return blows and harsh language, but to meet force with kindness and with love. The parent who did not depend on love to influence and mold the character of the child rather than force would be regarded not as a real parent but a brute. Force is worse than useless in developing the conduct of the child. It is true that by means of force the little child may be awed by superior brute power, but he gives way only under protest, and the violence that he suppresses in his hand or tongue finds refuge in his heart. Violent acts are not evil—they are a manifestation of evil. Good conduct is not goodness. It is but a manifestation of goodness. Evil and goodness can only be conditions of the inmost life, and human conduct, while it generally reflects this inmost life, may be so controlled as not to manifest the real soul that makes the man.

Every child needs development, needs training to fit him to live in peace and right relations with his fellow man. Every intelligent and right-thinking person knows that this development must be through love, not through violence and force. The parent who would teach his child to be kind to animals, not to ruthlessly kill and maim, would not teach this gentleness with a club. The intelligent parent would not use a whip to teach a child not to beat a dog. The child is not made into the good citizen, the righteous man, by pointing out that certain conduct will lead to punishment, to the jail or the gallows. The beneficence of fear was once considered a prime necessity in the rearing of the child, and this theory peopled the earth with monsters and the air with spooks ready to reach down and take the helpless child when he wandered from the straight and narrow path; but this method of rearing children does not appeal to the judgment and humanity of to-day. The conduct of children can only be reached for good by pointing to the evil results of hatred, of inharmony, of force, by appealing to the higher and nobler sentiments which, if once reached, are ever present, influencing and controlling life. The code of hatred, of violence and force, too, is a negative code. The child is given a list of the things he must not do, exactly as the man is furnished a list of the acts forbidden by the state. At the best, when the limits of this list are reached and the forbidden things are left undone, nothing more is expected or demanded. But no code is long enough to make up the myriad acts of life. Kindness or unkindness can result in a thousand ways in every human relationship. If the child or the man observes the written code through fear, the unwritten moral code, infinitely longer and more delicate, will be broken in its almost every line. But if the child or the man is taught his right relations to the world and feels the love and sympathy due his fellow man, he has no need of written codes; his acts, so far as those of mortals can be, will be consistent with the life and happiness of his fellow man. And this not through fear, but because he bears the highest attitude toward life.

WITH OUR LONG HEREDITY and our imperfect environment, even if the organized force of the state should disappear, even if the jails and penitentiaries should close their doors, force would only completely die in course of time. Evil environment and heredity may have so marked and scarred some men that kindness and love could never reach their souls. It might take generations to stamp out hatred or destroy the ill effects of life; but order and kindness most surely would result, because nature demands order and tolerance and without it man must die. No doubt here and there these so-called evil ones would arouse evil and hatred in return, and some sudden act of violence would for a time occasionally be met with violence through mob law in return. But uncertain and reprehensible as mob law has ever been it is still much more excusable and more certain than the organized force of society operating through the criminal courts. Mob law has the excuse of passion, of provocation, not the criminal nature of deliberation, coldness and settled hate. Mob law, too, generally reaches the object of its wrath, while evidence is fresh and facts are easily understood and unhampered by those rules and technical forms which ensnare the weak and protect the strong. And unjust and unwise as the verdicts of mob law often are, they are still more excusable, quicker, more certain and less erring than the judgments of the criminal courts.

But neither civil law nor mob law is at all necessary for the protection of individuals. Men are not protected because of their strength or their ability to fight. In the present general distribution of weapons, in one sense, every man's life is dependent on each person that he meets. If the instinct was to kill, society as organized presents no obstacle to that instinct. When casual violence results it is not the weakest or most defenceless who are the victims of the casual violence of individuals. Even the boy at school scorns to war upon a weaker mate. The old, the young, the feeble, children and women, are especially exempt from violent deeds. This is because their condition does not call for feelings of violence, but rather awakens feelings of compassion, and calls for aid and help. The non-resistant ever appeals to the courageous and the manly. Without weapons of any kind, with the known determination to give no violence in return, it would be very rare that men would not be safe from disorganized violence. It is only the state that ever lays its hands in anger on the non-resistant.

Neither would non-resistance in the state or individual indicate cowardice or weakness or lack of vital force. The ability and inclination to use physical strength is no indication of bravery or tenacity to life. The greatest cowards are often the greatest bullies. Nothing is cheaper and more common than physical bravery. In the lower animals it is more pronounced than in man. The bulldog and the fighting cock are quite as conspicuous examples of physical bravery as the prize-fighter or the soldier. The history of all warfare shows either that physical bravery is not an indication of great excellence or that supreme excellence is very common, in fact almost a universal possession. Under the intoxication of patriotism, or the desire for glory, or the fear of contempt, most men will march with apparent willingness into the face of the greatest danger. Often it requires vastly more courage to stay at home than to enlist— more courage to retreat than to fight. Common experience shows how much rarer is moral courage than physical bravery. A thousand men will march to the mouth of the cannon where one man will dare espouse an unpopular cause. An army well equipped and ready for action has less terror for the ordinary man than the unfavorable comment of the daily press. True courage and manhood come from the consciousness of the right attitude toward the world, the faith in one's own purpose, and the sufficiency of one's own approval as a justification for one's own acts.

This attitude is not that of the coward, for cowardice is really disapproval of self, a consciousness of one's own littleness and unworthiness in the light of one's own soul, which cannot be deceived.

INTELLIGENT MEN ARE WILLING to accept many truths that they believe are not fitted for the universal acceptance of mankind, and however they may feel that punishment is wrong they still urge that it will not do to teach this doctrine to the great mass of men and to carry its practice into daily life. But sooner or later all conduct and all life must rest on truth. It is only fact that can form a basis for permanent theories that tend to the preservation of the race. No one is too poor, or too young, or too vicious to know the truth, for the truth alone is consistent with all the facts of life, and this alone can furnish any rule of life. The truth alone can make free. When society is taught the truth that it is wrong to punish, to use force, to pass judgment on man, it will have no need for jails. The man who really knows and understands this truth can have no malice in his heart, can use no force and violence against his fellow, but will reach him with love and pity. The man or society that understands this truth will know that so-called crime is only so-called crime; that human conduct is what the necessities of life make of the individual soul. Then in reality, as now only partially, men will turn their attention to the causes that make crime. Then will they seek to prevent and cure, not to punish and destroy. Then man will learn to know that the cause of crime is the unjust condition of human life; that penal laws are made to protect earth's possessions in the hands of the vicious and the strong. Man will learn that poverty and want are due to the false conditions, the injustice which looks to human law and violence and force for its safeguard and protection. Man will learn that crime is but the hard profession that is left open to a large class of men by their avaricious fellows. When new opportunities for life are given, a fairer condition of existence will gradually be opened up and the need for violence and the cause of violence will disappear.

Instead of avenging a murder by taking a judge, sheriff, jurors, witnesses, jailer, hangman, and the various appendages of the court,—by taking these and staining their hands with blood and crime, the world will make the original murder impossible, and thus save the crimes of all. Neither will the vicious control without the aid of law. Society ever has and must ever have a very large majority who naturally fall into order, social adjustment and a rational, permissible means of life. The disorganized vicious would be far less powerful than the organized vicious, and would soon disappear.

Punishment to terrorize men from violating human order is like the threat of hell to terrorize souls into obedience to the law of God. Both mark primitive society, both are degrading and debasing, and can only appeal to the lower instincts of the lower class of men. Most religious teachers have ceased to win followers by threats of hell. Converts of this sort are not generally desired. The religion that does not approach and appeal to men along their higher conduct is not considered worthy to teach to man. And those souls who cannot be moved through the sentiments of justice and humanity, rather than threats of eternal fire, are very, very rare, and even should such a soul exist the fear of hell would cause it still further to shrivel and decay.

Hatred, bitterness, violence and force can bring only bad results—they leave an evil stain on everyone they touch. No human soul can be rightly reached except through charity, humanity and love.

Crime: Its Cause and Treatment

STUDENTS OF CRIME AND punishment have never differed seriously in their conclusions. All investigations have arrived at the result that crime is due to causes; that man is either not morally responsible, or responsible only to a slight degree. All have doubted the efficacy of punishment and practically no one has accepted the common ideas that prevail as to crime, its nature, its treatment and the proper and efficient way of protecting society from the criminal.

The real question of importance is: What shall be done? Can crime be cured? If not, can it be wiped out and how? What rights have the public? What rights has the criminal? What obligations does the public owe the criminal? What duties does each citizen owe society?

It must be confessed that all these questions are more easily asked than answered. Perhaps none of them can be satisfactorily answered. It is a common obsession that every evil must have a remedy; that if it cannot be cured today, it can be tomorrow; that man is a creature of infinite possibilities, and all that is needed is time and patience. Given these a perfect world will eventuate.

I am convinced that man is not a creature of infinite possibilities. I am by no means sure that he has not run his race and reached, if not

---

Crime: Its Cause and Treatment (New York: Thomas Y. Crowell Co., 1922) is Darrow's most exhaustive treatise on the subject. The present selection comprises the book's last chapter, "Remedies" (pp. 273–85).

passed, the zenith of his power. I have no idea that every evil can be cured; that all trouble can be banished; that every maladjustment can be corrected or that the millennium can be reached now and here or any time or anywhere. I am not even convinced that the race can substantially improve. Perhaps here and there society can be made to run a little more smoothly; perhaps some of the chief frictions incident to life may be avoided; perhaps we can develop a little higher social order; perhaps we may get rid of some of the cruelty incident to social organization. But how?

To start with: it seems to me to be clear that there is really no such thing as crime, as the word is generally understood. Every activity of man should come under the head of "behavior." In studying crime we are merely investigating a certain kind of human behavior. Man acts in response to outside stimuli. How he acts depends on the nature, strength, and inherent character of the machine and the habits, customs, inhibitions and experiences that environment gives him. Man is in no sense the maker of himself and has no more power than any other machine to escape the law of cause and effect. He does as he must. Therefore, there is no such thing as moral responsibility in the sense in which this expression is ordinarily used. Punishment as something inflicted for the purpose of giving pain is cruelty and vengeance and nothing else. Whatever should be done to the criminal, if we have humanity and imagination, we must feel sympathy for him and consider his best good along with that of all the rest of the members of the society whose welfare is our concern.

While punishment cannot be defended, still self-defense is inherent in both individuals and society and, without arguing its justification, no one can imagine a society that will not assert it and act for its defense. This will be true regardless of whether the given society is worth preserving or not. Inherent in all life and organization is the impulse of self-preservation. Those members of society who are sufficiently "antisocial" from the standpoint of the time and place will not be tolerated unduly to disturb the rest. These, in certain instances, will be destroyed or deprived of their power to harm. If society has a right attitude toward the subject, if it has imagination and sympathy and understanding, it will isolate these victims, not in anger but in pity, solely for the protection of the whole. Some there are who ask what difference it makes whether it is called punishment or not. I think that the attitude of society toward the criminal makes the whole difference, and any improvement is out of the question until this attitude influences and controls the whole treatment of the question of crime and punishment.

If doctors and scientists had been no wiser than lawyers, judges, legislatures and the public, the world would still be punishing imbeciles, the insane, the inferior and the sick; and treating human ailments with incantations, witchcraft, force and magic. We should still be driving devils out of the sick and into the swine.

Assuming then that man is governed by external conditions; that he inevitably reacts to certain stimuli; that he is affected by all the things that surround him; that his every act and manifestation is a result of law; what then must we and can we do with and for the criminal?

First of all we must abandon the idea of working his moral reformation, as the term "moral reformation" is popularly understood. As well might we cure the physically ill in that way! Man works according to his structure. He never does reform and cannot reform. As he grows older his structure changes and from increase of vitality or from decrease of vitality his habits, too, may change. He may likewise learn by experience, and through the comparing and recalling of experiences and their consequences may build up rules of conduct which will restrain him from doing certain things that he otherwise would do. Anything that increases his knowledge and adds to his experience will naturally affect his habits and will either build up or tear down inhibitions or do both, as the case may be. If he has intelligence he knows he is always the same man; that he has not reformed nor repented. He may regret that he did certain things but he knows why and how he did them and why he will not repeat them if he can avoid it. The intrinsic character of the man cannot change, for the machine is the same and will always be the same, except that it may run faster or slower with the passing years, or it may be influenced by the habits gained from experience and life.

We must learn to appraise rightly the equipment of every child and, as far as possible, of every adult to the end that they may find an environment where they can live. It must never be forgotten that man is nothing but heredity and environment and that the heredity cannot be changed but the environment may be. In the past and present, the world has sought to adjust heredity to environment. The problem of the future in dealing with crime will be to adjust environment to heredity. To a large extent this can be done in a wholesale way. Any improved social arrangement that will make it easier for the common man to live will necessarily save a large number from crime. Perhaps if the social improvement should be great enough it would prevent the vast majority of criminal acts. Life should be made easier for the great mass from which the criminal is ever coming. As far as experience and logic can prove anything, it is certain that every improvement in environment will lessen crime.

Codes of law should be shortened and rendered simpler. It should not be expected that criminal codes will cover all human and social life. The old method of appealing to brute force and fear should gradually give place to teaching and persuading and fitting men for life. All prisons should be in the hands of experts, physicians, criminologists, biologists, and, above all, the humane. Every prisoner should be made to feel that the state is interested in his good as well as the good of the society from which he came. Sentences should be indeterminate, but the indeterminate sentence of today is often a menace to freedom and a means of great cruelty and wrong. The indeterminate sentence can only be of value in a well-equipped prison where each man is under competent observation as if he were ill in a hospital. And this should be supplemented with an honest, intelligent parole commission, fully equipped for thorough work. Until that time comes, the maximum penalty should be fixed by the jury, the parole board retaining the power to reduce the punishment or parole. No two crimes are alike. No two offenders are alike. Those who have no friends on the outside are forgotten and neglected after the prison doors have been closed upon them. Some men now are confined much too long; others not long enough.

No doubt, owing to the imperfections of man, this will always be the case.

At present no penal institutions have the equipment or management to provide against such shortcomings. They never can have it while men believe punishment is vengeance. When the public is ready to provide for the protection of society and still to recognize and heed the impulses of humanity and mercy, it will abolish all fixed terms. As well might it send a patient to a hospital for a fixed time and then discharge him, regardless of whether he is cured or not, as to confine a convict for a definite predetermined time. If the offense is one of a serious nature that endangers the public, the prisoner should not be released until by understanding or education, or age, or the proper form of treatment, it is fairly evident that he will not offend again. When the time comes, if it is the day of his incarceration, be should be released. The smallest reflection ought to teach that for many crimes, especially for many property crimes, it is hopeless to release a prisoner in an environment where he cannot survive. An environment adjusted to his heredity must be found by the state.

All indignities should be taken away from prison life. Instead the prisoner should be taught that his act was the necessary result of cause and effect and that, given his heredity and environment, he could have done no other way. He should by teaching and experience be shown where he made his mistakes, and he should be given an environment where he can live consistently with the good of those around him.

Various reforms have been urged in the treatment of criminals and in criminal procedure in the courts. Most of these impress me as possessing no fundamental value. It is often said that the accused should be given an immediate trial; that this and subsequent proceedings should not be hindered by delay; that the uncertainties of punishment furnish the criminal with the hope of escape and therefore do not give the community the benefit of the terror that comes with the certainty of punishment that could prevent crime. I can see no basis in logic or experience for this suggestion. It is based on the theory that punishment is not only a deterrent to crime, but the main deterrent. It comes from the idea that the criminal is distinct from the rest of mankind, that vengeance should be sure and speedy and that then crime would be prevented. If this were true and the only consideration to prevent crime, then the old torture chamber and the ancient prison with all its hopelessness and horror should be restored. Logic, humanity and experience would protest against this. If there is to be any permanent improvement in man and any better social order, it must come mainly from the education and humanizing of man. I am quite certain that the more the question of crime and its treatment is studied the less faith men have in punishment.

England and Continental Europe are often pointed to as examples of sure and speedy justice. The fact that there are more convictions and fewer acquittals in England in proportion to the number of trials does not prove that the English system is better than ours. It may and probably does mean that ours is better. Here the accused has more chance. There the expense, the formality, the power of the court all conspire to destroy every opportunity of escape, regardless of innocence or guilt. Even the fact that there are fewer crimes committed in England does not prove that the system is best or that it prevents crime. An old country with its life of caste lacks the freedom and equality that naturally produce defiance of rules and customs and lead to breaches of the law. Other things being equal, a greater degree of freedom leads to more violations of rules and greater resisting power among the poor than a lesser degree of freedom. It does not necessarily follow that the country is best where the people are the most obedient. Complete obedience leads to submission, to aggression and to despotism. Doubtless China has fewer crimes than England. The power of resistance is so crushed that no one thinks of defying a master, resenting an injury, violating a rule, claiming any personal rights or protesting against caste, age, or privilege.

Always there are certain men who believe that all reform in criminal procedure must come by abolishing juries and submitting every question to a court. Those who are rich and strong and the lawyers who advocate their interests are mainly arrayed on this side. The poor and rebellious, with those who naturally or otherwise advocate their cause, stand for the juries as against the courts. Those who strive to be fair are often misled from a lack of experience and little judgment of human nature. The public is always against the accused. The press is against him. The machinery of the law is against him. The dice are loaded for his conviction. Some people have childish faith in the courts. But judges are neither infinitely wise nor infinitely good; they come from the ranks of lawyers and for the most part from those who have been long engaged in defending property rights; they are generally conservative; they are not independent of public opinion; almost invariably they reflect public opinion, which means the public opinion of the community in which they live. Few of them have much knowledge of biology, of psychology, of sociology, or even of history.

One curse of our political life comes from the fact that as soon as a man has secured an office, he has his eye on another and his whole effort is to please the people, that is, the people who express themselves the most easily. Very few judges rise to a great degree of independence or defy popular clamor. A jury is less bound by public opinion; their responsibility is divided; they are not as a rule seeking office; while swayed by the crowd they are still more independent than judges and with them the common man, the accused, has a better chance.

No doubt judges are abler, better educated, more accustomed to weighing evidence and able to arrive at a more logical conclusion than most juries. Still none of these qualities necessarily leads to just findings. Questions of right and wrong are not determined by strict rules of logic. If public opinion could come to regard the criminal as it does the insane, the imbecile, or the ill, then a judicial determination would be the best. But as long as crime is regarded as moral delinquency and punishment savors of vengeance, every possible safeguard and protection must be thrown around the accused. In the settling of opinions and the passing of judgments, mob psychology is all-powerful and really, in the last analysis, every human question comes down to the power of public opinion.

The first thing necessary to lessen crime and to relieve victims from the cruelty of moral judgments is a change of public opinion as to human responsibility. When scientific ideas on this important subject shall be generally accepted, all things that are possible will follow from it. Some headway has already been made in the direction of considering heredity and environment. Theoretically we no longer hold the insane responsible, and some allowance is made for children and the obviously defective. The discouraging thing is that the public is fickle and changeable, and any temporary feeling overwhelms the patient efforts of years. In the present mad crusade against crime consequent upon the Great War, penalties have been increased, new crimes created, and paroles and pardons have been made almost impossible. The public and press virtually declare that even insanity should not save the life of one who slays his fellow. Repeatedly the insane are hanged without a chance, and sentences of death are pronounced, where before, a term of years, or life imprisonment would have been the penalty for the offense. Individual men and collections of men are ruled not by judgment but by impulse; the voice of conscience and mercy is always very weak and drowned by the hoarse cry for vengeance.

As long as men collectively impose their will upon the individual units, they should consider that this imposition calls for intelligence, kindliness, tolerance and a large degree of sympathy and understanding. In considering the welfare of the public: the accused, his family and his friends should be included as a part. It need not be expected that all maladjustments can ever be wiped out. Organization with its close relation of individual units implies conflict. Nevertheless, the effort should be to remove all possible inducement for the violent clashing of individuals and to minimize the severity of such conflicts as are inevitable.

The Ordeal of Prohibition

IT TOOK MANY MONTHS for the inhabitants of the United States to realize that (at least theoretically) the country had gone dry. The Eighteenth Amendment and the Volstead Act[1] were passed without submission to the people, who had been educated for nearly a century and a half to believe that they were the supreme power in the government of the land. A radical and revolutionary change in policy was made as a war measure, at a time when the great majority of citizens were engrossed in graver matters, and when none but a few zealots considered Prohibition important. While the legislation designed to put it into effect was pending, a large number of our young men were fighting in France and the whole country had its thoughts on the war. It was a favorable time for zealots to do their work.

But all that is now past. By whatever means it was done, and however slight may have been the understanding of the people, the fact is that

This essay first appeared in the *American Mercury* 2 (August 1924): 419–27. It is perhaps Darrow's most incisive treatment of the subject, arguing that Prohibition is one more instance of a long array of ineffective moral legislation. For other of Darrow's writings against Prohibition, see *Resolved: That the United States Continue the Policy of Prohibition as Defined in the Eighteenth Amendment* (1924), a debate with John Haynes Holmes (rpt. in *Verdicts out of Court*, pp. 106–23); "Our Growing Tyranny," *Vanity Fair* 29 (February 1928): 39, 104; "Prohibition Cowardice," *Vanity Fair* 31 (September 1928): 53, 100; "Why the 18th Amendment Cannot Be Repealed," *Vanity Fair* 37 (November 1931): 62, 84; and, most exhaustively, *The Prohibition Mania* (1927; with Victor S. Yarros).

Prohibition is entrenched today in the fundamental law of the nation, and, what is more important, that there are many men and powerful organizations who feel it to be their duty to enforce it. The impossibility of its complete repeal has only slowly dawned upon the American people. Even to modify the Volstead Act would require a political revolution; to repeal the Eighteenth Amendment is well-nigh inconceivable. Eleven or twelve million voters, properly distributed amongst the States that naturally support Prohibition, will suffice to keep it on the books. But does this mean that it will remain in force forever? Does it mean that millions of people who have no sense of wrong in making, selling or using intoxicating liquors will be subject for all time to drastic penalties and tyrannical judgments?

The question can be best answered by a glance at the history of the methods by which laws have been made and repealed in the past. Against the rash doctrine of the unthinking, so often heard today, that so long as a law is on the books it must and shall be enforced, stands the almost universal experience of mankind. Probably no one who ever actually studied the growth and change of law and understood the true nature of government has ever held that so long as a statute is on the books it should be enforced. All such students know that it is an idle statement, made by men who are ignorant of history, or who are excessively eager to enforce some particular law.

Most laws grow out of the habits and customs of the people. These customs grow into mores and are finally embodied in laws. Long before statutes are passed, the great mass of men have formed their attitudes and ways of living and the statutes are simply codifications of existing folkways. Now and then, however, this natural process is changed. Some active minority, moved by religious zeal, political intolerance or special interest, finds itself able to pass a law that has not originated like the others in the customs and habits of the people. Such laws are often extremely arrogant and oppressive; they violate the conscience, the practice and the beliefs of a large number of the citizens of the state. No better illustration can be found than the body of statutes which shaped and directed the Inquisition. These were laws meant to enforce religious doctrines; they were passed alternately by Catholics and Protestants, depending upon which was in power at the time. During the three or four hundred years of violence and bloodshed that followed, many millions of human beings were directly put to death by execution or indirectly by war, and they comprised many of the best, the most intelligent, and the noblest people of the earth. The reign of terror devastated large portions of Europe and threatened completely to destroy freedom of thought and speech. Very few people in any country today would advocate the revival of any of these fierce and bloody laws. Civilization looks back upon them in amazement and horror. It feels a deep relief that the Inquisition is dead. But it forgets the method by which the laws underlying the Inquisition were got rid of.

It took religious persecution more than a hundred years to die in Europe. It lingered in some countries long after it was dead in others. It was not disposed of at last by repealing the various civil and canonical laws under which hundreds of thousands had been burned at the stake and tortured in the most horrible ways; it perished through the growth of scientific knowledge and rationalism, in the churches and out. Gradually the inquisitors themselves refused to enforce the laws. They framed for themselves all sorts of excuses and evasions, until finally they began to take their appointments and draw their salaries without any thought of performing the bloody services for which their offices were created. The Inquisition died because it was outgrown. In some places, long after the persecutions were ended, the laws were repealed, but not always, not everywhere; sometimes they were allowed to remain on the books. Some of them, indeed, have never been formally repealed to this day. But there are few bigots now living who would urge that men should be burned or tortured because they disagreed with a theological dogma. Even the most unintelligent would not seek to resurrect the torture chamber on the ground that it is a sacred duty of government to enforce all laws, however foolish, so long as they remain on the books.

Along with these laws, and really a part of them, was the code which punished the crime of witchcraft. This, like the code of the Inquisition, was a part of both the civil and the canonical law. The statutes were numerous and brutal in the extreme. They provided for torture, for burning, and for even more horrible modes of killing. After the death of the witch, his or her estate was confiscated. These cruel and barbarous laws were in effect all over Europe and spread to America; they were in force, at one place or another, for three hundred years. Now and then some judge or ecclesiastic who was more enlightened and humane than the others refused to put witches to death, and so prosecutions would tend to fall off. But at some subsequent time they would be resumed again by a sudden flaming of religious fanaticism. Joan of Arc was one of the noblest victims of this fanaticism. Would our modern Prohibitionists have approved of her death on the ground that the law was on the books? Would they have solemnly mouthed the foolish phrase that "the best way to get rid of a bad law is to enforce it?"[2]

Cotton Mather wrote a history of witchcraft. It was introduced to the English public by Richard Baxter, who declared in his preface that "a man must be a very obdurate Sadducee who would not believe in it."[3] The book was extensively circulated in America and had a great influence in spreading the belief in witchcraft and in supporting the drastic laws which were passed against it here. Now and then some enlightened clergyman, such as Hutchinson,[4] denounced witchcraft as a delusion, but the belief in it became almost universal. Gradually, however, either because of weariness in the shedding of blood or a rising skepticism, the prosecutions began to abate. Three witches were executed in England in 1682 and one in 1712. These were the last who died under those fanatical, horrible laws outside of Spain, where the mania lingered into the next century.[5] Many began to disbelieve; juries refused to convict; pamphlets and books appeared against the prosecution of witches. The law remained on the books,—but it was dead. It perished from lack of use, not from repeal. John Wesley, writing on the subject in 1760, regretted its disuse. He admitted that most learned men, by that time, disbelieved in witches, but he still contended that witchcraft was a fact. He regarded the general disbelief "a compliment which so many that believe the Bible pay to those who do not believe it," and said that the "giving up of witchcraft is in effect giving up the Bible."[6]

The story of witchcraft in America is not so long. Up to the year 1692, there had been perhaps a dozen trials and not over two or three executions. Most of the prosecutions occurred in 1692. They were almost all in Salem, Massachusetts, the first ones occurring early in the year under an old English law that was still in force but had lain dormant in the Colonies. In the same year Massachusetts passed a new act defining and punishing the crime. In this year some twenty people, mostly women, were convicted and executed in Salem. Accusations passed from one to another until no one was safe; finally a charge was made against a prominent and influential woman of Salem, the wife of a clergyman. Everyone began to fear accusation. In 1693, a number of people were placed on trial in Salem. The evidence was not substantially different from the evidence in 1692, but the jury refused to convict. No further trials occurred in Massachusetts, but the law was not repealed until two years later.

It should be noted that the juries that acquitted in 1693 were made up of the common people, while the juries that acquitted in 1692 were made up of freemen, who were necessarily church members and therefore not so likely to act as independently and humanely as jurymen selected from the body of the people. Winfield S. Nevins, in his "Historical Sketch of Witchcraft in Salem," says that after the first acquittal in 1693 "every effort was made by the authorities for three months longer to secure convictions. The officials never relaxed their efforts until the juries composed of the common people had refused repeatedly to convict."[7]

II

The long code of laws in America which have passed into history under the name of the Blue Laws furnish another illustration of the way in which fanaticism burdens the statute-books with oppressive legislation, and also of the way in which the common sense of the people finally disposes of it. It would be hard to find a variety of conduct that the Blue Laws did not attempt to regulate or any expression of pleasure that was not frowned upon or forbidden. They forbade women to dress their hair in a way that would attract attention, or to wear ribbons or silks. They forbade attending theatres; all kinds of travel on Sunday, except going to and from church; sleeping in church, not attending church, and the playing of any game of any sort on Sunday. They regulated the diet of the people, and of course regulated it so that they could eat nothing which tasted good or was expensive. They constituted, in brief, a desperate crusade against joy. Their theory was that good people would have their pleasures after death, and that the less joy they indulged in on earth the more they would get in the hereafter.

These laws made it the duty of all men to deliver offenders to the police for punishment. They made spies and informers of every citizen, and those who failed to serve did so at their peril. Dancing was forbidden; children were forbidden to walk the streets and fields on Sunday, for "they misspend that precious time, which tends to the dishonor of God and the reproach of religion, grieving the souls of God's servants." Parents were required to punish any child over seven years old for these offenses and to report it to the authorities in case punishment accomplished no result. In order that the Sabbath should be strictly observed it was provided that Saturday night, after sundown, was a part of the Lord's Day, but that the Sabbath did not end at sunset on Sunday, but continued until midnight. Death for cursing or striking parents was decreed by the Massachusetts Colony in November, 1646, if done by a boy or girl over sixteen years old. It was enacted that "any son which will not obey the voice of his father or the voice of his mother and when they have chastened him will not harken unto them, then shall his father and mother, being his natural parents, lay hold on him and bring him to the Massachusetts Assembly in the Court, and if it is proven in Court that their son is stubborn and rebellious, and will not obey their voice and chastisement, but lives in sundry, notorious crimes, such a son shall be put to death."

Politicians, Better Government Associations and Law Enforcement Leagues loudly proclaimed that all these laws must be obeyed, that so long as they were on the books they must be enforced. They are, however, not enforced today—even though many of them have not been repealed. Theatres were forbidden in Boston, but there were plenty of playhouses in New York and the well-to-do who lived in Boston and believed in enforcing the law went to New York and attended the theatre there, just as they now go to Havana, Canada, Mexico and England for a drink. Later, theatres were built in Boston, at first under the pretense that they were not theatres at all, but only lecture-halls. In them songs were sung and women walked on tight ropes. The people grew bolder and bolder as their natural impulses asserted themselves. The performers were prosecuted, but the juries acquitted them and judges began distinguishing what the law meant until it finally meant nothing.

Most of the other Blue Laws died the same way. The law compelled going to church on Sunday, but many people would not go. The law forbade sleeping in church, but they slept. Women wore ribbons and silks and curled their hair in spite of the law. Children were children, and played on Sunday. Occasionally, after they had been long ignored, under the impetus of a general housecleaning, some of the old statutes were repealed. But many remain on the books today; they are not worth repealing, for they are dead. They are like the rudimentary muscles which abound in the human body; they once did some kind of service, but the rest of the muscles found a way to get along without them, so they became useless and atrophied. They were not removed by a surgical operation, for it would have been difficult and superfluous.

The Poor Laws of England which were more or less in force for three hundred years—from the Sixteenth Century to the beginning of the Nineteenth—furnish abundant evidence of the way that arbitrary and cruel legislation may be forced upon the books by an active party serving its own interests. And, together with the Labor Laws of the same period, they show also the method by which the people get rid of such statutes. "Begging and idling" were strictly forbidden except upon special license by the authorities. "Sturdy beggars"—that is, persons who were able to work but idled away their time—came under the fierce condemnation of the law. Punishment of death for the third offense was enacted and thousands of people suffered execution. Still, in spite of the statutes and their steadily increasing penalties, it gradually grew impossible to convict, and they finally fell into disuse long before their repeal.

In 1530 Parliament passed a law confessing the failure of all other laws to accomplish the object aimed at; its preamble was as follows:

> Whereas, in all places throughout this realm of England, vagabonds and beggars have long time increased and daily do increase, in great and excessive numbers by the occasion of idleness, mother and root of all vices, whereby hath insurged and sprung and daily insurgeth and springeth continual thefts, murders and other heinous offenses and great enormities to the high displeasure of God, the inquietation and damage of the King's people and the disturbance of the common weal of this realm. And whereas many and sundry good laws . . . have been before this time devised and made . . . for the most necessary and due reformation of the premises, yet that notwithstanding the said numbers of vagabonds and beggars be not seen in any part to be diminished, but rather daily augmented and increased into great routs and companies as evidently and manifestly it doth and may appear.[8]

Although this law provided for excessively barbarous punishments, it had no effect, and five years later Parliament passed another law, one section of which read:

> . . . that if any of the aforesaid ruffelers, sturdy vagabonds and valiant beggars, after such time as they have been once apprehended, taken and whipped, . . . happen to wander, loiter or idley to use themselves and play the vagabonds and willingly absent themselves from such labor and occupation as he or they shall be appointed unto . . . that he or they being again apprehended and taken of suspicions of idleness, . . . shall be brought before the next justice of peace, and upon due examinations and proof of the continuance of his said loitering, wandering in idleness or vagabondage shall be not only shipped again and sent into the [place] . . . whereunto he was first appointed, but

also shall have the upper part of the gristle of his right ear clean cut off, so as it may appear for perpetual token after that time, that he hath been a contemner of the good order of the commonwealth . . . [and for a third offense] then every such sturdy vagabond and valiant beggar so found guilty as contemned shall have judgment to suffer pains and execution of death as a felon and as enemies of the commonwealth and to lose and forfeit all their lands and goods as felons do in all other causes within this realm. . . . [9]

But even this law had no effect. The statutes were constantly neglected and new legislation was passed without better results. Finally, the whole body of it fell into complete disuse. But it was not repealed until 1834![10]

With the rise of trades unionism in England drastic measures were taken against rebellious workmen. For one laborer to solicit another to join him in a strike was made a felony. Organizations of workingmen were driven into the woods and waste places to carry on their activities. These laws were made and enforced by landholders and by others who wished free competition between individual workingmen, that wages might be low; but in spite of jails and scaffolds the labor organizations grew and flourished until all the laws were nullified by disuse. It was only long afterward that they were repealed.

III

The English criminal code is filled with examples of the process of getting rid of legislation by disuse. Up to the beginning of the last century more than two hundred offenses were punishable by death in England, including loitering and loafing, petty larceny and poaching. The scaffold had its thousands of victims, but crime increased. Finally juries refused to convict, judges found excuses, the laws became dead letters, and eventually they passed into the rubbish heap. They were repealed in the end because they encumbered the books and no longer had any vital force. The humanizing of the English penal code came from the fact that juries would not convict. They were too humane and decent to obey the laws.

The history of the past is carried into the present. All our codes are filled with obsolete laws. The Fugitive Slave Law was never obeyed in the North; it took more than a law to compel a humane white man to send a black man back to slavery. The Sunday laws today in many states of the Union forbid the publication of newspapers, the running of trains and street cars, riding and driving for pleasure, attending moving picture shows, playing any game, the starting out of boats on voyages, or the doing of any work except works of necessity. Nearly all these laws are dead, though they still remain on the books. They are dead because they do not fit the age. They are not now a part of the customs, habits and mores of the people. They could not be enforced.

After the Civil War the Constitution was amended to abolish slavery and provide equality between whites and blacks. Congress and most of the Northern States thereupon passed explicit legislation forbidding any discrimination between the races in public places, such as hotels, theatres, railroad trains, street cars, restaurants and the like. But these laws, as everyone knows, are now openly ignored. The Negro does not go to the good hotels; he does not have good seats in the theatre; he does not enter the best restaurants; is not permitted to mingle with the whites, or to get what the whites believe belongs exclusively to them. This is not only true in the South; it is rapidly becoming a fact in the North. Custom and habit override the law because of the deep prejudice of the white against social equality with the black. Any effort to enforce these laws would bring serious consequences either North or South, and would no doubt injure the condition and standing of the black man, which can only be improved by a long process of education and growth. It cannot come from passing laws. All sorts of gambling is forbidden by the statutes of the various States. This includes betting and playing cards for money or prizes; it includes raffles even at church fairs. Yet most Americans gamble in some way or other—and are not prosecuted.

The Anti-Trust Act is a notorious example of legislation that is not enforced and cannot be enforced. Only a few prosecutions have ever been brought under it, and even when a prosecution has been successful ample means have been found to accomplish the desired ends in spite of the law. It has never kept Big Business from organizing and combining. It never can or should. Nevertheless, Big Business, through complaisant law officers and courts, has been able to enforce it against organizations of workingmen that engage in strikes. This is done in spite of the fact that it was passed in the interest of workmen and consumers and to control Big Business.

No one who has property believes in the tax laws. No one obeys them or pretends to obey them. When speaking of these laws no one shouts from the housetops the silly doctrine that a law must be enforced because it is on the books. No one even quotes the foolish statement of General Grant that the "best way to repeal a bad law is to enforce it." No doubt Grant was a good soldier, but he was never suspected of being a philosopher or an historian. The way to get rid of a bad law, which means a law obnoxious to large masses of people, is not by trying to keep it alive, but by letting it die a natural death. This is the way that society has always followed in dealing with unjust laws. The tax laws are a part of our civil and criminal codes, yet those who shout the loudest for enforcing Prohibition never pretend to obey them. When a man argues that a law must be enforced so long as it is a law, or that the best way to repeal a bad law is to enforce it, he is talking about some law he wants enforced and not about a law that he believes is tyrannical and unjust.

IV

The laws of the ancient world were modified and repealed in the same manner that is followed in the modern world. In Livy's "History of Rome" is an interesting sketch of the cult of Bacchus, a movement which grew up in obscurity, but about the year 200 B. C. became so strong as to attract the attention of the Roman rulers.[11] Livy says that a Greek of mean condition first introduced it into Etruria. This Greek was "a low operator in sacrifices and a soothsayer." After gathering a small body of disciples about him he proceeded to hold secret meetings and practice nocturnal rites. He soon had large numbers of followers, both men and women. They were accused not only of performing new and forbidden religious ceremonies, but also of drinking, debauching and practicing all sorts of vices. It was charged that from them proceeded counterfeit seals, false evidence, poisoning, the burning of buildings and secret murders. A member of a noble family joined the sect and this attracted the attention of the rulers. Laws were passed providing for the burning of its temples, the exile and imprisonment of members, and the execution of its leaders. The government undertook to stamp out the cult in Rome and the provinces, and in the effort to destroy it indulged in the kind of crusade of hatred and violence which everywhere follows a blind and bigoted political or religious frenzy. Thousands of devotees were put to death, many others were thrown into prison, and yet others were driven from Rome. But all of these measures failed to destroy the cult. It survived the most drastic laws. In the face of all opposition it grew and flourished until the general break-up of all the old religions in Rome after the introduction of Christianity.

About the year 20 A. D., Tiberius, Emperor of Rome, issued his edict expelling the Jews. The most drastic measures were taken, involving the destruction of their temples and their religious emblems and their own imprisonment and death. But the Jews stayed in Rome. Twenty years later, under Claudius, they were attacked by the same laws and suffered the same outrageous persecutions and an attempt was again made to drive them from the city. Many of them fled, but the majority stayed. They have remained ever since and are there in large numbers now. They have had to face similar drastic and barbarous laws and persecutions in most European countries, but nearly everywhere the Jewish population has steadily increased.

Nero commenced persecuting Christians in Rome about the year 66. Almost every conceivable form of cruelty was adopted to stamp out their religion. The government sought to destroy Christianity not only because it was hostile to the ancient gods but because it was regarded as treasonable to the state. Christians were thrown to the wild beasts in the arena, nailed to the cross, and covered with the skins of wild beasts to be torn to pieces and devoured by dogs. In spite of all this they persisted bravely and fanatically, and finally a feeling of compassion for them arose in Rome. The decrees were not repealed, but the persecutions died out. They were revived by Domitian in the year 93. Again, the Christians bravely withstood all the terrible ordeals of persecution until the people grew weary in the attempt to destroy them. For a time they were not molested; then Trajan revived the persecution in the year 112. It ran its course, and then, finally, the Christians were left to pursue their way. After the year 177, they were unmolested for nearly a hundred years. Then, under Decius, the laws still on the books were again invoked, resulting in a persecution more bitter and cruel than ever before. During all this time no law was repealed. Enforcement was simply broken down by the devotion of a sect that had faith in its cause.

About the year 310, under the Emperor Galerius, a final attempt was made to stamp out Christianity from the Empire. Like the others, it was met by the stubborn resistance of a religious organization that had grown strong by persecution, and had rapidly increased in numbers year after year. Galerius soon grew tired of the persecution, declared openly that the law was a failure and could not be enforced, granted clemency to the Christians, and left them free to enjoy and spread their faith. If during all these years, they had believed that the law should be enforced so long as it was on the books, Rome, and probably the rest of the Western world, would not today be Christian, even by profession. The repeated attempts of part of a community to control the beliefs, the conduct and the habits of men who had an instinctive feeling that they were right, and the utter failure of all such attempts, gave birth to the aphorism, "the blood of the martyrs is the seed of the church."[12]

V

It is much easier to pass a new law than to repeal an old one. Legislation which represents special interests or is demanded by organized associations which make a great show of power before law-making bodies is seldom met by strong opposition. The force which demands the law is active and persistent; its insistence leads politicians to believe that a large mass of men is behind it. But when the statute goes into effect it may create serious oppression and violent disorder; it may come into conflict with the desires and prejudices of the majority of the people affected by it. But, once it is on the books, an active minority can easily prevent its repeal. It is only by the steady resistance of the people that it is eventually destroyed.

In spite of the common opinion, this method has always been the ruling one in getting rid of bad laws. It is Nature's way of letting the old die by opposition, neglect and disuse. If it were not in operation there could be no real progress in the law. If history were not replete with illustrations, if philosophy did not plainly show that this must be the method of society's growth, it would be easier to understand the people who so glibly argue that, whatever the cruelty or the hardship, the law must be enforced while it is on the books. A law cannot be taken off the books while it is complacently obeyed. Constant protest is the only manner that history offers the common people of having their way in the making and administration of the law.

All this, of course, does not mean that all laws are or should be habitually violated. The larger part of our criminal code represents the ideas of right and wrong of nearly all our people. But the sumptuary laws that regulate individual conduct and custom are never believed in by the great mass of the people. Men, unfortunately, are in the habit of being influenced by aphorisms and catchwords. We continually hear of "Law and Order," as if they always went together and law came first. As a matter of fact, order is the mother of law, and the law which seriously overturns habits and customs does not promote order, but interferes with it instead. The enforcement of an unpopular law by drastic threats, by increasing penalties, by more cruelty, is not the administration of justice; it is tyranny under the form of law.

James C. Carter, one of the ablest of American lawyers, in a lecture delivered at the Harvard Law School, said:

> When a law is made declaring conduct widely practiced and widely regarded as innocent to be a crime, the evil consequences which arise upon attempts to enforce it are apt to be viewed as

the consequences of the forbidden practice, and not of the attempt to suppress it; and it is believed that the true method of avoiding or doing away with these consequences is to press the efforts at enforcement with increased energy. But when a mistake has been made, its consequences can not be avoided by a more vigorous persistence in it. . . . An especially pernicious effect is that society becomes divided between the friends and the foes of repressive laws, and the opposing parties become animated with a hostility which prevents united action for purposes considered beneficial by both. Perhaps the worst of all is that the general regard and reverence for laws are impaired, a consequence the mischief of which can scarcely be estimated.[13]

A great part of the misconception about the power of law comes from the assumption that the social group is held together by law. As a matter of fact, the group came into being long before the statutes. It formed itself automatically under the law of the survival of the fittest. The group is always changing in accordance with this natural law. Even statutes and courts are powerless when they stand in its way. To quote again from Mr. Carter:

The popular estimate of the possibilities for good which may be realized through the enactment of law is, in my opinion, greatly exaggerated. Nothing is more attractive to the benevolent vanity of men than the notion that they can effect great improvement in society by the simple process of forbidding all wrong conduct or conduct which they think is wrong, by law, and of enjoining all good conduct by the same means; as if men could not find out how to live until a book were placed in the hands of every individual, in which the things to be done and those not be done were clearly set down.[14]

All laws are made, altered and amended in the same way. When a large class does not respect them, but believes them to be tyrannical, unjust or oppressive, they cannot be enforced. It is a popular idea that the majority should rule. But this does not mean that the people should vote on every question affecting human life, and that the majority should then pass penal statutes to make the rest conform. No society can hold together that does not have a broad toleration for minorities. To enforce the obedience of minorities by criminal statute because a mere majority is found to have certain views is tyranny and must result in endless disorder and suffering.

When the advocates of Prohibition urge that all laws must be enforced, they really refer only to the Prohibition laws. They do not refer to the numerous other laws in every State in the Union that have never been enforced. Even the drastic Volstead Act has not prevented and cannot prevent the use of alcoholic beverages. The acreage of grapes has rapidly increased since it was passed and the price gone up with the demand. The government is afraid to interfere with the farmer's cider. The fruit grower is making money. The dandelion is now the national flower. Everyone who wants alcoholic beverages is fast learning how to make them at home. In the old days the housewife's education was not complete unless she had learned how to brew. She lost the art because it became cheaper to buy beer. She has lost the art of making bread in the same way, for she can now buy bread at the store. But she can learn to make bread again, for she has already learned to brew. It is evident that no law can now be passed to prevent her. Even should Congress pass such a law, it would be impossible to find enough Prohibition agents to enforce it, or to get the taxes to pay them. The folly of the attempt must soon convince even the more intelligent Prohibitionist that all this legislation is both a tragedy and a hoax.

A wise ruler studies the customs and habits of his people and tries to fit laws and institutions to their folkways, knowing perfectly well that any other method will cause violence and evil; he knows that fitting laws to men is like fitting clothes to men. The man comes first and both the laws and the clothes should be fitted to him. Instead of increasing penalties, stimulating cruelty, and redoubling the search for violators, he should take a lesson from Trajan, the Roman Emperor, as shown by his correspondence with Pliny. About the year 112, when the campaign against the Christians was in full sway in the Empire, Pliny, who was the governor of a province, wrote to Trajan for instructions as to how to carry on the prosecutions. The Emperor replied: "Do not go out of your way to look for them."[15]

Crime and the Alarmists

READERS OF NEWSPAPERS AND periodicals are constantly regaled with lurid stories of crime. From time to time with great regularity these tales are pieced together to produce the impression that waves of crime are sweeping across the land. Long rows of figures generally go with these tales which purport to tabulate the number of murders, hold-ups, burglaries, etc., in given areas, and sometimes comparisons are drawn with other countries and with other periods. The general effect is always to arouse anger and hatred, to induce legislatures to pass more severe laws, to fill the jails and penitentiaries, and to furnish more victims for the electric chair and gallows. It is a commonplace that cruel and hard punishments cannot be inflicted unless the populace is moved by hatred and fear. The psychology of fighting crime is the same as the psychology of fighting wars: the people must be made to hate before they will kill. This state of mind prevents any calm study of facts or any effort to seek causes or even to consider whether causes for crime may exist.

No one need be surprised that crime is so seldom the subject of objective study. It has not been very long since men thought that the whole

First published in *Harper's* 153 (October 1926): 535–44, this essay seeks to address the hysteria surrounding the findings of the Chicago Crime Commission, which some commentators interpreted as indicating a radical increase in criminal activity. The publications to which Darrow seems to be referring are the Chicago Crime Commission's *Annual Report* (1920f.). It later published a journal, *Criminal Justice* (1927–54).

physical world was operated by miracles. The motion of the earth and sun, the procession of day and night, the seasons of the year, the waves and wind, the flood and drought, the seed time and the harvest—all were defined by no natural laws, but all were dependent upon the whim and caprice of some other-worldly power. Even when some natural law of causation was believed to account for the phenomena of the physical world, the conduct of man was still supposed to lie outside this realm. Sickness and disease meant the possession of the individual by devils, and these could be driven out only by punishments and incantations. The ordinary treatment of disease was by magic and sorcery. For eighteen centuries, over most of Europe, medical men were punished often in the most terrible ways for seeking to find out the causes of disease and for attempting to treat illness by scientific methods. It was the greatest heresy to deny that sickness was due to sin and that pestilence and plague came as a divine visitation of angry gods to afflicted communities. And yet, in spite of restrictive measures and stern persecutions, the doctors persisted, until now no one questions that disease and pestilence are due to natural causes which must and can be removed if the patients are to be cured and infection prevented.

Insanity, too, was for many centuries thought of as possession by devils, and the punishment of the afflicted individual was the favorite treatment for driving out the demon. Hundreds of thousands of unfortunate insane men and women have been put to the severest tortures even down to the most recent times. Sorcery, witchcraft, and magic were the only methods of treatment permitted and the physician was obliged to risk his liberty and life in treating insanity as a disease, and seeking to understand the causes back of the phenomenon.

To-day, no one doubts that disease and insanity can be traced to natural causes and that both can be cured only by discovering the cause and applying the remedies which have been arrived at by careful and objective study of the disease.

The realm of miracle and magic has constantly grown smaller as natural law has come to be better understood. Crime, like insanity and sickness, is a departure from ordinary conduct; but most of the world clings to the belief that it can only be treated as a manifestation outside the realm of natural law. The old indictments read that "John Smith, being possessed of the devil, did wilfully kill," etc., etc. The modern indictments do not mention the devil, yet we still believe that crime is not due to causes, but is an arbitrary act unrelated to the criminal's past. We believe that the criminal should be made to suffer punishment for his act as a matter of "justice" and likewise that the only way to deter others from crime is to make them fear punishment.

In support of the theory that severe punishment with all its attendant horrors, and the psychology of general fear which goes with it, is the only admissible treatment of crime, tables of so-called statistics are always freely called into play. What these figures would prove in this behalf, even if they were dependable, is not easy to conceive.

It is only during a few years that any effort has been made in the United States to gather statistics on the subject of crime. From the nature of our political organization, this movement began with isolated states and cities, and even up to the present time statistics can be obtained from relatively only few and small areas. In the main these figures have been collected by police departments, coroners' offices, clerks of courts, Grand Juries, prison superintendents, and sometimes by outside agencies. In short, as the system was built up the methods of gathering statistics have developed in a hit or miss fashion. Naturally, as in all similar cases, the additional work thrown upon the various officials was done carelessly and imperfectly. As time has gone on, however, the collection of data has been improved. The growing care in gathering statistics in itself might easily lead to the conclusion that crime in the United States is on the increase. But still in very few places has there been any attempt to place the collection of data in the hands of intelligent people trained for such a task.

Every student of crime who has commented on these statistics gathered by various agencies has reached the conclusion that in their present state they are of little if any value. In no field has it been more clearly shown that there is a vast difference between the mere gathering of figures and an *intelligent interpretation* of the statistics after they have been collected. Public speakers, magazine writers, and newspapers are periodically presenting long arrays of figures to prove that there is an epidemic of crime in some part of the United States. As a rule there is not the slightest relation between the figures and the conclusions drawn. For example, the figures which are sometimes quoted with regard to the increase of the crime of rape are noteworthy illustrations of the care that must be taken in interpreting criminal statistics. Any one reading the startling statement that in New York state 146 persons were convicted of rape in the decade between 1880 and 1889, while 1297 were convicted of rape in the decade between 1910 and 1919 would be amazed if not horrified at the increase in the sexual passion and its manifestations in this period. Still, their condemnation of their fellows may be somewhat abated when they learn that in the decade showing the largest number of convictions for rape the age of consent had been raised from ten years of age to eighteen. Let us take another case: 991 persons were found guilty of violating motor laws in Michigan in the three-year period from 1906 to 1909. The number increased to 29,393 in the three-year period from 1919 to 1922. Before reaching the conclusion that this is positive evidence of the increasing recklessness of automobile owners and drivers or of the younger generation it might be well to consider the increase in the general use of automobiles from 1909 to 1922.

Alarmists also forget that the number of violators of law has something to do with the number of laws. Every new criminal statute brings a new grist of crimes. This is well illustrated in the Volstead Act and the state legislation covering the same subject. Prisons are now filled with inmates who have only done something which a few years ago was perfectly legal.

Or, again, it is freely asserted that the late comers to the United States commit more crimes than the descendants of the earlier settlers. Those who make this statement forget to take into account the fact that practically all of the later immigrants live in our large cities and industrial centers. It is beyond question that our large urban areas produce more disorder, maladjustment, and crime than our rural communities. And this is true, irrespective of the race or nationality of the people who live under these crime-breeding conditions.

Likewise, the colored population is charged with a share in the commission of crime quite out of proportion to their number. This, too, should always be considered in connection with the fact that in the North they live in industrial centers and in restricted, crowded areas and that colored people, owing to race prejudice and poverty, are much more apt to be accused and convicted than whites.

II

All this amounts to saying that the agencies which gather statistics of crime and those who quote these statistics in our newspapers and magazines use all sorts of standards and definitions and overlook explanatory facts which make their conclusions valueless. For instance, in classifying murders some agencies base their conclusions on the police reports, some on the coroner's inquests, some on indictments, and others on convictions. Statistics taken from these various sources differ so widely that they seem almost to have no relation to each other. As a rule, the people who quote statistics to prove their theories simply cite figures without giving their source and without in any way analyzing them to find out what they mean.

In my recent studies in this field I have observed that many books and articles, while calling attention to the uncertainty of figures on crime, at the same time quote the statistics furnished by the Chicago Crime Commission as being the best statistics on crime in the United States now available. Perhaps these are the best. If they are, it is all the more reason for examining them carefully to see just how reliable are the "best" statistics on crime. Let us, then, consider the reports of the Chicago Crime Commission.

In the first place, let me say that I have no idea that those in charge of the Chicago Crime Commission would pretend to give their statistics any such interpretation and validity as has widely been credited to them. They have gathered statistics on crime in the best way they could, conditions being what they are, and in most cases they have simply given them to the public. In the remarks which follow I have no intention of criticizing the work of the Chicago Crime Commission as such, but I only wish to use their reports as an example of the extreme care necessary when drawing inferences from statistics relating to crime.

The Chicago Crime Commission was organized in 1919 to combat what was said to be a crime wave. In the main it is backed by the Chicago Association of Commerce and leading business men of the city. It has published several annual reports and a number of pamphlets, all dealing with crime in Chicago. The question is—what light do these reports throw on this problem in the city of Chicago, and, by implication, on the problem in the country at large? Is crime decreasing or increasing? Is there a crime wave?

Let us look at the figures which the Commission has collected on burglary, robbery, and murder. The Commission reports that so far as burglary is concerned there has been a steady decrease from the year 1919 to the present time. For example, in December, 1919 there were approximately 550 burglaries in Chicago, while in the month of December, 1925, there were approximately only 100 cases. As to robberies the figures are likewise impressive. For December, 1919, the number of robberies was approximately 350. In December, 1925, this number had decreased to approximately 200. In both cases the month of December is cited because this month shows the highest number of offenses of this type of any month during the year. The total numbers for the whole year period indicate substantially the same general trend, *i.e.*, for both robbery and burglary there has been a marked and steady decrease during the seven-year period covered by the reports of the Commission.

I have made no effort to verify the figures given out by the Commission for the number of burglaries and robberies, nor in any way have I attempted to ascertain how they were arrived at otherwise than that they were taken from the annual reports of the police department.

However, we assume from these figures, showing as they do such a marked decrease in the number of burglaries and robberies, that when the newspapers and orators talk about the "crime wave" in Chicago their remarks are evidently directed to what they call "murders." For example, one of the most esteemed judges on the bench in Chicago is quoted as having said before the St. Louis Bar Association that "there are at large and unafraid in the United States at least 135,000 crimson-handed women and men who have unlawfully taken human life," and that the number of those who live by crime is "increasing with incredible rapidity." Where these figures came from we are not told; however, on other occasions the judge has referred to the reports of the Chicago Crime Commission. It is possible that the figures on "murder" given out by this Commission may have furnished him with some basis for his estimate, although the Crime Commission does not pretend to tell how many of the murderers now at large are "unafraid."

Be this as it may, the fact remains that Chicago has been held up to view throughout the United States for its large number of murders, and it is also true that the reports of the Chicago Crime Commission have been widely quoted to support this fact. Let us, then, carefully examine their figures on murder. It may prove a valuable lesson in the interpretation of criminal statistics. The Commission has made available to the public statistics on murder in Chicago for the years 1919 to 1924:

Year.	No. of Murders.
1919	330
1920	194
1921	190
1922	228
1923	270
1924	294

From these figures the reader might draw the conclusion that the number of murders in Chicago had steadily increased from 1921 to 1924. However, before drawing any such conclusion, or before allowing ourselves to believe that any such numbers of murders have occurred in any year let us find out how these statistics were compiled.

With the exception of the year 1919 the figures for the number of murders in Chicago as recorded by the Chicago Crime Commission were taken solely from the reports of the Coroner's office; 1919 being the first year of the Commission's work, the figures were taken from various sources including the Coroner's office. For the sake of accuracy it should be stated that the jurisdiction of the Coroner extends over the whole county in which Chicago is located. It is the duty of the Coroner to call a jury to determine the cause of death in all cases where it appears that death might not be due to what is termed natural causes. This office, of course, has been created in order to have some agency to investigate cases where death *might have* been brought about by foul means. The investigation is made very soon after the death is reported, necessarily without great care, and with the end in view that where there is even a possibility of homicide somebody should be held to the Grand Jury for further investigation. The Chicago Crime Commission's reports, then, as to the number of "murders" in Chicago in any given year are based upon the fact that the Coroner's jury has in a certain number of cases made a finding of "murder" with a recommendation that the "guilty persons" be held pending further investigation and examination by the Grand Jury.

Let us continue our investigation of these cases which, during these various years, the Coroner's jury reported as "murder." For purposes of convenience let us take the two years 1922 and 1923 in which the Commission reported 228 and 270 murders respectively. We may take these two years simply as representative years of the period covered by the work of the Commission. The records of the Clerk of the Criminal Court of Cook County show that the number of persons indicted for murder by the Grand Jury in Chicago (Cook County) for the year 1922 was 178. The number of persons indicted for manslaughter was 30. In the same year (1922) 38 persons were convicted of murder and 28 of manslaughter. In the year 1923 the number of persons indicted for murder by the Grand Jury was 179. The number indicted for manslaughter was 46. The number of convictions for murder was 44 and for manslaughter was 18. Thus in the two years 1922 and 1923 the total number of "murders" *reported* by the Chicago Crime Commission (Coroner's Jury) was 498. Whereas in the same two-year period the total number of *indictments* for murder by the Grand Jury was 357 and the total number of *convictions* for murder was 82.

Let us see if we can find out with reasonable certainty what became of the 416 "murderers" reported by the C. C. C. who were not convicted during the years 1922 and 1923. In the first place we already know that in 141 cases the Grand Jury refused to indict. Then of those who were indicted for murder by the Grand Jury in this two-year period according to the reports of the C. C. C., we find that out of a total of 326 defendants—the total number which *they* report as having been indicted during the period under consideration—138 were convicted; 48 were dismissed by the State's Attorney without prosecution; 41 were stricken off the docket with leave to reinstate (which order almost always means dismissal); 99 were found not guilty.

The first point to be made about these figures concerns the matter of the number of convictions for "murder." The total number of convictions for murder for the two-year period 1922–3 as shown by the records of the Clerk of the Criminal Court, was, as we have already stated, 82. The Crime Commission shows the number of convictions for murder for the same period to be 138. How shall we account for this difference of 56? Of course it is possible that all indictments are not disposed of by the courts in the same year in which they are returned. Each year, no doubt, some cases are tried, the indictments for which were returned in the preceding year; but this would make no notable difference when the figures are taken for a two-year period. The discrepancy between the two sets of figures is mainly to be accounted for by the fact the Crime Commission in making its tabulation of "murders" does not distinguish between manslaughter and murder. All are listed as murder. As a matter of fact during these two years there were 46 convictions for manslaughter. Manslaughter, by no possible definition of the term, is synonymous with murder, although a verdict of manslaughter may be found under an indictment for murder in cases where death was caused without malice, or through accident due to gross carelessness.

It is at once manifest that there can be no possible excuse for the various statements which are so glibly and carelessly made as to the number of "murders" in Chicago during any given year. The number of "murders" put down by the Crime Commission for the years 1922 and 1923 was 498. The number convicted for murder during the same period was 82, or less than one-sixth the number constantly heralded to the world. It will not do to say that the State's Attorney and his assistants are dishonest and incompetent, and no one pretends to account for the discrepancy in the above figures in this way. The story has been practically the same in all administrations in Chicago, and no doubt in other cities as well. No one can pretend that the findings of the Coroner's jury gives any sort of evidence of the actual number of murders. On the contrary, there is every reason for taking the number of convictions as the real basis for estimates of the number of murders during any given period.

Even indictments returned by the Grand Jury, although far superior as a basis for statistical computation to the reports of the Coroner's jury, do not furnish any accurate evidence of the number of murders in a city like Chicago. It is a well-known fact that although the evidence presented to the Grand Jury may be rather carefully prepared, nevertheless, the Grand Jury investigation is purely one-sided and almost entirely under the control of the State's Attorney or his deputies. The defendant is never present nor is he represented. In the two years which we have been considering there were 357 indictments for murder in Chicago—or, rather, in Cook County, the jurisdiction covered by the Coroner and the Criminal Court. As we have said, these 357 indictments resulted in 82 convictions for murder; 89 of these indictments were dismissed by the State's Attorney after full consideration. This left a little over one half the number shown by the Coroner on which the State's Attorney even asked a trial. And out of these only 82 were convicted of murder while 99 were found not guilty of any crime.

It should be clear that no person can possibly use the figures of the Crime Commission as an indication of the number of murders in Chicago without the most serious reflection upon the Grand Jurors and upon the State's Attorney, to say nothing of the Judges of the Criminal Courts. And no one pretends to make any such charges.

III

But perhaps some one will think that the foregoing simply represents a more or less adroit juggling of figures in the interest of proving my point. Statistics are notoriously slippery affairs. To be fully certain what these figures mean it would be necessary to take the complete history of each individual case from the time it left the Coroner's office until it was finally disposed of by the courts (assuming that it got that far). Obviously, limitations of space will not allow any such exhibit in this place. However, suppose we take at random one month during this two-year period and see the character of the "murder" cases reported during that month and what befell them. The following cases are those listed by the Chicago Crime Commission and the Coroner's juries for the month of March, 1923. During this month there were 26 cases of "murder" involving 29 defendants reported by the C. C. C. The cases listed seriatim are:

Case 1. Thomas Rutledge shot by Forrest Hand during a quarrel over the deceased's wife (all parties colored). Plea of guilty. Sentenced to 14 years in the penitentiary.

Case 2. Hattie Morgan throat cut by Robert E. Morgan (both colored). Plea of guilty. Sentenced to 20 years.

Cases 3 and 4. Antonio Giambaluo shot in a duel with Joseph Salamitano. Both parties killed in the duel. (Both reported as "murders.")

Cases 5 and 6. Paul Radin shot by Albert Green when Green was shooting at William Kinsella (also killed) during a quarrel at a meeting of the Butchers' Union. Defendant found not guilty on both charges.

Case 7. Wilbert Andrews shot by Owen Thomas who was sentenced on a plea of guilty of manslaughter.

Case 8. Alice Powers shot by Elmer Bostic. Verdict—guilty, but insane.

Case 9. Allen Walker stabbed by Burton Andrews (both colored). Verdict of manslaughter.

Case 10. James Lockett stabbed by Raymond Perkins (both colored). Verdict—guilty of manslaughter.

Case 11. Donald Whitner shot by James Brooks. Dismissed.

Case 12. Michael McGinnis shot during a quarrel. Four defendants (three women and one man) all found not guilty.

Case 13. John Nicolin thrown over a porch railing during a quarrel with Theodore Past. Verdict—not guilty.

Case 14. Ella Wollson throat cut by Edna Robinson (her daughter) who then committed suicide.

Case 15. Orfie Rizzato killed in a fist fight in a saloon by Sam Sanadrea. No indictment.

Case 16. Donata Frazzolari shot by insane brother-in-law who then committed suicide.

Case 17. Gaspar Lombardi struck by unknown vehicle. Unsolved.

Case 18. Walter Henning shot by unknown persons. Unsolved.

Case 19. Unknown white baby found under elevated railway in a pile of ashes. Coroner's verdict—died from neglect at birth. Unsolved.

Case 20. Joseph Basile shot by Phillip Leonette. Unsolved.

Case 21. George Wesley killed by blow on the head by persons robbing a laundry. Unsolved.

Case 22. Frederico Amadio shot by unknown persons in the rear of his home. Unsolved.

Case 23. Asap Shultz shot by an unknown colored man during a holdup. Unsolved.

Case 24. Unknown white baby. Neglect at time of birth. Found in rear of building. Unsolved.

Case 25. Julia Sinks, 18-year-old colored girl, struck on head with hatchet by unknown persons. Unsolved.

Case 26. Frank Liber killed by unknown automobile. Unsolved.

In this list of 29 possible defendants all of them were classed as "murderers" by the Coroner's Jury and the Chicago Crime Commission. And yet it is extremely unlikely that more than two of them (Cases 21 and 23) were really cases of out and out murder, and both of these were unsolved. Is this feeble list for March, 1923, the red-handed menace that is so luridly pictured as an army in mortal combat with organized society? Rather it is a fair sample of the results of poverty, hard luck, ignorance, maladjustment, and destiny that in some form come to light in every great city filled with the flotsam and jetsam of humanity. It is a condition, and it needs careful study to find out what should be done and what can be done. It does not call for blind hatred and stern revenge.

What general conclusions can be drawn from the object lesson just exhibited in our analysis of the statistics on crime compiled by the Chicago Crime Commission? One thing is certainly clear—no intelligent person can examine carefully the statistics which are at present available and come to any satisfactory or defensible conclusion as to the number of crimes committed in the United States, or whether they are increasing or diminishing in proportion to the population, or the cause of any increase or diminution. The study of statistics in regard to crime, as in many other matters, leaves one in a hopeless maze. It will take years of careful preparation and thorough, unbiased gathering of objective statistics before any general conclusion can be reached in this way. It is, however, safe to say that statistics do not show that there is an increasing trend of crime in America. On the whole, it probably remains fairly stationary—with variations up and down now and then due to all sorts of reasons. Probably, on the whole, there is a tendency downward, especially if allowance is made for the new crimes that are constantly being created by statute and which add materially to the tables of law violation.

The growing use of the automobile has had a positive tendency to increase crime materially. It is a new lure that is hard to withstand. Men and women mortgage their homes and their beds to get them, and of course boys borrow and steal them. The indiscriminate use of the automobile in crowded cities has added largely to the coroner's returns, and many accidents appear in the tables as murders, although the only element even of homicide is careless or reckless driving. Sometime life may adjust itself to the automobile, but it will be a long time before men, women, and children can withstand the lure and before the accidents incident to the use of the automobile be materially reduced.

The Volstead Act and kindred state laws have furnished a great many additions to the reports of crimes. Many of these are classed as murders, many others as unlawful buying and selling. It is inevitable, in a mixed people like ours, with their diversity of habits and customs, that a drastic, tyrannical law, which makes criminal acts that carry with them no feeling of wrong, can have any other effect than to add to the list of crimes. Prohibition will continue to reap this harvest until it is settled whether the government shall recognize the habits of its citizens or whether the people shall be compelled by brute force to yield what they have long believed to be their rights.

Those who believe in sterner laws and harsher treatment of criminals are always drawing comparisons between America and England. Different parts of England show marked differences in the statistics of crime. Liverpool, for example, shows more burglaries than New York, and about the same as Chicago, and nearly twice as many murders and other serious felonies as London. The difference is most likely accounted for by the seaport location of Liverpool which adds to the mixture of races and peoples. Still, it is true that there are many more felonies in the United States than in England in proportion to the population. This condition cannot be accounted for by the severity of punishment in England. In many important instances the American penalties are much harsher and more brutal. The executions in England are fewer in proportion to the population than in America and, in cases where death sentences are pronounced, a much larger proportion receives clemency there than here. From all that can be gathered, it is probable that China has a smaller crime rate than England, though it is not possible to find statistics of crime for China. Regardless of the question of crime, few Americans believe that England is, on the whole, a more desirable place for living than America, much less is China.

Other things being equal, all new countries have a higher crime rate than old ones. This is due to many reasons, not all of which apply in all new countries. The residents of England are a homogeneous people. This is true of all old countries. They lack many of the inducing causes that lead to crime. The English people have been made alike by centuries of molding and welding. They have from long association formed common customs, habits, and views of life; in other words, folkways—which make them one people. An old country inevitably develops a sort of caste system; each person takes his place without hope of change or advancement. The individual grows to accept his lot in life.

When we remember that crime means the violation of law, which in turn means getting out of the beaten path, it is easy to see why it is more common in new countries, where the paths are faint and not strongly marked, than in old countries where the paths are deep. It is only one hundred and fifty years since the United States gained its independence. It then had some 3,000,000 people. Since that time it has grown to about 115,000,000. This necessarily means that it has drawn from almost every country of the earth. These people have brought all kinds of religions, social customs, political ideas, temperaments, and ambitions. Probably no such heterogeneous combination was ever before brought together upon the earth. Most of these people came here to improve their condition, to get out of their caste. Their children are still hopeful that they may rise. The subduing of natural resources has built our great cities and filled them with a babel of tongues and a medley of temperaments, and with every religious, social, and political idea in the world. The higher wages and better opportunities have made the people venturesome and aggressive. The larger individual freedom and greater independence of individual action have made collisions more inevitable and severe.

Most of the crime in the United States comes from our industrial centers. Our cities have always been settled by a mixture of the peoples of the world with varied feelings and emotions, and with the individual customs and habits of their native lands. In the main these have been the poor of Europe. They have come with new hopes and ambitions, moved by intense desires. The industrial cities have been alternately prosperous and idle. Aside from the natural emotions of love and fear and hate, there has been the constant battle with employers and between union and non-union men. Such a medley of conflicting peoples and emotions has always been a prolific soil out of which violations of habits, customs, and laws inevitably grow. No other country has ever had so many antagonisms, such a fertile soil for combat and discontent. Australia and Canada, although new countries, have in the main a homogeneous people and a rural population. The statistics of crime of the rural communities of the United States are not unlike the statistics of rural communities in Canada and the other countries of the world.

The population of the United States has been constantly augmented by the poor of other countries. These have left an old social organization with fixed habits and have been thrown into a social environment new and strange. Such a condition has always been disorganizing to every group. Old customs and folkways which act as restraints are left behind, and inevitable disorganization is the result. The study of our recent immigrants shows the difficulty of new adjustments and the disintegration and misfortune that comes to individuals and groups.

It is not the terror of brutal punishment that holds the units of society in their place. It is customs and habits. It is long familiarity with the beaten paths. People think and act and live as they are wont. They stay in grooves. Any sudden change jolts them from their ways and sets them loose to find or make other paths. To believe that men are kept in a certain line by fear is a crude conception at variance with experience and psychology alike.

Imperfect as all our statistics are confessed to be, it is doubtless true that the dangerous age for boys in reference to crime is constantly growing younger. It is safe to say that almost all crimes are committed by boys in their early teens or by those who began in effect a criminal career at that age. Saving criminals is, in the last analysis, only saving children; and saving children means not only saving criminals but their victims, too. Most of the criminals come from the cities and most of them were born and reared in the poor and crowded districts where they had little chance to develop into anything but criminals. A little knowledge of biology, psychology, and life makes this plain to understand. No well-informed person believes that one is born a criminal or with even a tendency to crime. If so, crime would not be of the individual's own choosing nor his end be due to his own volition. No child is born a criminal. He may be born weak or strong and, therefore, his power of resistance be more or less; but the course he takes is due to training, opportunity, and environment. The protection of the child or the grown person comes from habit. Religion may teach precepts, but this means nothing without habits. The school may give a certain kind of education, but unless this creates habits which fit the child for life it is of no avail.

Most of those who follow a criminal career have had little education and cared little for books. Most of them could not be fitted for professions by education; their only chance was some sort of work. They passed the school age without becoming scholars, and the schools have given them nothing in the place of what is generally called an education. When very young they began a life that almost inevitably leads to crime. If it is the duty of the state or any organized institution to provide for the education of the youth, then the most important thing is to fit them for the job of living. Many boys come to the adolescent age with only scant education in books and no education that fits them for any self-reliant life. For the large class who have no taste for books society furnishes no training in the schools. These boys are thrown on their own resources with no occupation that will furnish them a chance to live. The schools could as well teach manual trades as books, and a large part of those who cannot succeed with books could do well in working with their hands. There is no more reason why schools should prepare one to succeed in a profession than why they should teach certain ones a useful trade. Most boys like to use their hands, and the proper training for trades should be begun when very young. It is seldom that a mechanic enters on a life of crime. He forms habits that keep him safe.

The child is born with the same instincts that move all other animals. When he wants something he feels the urge to take it in the easiest way. It is only training that teaches him that he may get things one way, but not another. His training must be developed into habits. The life of a child is a conflict between primal emotions and social restrictions, and he must be fortified, not alone by teaching, but by habits, if he is to live by the rules that society lays down. Intelligent teachers and wise parents know what this means. It is only rarely that a boy carefully trained and fitted for life is sent to jail.

More and more the teacher and the psychologist are learning the importance of early training. Habits are formed when the child is young; these are easily fixed and hard to change. All statistics, if carefully gathered and thoroughly studied, lead to this conclusion, and logic and experience likewise show that this is true. To believe any other theory would be to deny the efficacy of moral and religious teaching and the effect of education and habit in the formation of character.

It is not difficult for the student to find the causes of crime. When they are found, it is not hard to prescribe for their cure. To ignore reason and judgment and all the finer sentiments that move men, to follow blind force and cruelty in the hope that fear will prevent crime and make all people safe, is bad in practice, philosophy, and ethics.

What to Do about Crime

I SHALL DISCUSS CRIME first, as to what it is and what is its cause, before I discuss what I think are the real remedies, if there are any. Before we talk about crime it is well enough to know what we mean by the word. A good many people don't know. They get their information, if they have any, from the newspapers. A criminal is a man who does something contrary to law and gets convicted. It doesn't really matter whether he actually does anything; he needs only to be convicted of some act that is contrary to a statute. It doesn't necessarily follow that he is bad or good—just that he did something that was forbidden by law. Of course there are so many fool laws that he might be too good to obey all of them. However bad he may be, unless he does something contrary to a statute and is convicted, he isn't a criminal. The fact that he has violated a law isn't in itself sufficient proof that he has done anything wrong. A legislature can not make right or wrong—that is, any legislature that I ever knew. I have worked in a law factory myself, so I understand something about them. To say that one is bad because he has done something that the legislature has forbidden him to do hardly satisfies

"What to Do about Crime" first appeared in the *Nebraska Law Bulletin* 6 (July 1927): 117–34 and was reprinted as a booklet (n.p., 1927). It is the transcript of an address before the Nebraska Bar Association on December 28, 1926, and sums up many of Darrow's views on crime: that it is not indicative of moral failing; that it is the strict result of cause and effect; that punishment in the conventional sense cannot "cure" crime; and that greater attention to the upbringing of children can prevent crime.

any ordinary person. Some of you may know some members of the legislature; and if so, there is enough said on that. Members of congress are just like them, only more so.

So you can not find out what is right or wrong by reading the statutes. You can find out what is dangerous and what is safe, but you can't find out what is right and what is wrong.

Some people believe that you can tell from religion what is right. That might do, but you have to pick out the right religion first. And that is some job. By the time a man carefully examines all of the different religions, he will have no time to do either right or wrong. He will be dead. Most people get their religion by inheritance rather than from study. They are more than apt to lose it by study. They get it because it is handed to them. One's religion is a question of where one was born. You happened to be born where the true religion is supreme. You are Americans and therefore Christian by way of Jerusalem. Even then, can you tell by religion what is right or wrong? You know that it is one thing to read the constitution or a statute and that it is another thing to construe it. That is where we lawyers drive in. The ordinary person can't tell what a statute or the constitution means. That is, the common people might think that it means what it says, but this is often not true. That is what the judges are for.

Religious creeds are subject to interpretation, too. There are very few of them that are clear. Otherwise we should not have so many different sects, probably over 300 or 400 in this country, differing on very important things in regard to the soul's salvation.

Do these creeds anywhere clearly indicate what is right and what is wrong? Let us take one of the Ten Commandments: "Thou shalt not kill." That seems easy, but is it? Does it tell you anything about what is right or wrong? It is a general commandment. What does it mean? Does it mean that you shall not kill any of the animals? The statute does not say you shall not kill anything but animals. It just says, "Thou shalt not kill." Nobody will believe it is wrong to kill animals as long as he likes to eat meat. If we didn't like to eat meat we would all say it was wrong. Well, does it mean human beings, when the commandment says, "Thou shalt not kill?" It doesn't mean that you can't go ahead with your part of the killing, when it is done by the State, or the Government.

Since the Volstead Act, the execution of some poor unfortunate is about the only way left to get a kick. War certainly is killing. Does the commandment mean "Thou shalt not kill" except in war? The commandment, by its terms, makes no distinction. Does it mean "Thou shalt not kill in war," when the whole Christian world has just been engaged for four years in killing each other? It certainly doesn't mean "Thou shalt not kill Germans or Frenchmen," or any people in particular.

It does not mean, "Thou shalt not kill by wholesale, but just retail." Of course the commandment simply says, "Thou shalt not kill." It doesn't give you any leeway at all. Does it mean retail killing? Everybody knows that it is right to kill in self-defense. That is, the law recognizes it, although the commandment does not. Everybody knows you can kill in self-defense. You may kill in defense of your family. You may kill in the defense of your home, unless it is invaded by a prohibition agent, and then he may kill. So we may say that we have amended the commandment so that it means, "Thou shalt not kill when you should not kill." Therefore it doesn't mean anything.

Now I could take all of the other ten commandments, if I could think of them, and go through them just the same way and show the same thing. So you can't answer the question by religious creed. Then how are you going to answer it? Some people say that everybody knows what is right or wrong; that the conscience tells us. Well, your conscience may tell you what is right and what is wrong, but what does your conscience know about it? What is your conscience? If the conscience tells us what is right and wrong, then everybody's conscience ought to tell the same thing and ought to do it accurately and clearly so that there would be some uniformity. But no two people have the same kind of conscience. Some people's conscience would bother them if they took a drink, and some people's conscience would bother them if they didn't take a drink. One woman's conscience will bother her if she goes out on the street without a veil. In Mohammedan countries you are entitled to four wives at once. Here you can have them only one at a time.

The Mohammedan's conscience doesn't bother him about his four any more than ours does about our one. Our consciences are not fixed; they don't bother us long, because our consciences are changing all the time. They have to, to keep up with the times. I remember, when I was a boy, that a girl's conscience bothered her if she went out on the street without a long dress. Now it would bother her if she should go out on the street with a long dress. She isn't used to it, that is all. Consciences change, so that now women go ahead and make the dresses shorter without its bothering their consciences at all. I have seen short dresses for so long that I have got used to it. I have got so used to it that I can look at a woman's face again. You can get used to anything. I remember when I was a boy in Ohio, we used to eat with our knives. I don't know how it is here. Some fellow came along and told us that we ought to eat with our forks. I remember what a hardship it was for me to get used to it. If I should undertake to eat with a knife now, my conscience would bother me; but it used to be all right.

Now, just what is conscience, anyway? You can't see it, as you can your nose. The doctors have dissected the human body and found the gizzard, but they have never found the conscience. Of course you can't see it. The conscience is a state of mind,—the way you feel about certain things. Where did you get it? You were not born with it. People are born without any ideas. Generally they die without any, too. They are born with plastic bits like putty in their heads and, later, impressions are made on that. Anybody that comes around makes a new impression. At first children don't know what is right or what is wrong; they just keep reaching out and getting things the best way they can, but someone begins educating their conscience and then it tells them what is right or what is wrong. Where do children get their ideas of right or wrong? Well, generally, at first, from their parents, who possibly knew nothing about it. When they grow older their teacher tells them. Then all of the neighbors contribute. By the time they all get through you have a fine conscience!—and it generally changes; there isn't any doubt about it.

Conscience, then, is a question purely of education. One can be educated to believe that anything is right or that anything is wrong. People have been so educated; but when it comes to finding out just what is right and what is wrong, then it isn't such an easy job.

Then how do we determine what is right or wrong? I will tell you how we determine it. We determine it by customs and habits. Men began to form habits long before they made laws. These habits became what was known as folkways. Men form these habits the same as animals do. Now the man who follows the habit is good, and the man who disregards or violates the habit is bad. The man who does something that the great mass of people don't do has done wrong. We are all constituted that way, and all our ideas of right and wrong are formed from and based upon custom and habit.

If any of you are interested in that subject and want to follow it further, read Dr. William Sumner's "Folk Ways."[1] The author isn't a Bolshevik; for forty years he was one of the leading members of the faculty at Yale. Of course you can find the same information in a great many other books. The best definition that I know of a man who does wrong is one that doesn't follow the common customs of the crowd; or, to put it in another way: In order to do right you must do what others do, think what others think and say what others say. It doesn't make any difference whether you think what is true, or what is high and good, you have to follow the bunch and do just as the others do. For men are like wolves; they run in bunches. If one wolf gets out of the bunch he gets into trouble. It doesn't matter whether he gets behind, ahead, or underneath; if he gets away from the rest he dies. So with human beings; we live in packs, and everybody else must agree with our ideas, and back them up by running with the pack. He who runs with the pack does right. Those who run against the pack do wrong.

Our ideas of right and wrong, then, grow out of habits. These habits are always changing; so the right and the wrong are determined simply by the time and place and are never fixed. They are always subject to change.

We are told that every man who violates a law should be punished. Punished, why? Because he violated the law? If punishing him would not bring any good to any human being on earth, then his punishment is pure vengeance. Some say that he must be punished because he has done wrong. That implies a good many things. Of course, then we raise the question as to whether anybody can help doing anything that they do. I am not going to discuss that question fully this afternoon. People have been discussing it for so long that it has become stale. But, as to whether there is anybody responsible for his conduct, let us see what man is. To start with, a human body grows from a single cell, one of some ten thousand in the body of the mother. There had to be a fertilization, by a sperm from the body of the father. The father had some billion of them. Nobody would pretend that the cells that were not fertilized could do right or wrong because they did not result in a human being. When a cell is fertilized a great deal has happened that cannot be changed. How much is determined in the cell? Of course it is determined whether we are to be white, black, or yellow; and once determined, there isn't any way to change it. It is determined whether you are to be male or female, and there is no way to change it; it is all in the cell. What is to happen to you, and how you are to come out in life, depends a good deal on whether you are black, white, or yellow. This may depend on where you are born. This, too, determines your religion and your social habits. You often hear people say that their grandmother's religion is good enough for them. Well, they are probably people whose grandmothers were more intelligent than they are. The last generation is really the oldest, because it has all of the past back of it, and really it should be more intelligent than its forebears. Your forefathers, away back in the past, may have had four wives at a time or just one at a time, depending on whether they were born in Turkey or elsewhere. The determination of sex determines to a large extent how people are coming out in life. A man has a much better chance to get in the penitentiary than a woman; though it seems that women are improving in that respect; there are twice as many going there now as formerly, and maybe it will be all right after a while.

But that isn't all that is settled in the cell. Your tendencies are probably settled. You may be of a nervous disposition, which might make you a drunkard or a poet. You may be of a stolid disposition which might make you a prohibitionist. You may be one of those individuals who act a good deal on impulse. Your emotional tendencies may be strong. Your inherent capacity is fixed in the cell long before birth.

So, up to the time that a person is born, you can't say that he has had very much to do with himself. You can't exactly blame a man because he didn't choose more intelligent parents. If he could have chosen, and was intelligent enough to do it, he perhaps wouldn't have been born at all. What happens after that? Some think that heredity, and others think that environment, is the more important in individual destiny. At any rate, things begin happening the instant a human being is born. He doesn't bring any ideas into the world with him. The kind of family he is born in has a good deal to do with what happens. The way he is brought up has everything to do with it. Everybody's ideas of right and wrong and the main things that govern in life, are fixed before they are ten or twelve years old. Some people later modify their ideas a little, but as a rule they are uniformly and almost invariably fixed in childhood, when we have not a single thing to do with it.

So, when one does this thing or that thing, differently from the things people generally do, it is pretty certain that he has either inherited a tendency to it, or that his environment was not the ordinary environment. Now let's go a little farther. There isn't a bit of excuse for punishment unless you believe that man is a free moral agent. I mean, punishment where you hurt somebody to help nobody else. You won't find any man of science who finds that man has very much of what is called free-will. There are some people who hold that there is a little bit of it, but not very much.

What has all this to do with crime? They used to punish people for being sick. Of course, to be ill was to be possessed of devils; one or more. The orthodox way of treating the sick was to take steps to cast out the devils. For ages that was the doctrine. If I had lived at that time I probably would have thought that way, too. There are lots of people who think so now. Slowly the world began to study disease. After the beginning of real investigation it was several hundred years before the medical profession was permitted to treat disease in a scientific way, or to dissect dead bodies. The religionists would not permit it, though the doctors kept on doing it until they finally conquered. I was reading the other day an interesting incident in that connection, which is the truth, although now it seems incredible. The use of morphine in alleviating pain was discovered only about a hundred years ago. The discovery was applied especially to women in childbirth. The orthodox view, vociferously supported by the clergy and orthodox laity, was that they must not do this; that it was meant that women should suffer in childbirth because, didn't Eve tempt Adam? Now how do you suppose people finally changed their minds? Some wise fellow looked over Genesis and found that when the Lord performed that first great surgical operation by taking a perfectly good rib out of a man to make a woman with, he put Adam into a deep sleep; so they said that the Lord was the first one to use an anaesthetic. For hundreds of years they fought the medical profession in every effort it made to treat disease. Everybody in the world today with any intelligence believes there is a cause for disease, and the wise surgeon tries to find out the cause. Then, if he can, he tries to cure the cause and thereby kill the disease. Nobody any longer says that people should be punished because they are sick. If people have pain we want to help them get rid of it, and we are determined to do everything we can to alleviate it.

Now, let us take our modern idea of cause and effect, in relation to crime and punishment. Our main idea now is to set criminals apart, put a lot of them in a pen. We call them criminals because we think they are not like us. I don't imagine their emotion is any different, but it isn't the same in all of us. We differ in the amount, and the balance of it. We all have every emotion that any human being ever had. We get emotions to kill, just the same as the man who does kill, but we have a balance that is somewhat better and governs the emotion; or the circumstances may be different. For myself, I have never killed anybody, but I have many times read obituary notices with great satisfaction. The fellow who actually kills has the same thing in his mind, but it balances up differently.

Medical scientists worked on insanity until they discovered what caused it, and began treating it as a disease due to causes. Today nobody advocates hanging an insane patient, or punishing him because he is sick. We have to shut him up because he would not be safe at large, but we treat him the very best that we can. When he is cured, if he ever is, we turn him out. Nobody believes people are insane because they want to be, or merely from pure cussedness. We know all of this is true in the physical world. We know that certain laws prevail. We know, for instance, that the earth goes around the sun. We know that in the organic world, everything operates according to law, and that there is a cause for everything. Can you imagine that anything could happen in this world without a cause? Of course, in many of the most important things of your life, you can't tell what the cause is. If anybody should ask you why you live here in Nebraska, many of you couldn't give a cause or reason. But none the less this world is a world of causes and effects, and all of our life is a sequence where one thing follows another; each thing follows what has gone before, and each follows the other because it inevitably must. If the same is not true of crime, then crime stands alone among all phenomena and manifestations as existing without cause.

Now, I am interested in the prevention of crime. I always have been. Of course my activities as what we call a criminal lawyer have led some people to think that I am interested in crime because I get money out of it. Well, one can't fully separate his consciousness from the idea of a fee. I imagine that the undertaker isn't entirely sorry, even when he buries his best friend, that he has sold a good coffin for $500.00, that cost him $10.00. He probably has mixed feelings. Anyway, I am no longer interested in trying such cases, so if I ever had any such interest, that interest has vanished. I am interested in running away from them, because I never did like work very well, and I have got to the time where I think I can pull through to the end without it. I am not longer interested in the actual trial of criminal cases, but I am more than ever interested in people; and more than in any other subject I am interested in determining how the world can get rid of crime. And I believe we can get rid of most of it if we treat it intelligently.

Almost no one has tried to find out the cause of crime. People think it is an individual act of free will, that has no relation to anything else in the past, present or future. They seem to think that the criminal just does it because he wants to do it. Now, let's see about it. You can't look into a man's mind and find out what is going on there, and if you could you might not find anything. You can only get a line on human beings and their activities by studying their conduct. The psychologists determine what is in a person's mind by finding what the person does; they study his behavior. It is safe to assume that back of every act was another one, and a process connecting it with the other, all making the necessary chain of cause and effect connecting up the thing that happens, whether it is crime or something else. If there is a cause of crime, and the cause or causes can be found, then an intelligent person could find a way to cure crime; for a cause must necessarily be followed by an effect, and instead of punishing we should cure the cause and get rid of the effect. If we kill the criminal, we get rid of that one manifestation of crime, and that is all.

You may go to any jail or penitentiary and you will find that the inmates are all of one class of people. You won't find three in a hundred that has any money, or ever had any, except for a brief period of time just before he got caught. I am safe in saying that without a doubt nine out of ten are poor and always have been. As a rule their parents were poor before them. But we will come to that later. There isn't money enough in any jail to pay a good lawyer to go through the whole institution. You lawyers all know that. That is why good lawyers are "civil" lawyers and not "criminal" lawyers. Good lawyers work for corporations where they can be honest and get the money. They are not interested in criminal business. There isn't anybody with experience that doesn't know that what I have said is true. Once in a while somebody gets in jail that has money—when he gets in—but they are so few that they are not worth talking about. First, then, they are all poor. Second, practically all of them are uneducated. That is, they haven't the education which we think is necessary to help us live. You almost never find an educated man in prison. If once in a while you do, it is because something special has occurred. You can hardly get a banker into prison. I am not against bankers, and I wouldn't send one to prison for anything except refusing me a loan or something like that. Then I might send him there, or some place else. But if you investigate the inmates of prisons you will find that half of them are sub-normal, that is, had less original capacity than ordinary persons. And when a fellow is below the average he is pretty far down, and you can't expect much of him, can you?

There are, then, two or three things, one or more of which are to be noted in connection with nearly all crimes and criminals. There are many exceptions, but I know of no remedy for everything, in any case. You can't get one hundred per cent of anything except Americanism, and you can get that only in Rotary Clubs and such organizations. If it is true that ninety per cent of all of the people in prison are poor, it ought to follow logically that there is some relationship between poverty and crime. If it is true that eighty per cent are ignorant, there must be some relationship between ignorance and crime. If fifty per cent of them are morons, then there ought to be some logical relationship between those two facts.

Here is another thing to consider: At least ninety per cent of all crimes are committed by people who are either children or began that kind of career when they were children. My interest, and yours, is in saving the criminal, and the victims of the criminal; and saving the criminal and his victims is nothing in the world other than saving the children. That ought to be worth while. Every father and mother ought to be interested in it, because nobody can tell when it will come home to him. Saving the children is nothing else than the establishment of proper habits, because later in life habits are fixed and it is almost never that they are changed. I believe that at least ninety per cent of the crime in the world can be cured by preventing its causes.

Crimes, like everything else, yield to classification. First, there are what might be called property crimes committed on account of property. As a usual thing, those who commit them have no property and never had any. Then there are crimes like murder, which are always especially played up in the newspapers and are talked about so much that people are afraid to stop off over night in Chicago. The crime of murder itself we can divide into different classes. There is first the type which generally occurs between the sexes, like a husband killing a wife and getting hanged or electrocuted, or a wife killing a husband and getting a chromo,[2] or lovers killing each other. We always have had that type and we always shall. Why? Because the feeling of passion is the deepest thing in life. It is right at the basis of life itself, and when something goes wrong with it, its victims do not care what happens; many times they wouldn't care even if they knew that they were to be hanged for it. If you have a woman after you with a gun, are you going to sit down and say reasonably, "If you kill me you will get hung?" She isn't interested in possible future consequences, nor deterred by fear of punishment; only in getting you, and I don't believe you are going to waste time remonstrating. A man, too, may get involved in some way, and, when he thinks it is all over, he doesn't care what may happen to him later; he wants to finish the job. There is no way of changing that. It will always be. We may get rid of some of these crimes of passion, but we will always have some of them with us. The other typical form of murder is that committed in the course of some other crime, such as burglary or robbery. What is that? Why, that starts out as a property crime. No such criminal ever originally intends to kill. The burglar doesn't intend to, but when he is in danger of getting caught he does so to protect himself. The old time murderer you used to read about, where a man deliberately and maliciously went out to kill, does not exist—is hardly discoverable. Most of the homicides are burglars, robbers and thieves, making up the grist which fills the jails and prisons. This can be prevented by opportunity and training.

Who is the criminal? Almost invariably he began as a boy. Even if not convicted until later, in most cases he has led that kind of life from childhood. He comes from the large cities. Almost invariably he started his criminal career in childhood. Generally, I might add, he is an orphan. If he isn't, he had no home, or what you might call no home. He very early began to get into trouble with the police. He went into vacant buildings to loaf or pilfer, and then he learned to go into occupied buildings. He has no education and no training. If any of you think that isn't true, investigate for yourself; but I know it is true, and so do any of you who are in any way familiar with the facts.

Men and women are not naturally criminals. Whenever they become so it is usually because they are born or reared in circumstances which made them such, and not because they just naturally want to be that way or because they just naturally choose that kind of career. They began as boys who had never gone to school to any extent. On the other hand maybe their parents had not been able to send them; or they may not have been able to learn. Now, of course, our idea of education is all nonsense. If I had time enough I would tell you why. What is education, anyhow? We think that all wisdom and learning comes to us from books. Does it? Maybe one can be educated without books. Lawyers ought to have the sort of education that is found in them; doctors should have it; and it wouldn't hurt a preacher to have some, though it might make him stop preaching. But a farmer doesn't need it. Need what? Well, book education. If they get it, it doesn't do them much good, and as a rule they don't get it. For nearly fifty years I have been practicing law. It is pretty nearly time to reform, don't you think? I have spent a large part of my time examining jurors and finding whether I wanted them or wanted to get rid of them. You know how that is! you get a case and a good share of the results depends on what kind of jurors you get. Now I have been examining jurors for all these years, and I am not so bad at it. If I can get a juror to answer enough questions I can tell about how his mind works—if it works. I have been asking them year after year where they were born, and why—the latter of which questions they can't answer. I ask them if possible what they read; and if they say that they do read, how much they read; and if they read a newspaper, and things like that. If I can find out something about their religion, that helps. In fact it helps a lot. Well, I ask them if they read and I have never found a juror yet that really can answer me. They'll say, "I read a paper, the sport news and some of that stuff; that is all." The average man doesn't read anything. He says, "I haven't any time to read." The college man doesn't read anything, either. He also says, "I haven't any time to read; now that I am out of college, I'm busy." I don't know any people who read very much, except myself. Once in a while I get into a house with a fine collection of books, and while my host is in the cellar I look over the titles to see what sort of books he has. I almost always find that the leaves haven't been cut.

What are all these schools for? Of course there are some things that even I don't dare talk about. I perhaps have my own ideas on my own religion and on schools. I think that almost all of the money spent on public schools is wasted. We shall be completely ruined pretty soon if we don't watch out, because nearly one-half of the taxes raised by direct taxation goes to the public schools. The trouble is that we don't get anything except sentimentality for it. As it is actually given, there is very little value in the teaching that one gets out of books. If one has a taste for books and a love of knowledge, he will become educated anyway; if he hasn't, no amount of formal education will give it to him. If the public schools were properly organized, they would give every child the fundamentals, and then let his capacities determine whether he should have more.

What is the important thing in education? There is just one important job that all of us have. That is the job of living and getting by, of getting through the world, and safely dead. Education should fit us for that job, but does it do it? I say it doesn't do anything for us. There isn't one child out of a dozen who goes out of our public schools that gets anything, at least beyond the primary grades, that fits him for his principal business in life. The child should be appreciated and understood by the teacher and by the parent and an effort made to find out what he is fitted for. I think every child can be taught something, if he hasn't been born an idiot, and even then he can be taught to weave baskets, or some other kind of work which will enable him to live a fairly happy life. Only a few people in this world, such as lawyers, can live by their wits. The rest of them have to work for a living. What equipment does a public school give them, for all of the money we pay out on them? The boy who makes a criminal is ordinarily one who can't learn the things found in books; but he goes to school anyway, and he gets along the best he can during his school years, and then he goes out into life; and what can he do to earn a living? Anything? Nothing. He has learned no trade. Such capacity as he has, has not been ascertained or developed. There is no place for him. He has not been trained to earn a living by work. So, naturally, he tries to live without working, and he winds up in prison, or dies on the gallows. His course is just as natural as that of his neighbor who starts in common school and goes on through college, and never offends against the accepted code.

What is it that keeps a man from stealing? A boy doesn't know anything about property and he will steal if he is where he can get anything. He usually doesn't know anything about statutes. He doesn't know anything about laws. It is instinctive in a boy to reach out and get whatever he wants. He must, of course, be taught that he can't get property that way. But what else is necessary? Why, he should be equipped to live. It is hard enough for any of us to live in this world; yes, it is hard enough. The boys who land in prison never had a chance to live. They are not all crazy; probably only a small percentage of them are crazy, in the true meaning of the word. But you must remember that they have been influenced by both heredity and environment. It is necessary that we create correct habits in the child as he grows up. Habits, if they are right—for that is a big word—must be formed not so much at school as at home. He ought to have some help in the public school. He ought to have an opportunity to learn something that would fit him for life. But most of the men who are going to jail are men who never did learn anything. They are not vicious, and they do the anti-social things largely because they don't know any better. Usually people don't commit crimes who are trained to do something else and who can use their energy to a better purpose. You may go into any jail or read any prison report and you will find that what I have just said is true. Whenever you follow criminals back to childhood you will find that they were all fundamentally the same kind of children, who couldn't under the circumstances have followed any career other than a criminal one. Is the child to blame? Here are two new-born children. Neither one of them has any knowledge of anything. One wasn't born wicked and the other good. They were born just alike and neither is to blame. How does one happen to land in high position—say in the United States Senate? How does the other happen to land in the penitentiary? Something happened after they began to be educated. If anyone tells you they were born that way, let me tell you that he doesn't know anything about biology. I have been interested in these questions all my life, and have looked into them to find out.

Now, the remedy is simple. That is the reason that nobody talks about it. It does not consist merely in simplifying the law; that is old stuff. It is not credible. I haven't heard of a case for twenty years where a conviction was avoided or reversed on a mere technicality. I would just as soon go into the trial of a case without even reading the indictment to see whether it is correct; we have forgotten technicality long ago. Criminal lawyers can't use technicalities. They are not allowed to. Neither are there any delays in a criminal trial; there are in the civil courts. In a case that is much discussed the average prosecutor always wants to get the accused indicted the next day after the crime, convicted the next, and hanged the third. They will string along an important civil case for years, but they must make haste with their criminal cases. Wherever you see a criminal case that has been a long time coming to trial, make up your mind that the prosecutor didn't want to try it, or feared that it might be reversed on appeal, or that there was some other good reason.

No, the remedy is much simpler, and therefore probably never will be adopted. You don't believe for a minute that if a man can make good watches or has any other good trade, he is going out on an excursion robbing buildings and holding up people or taking chances for his life? There are just two ways of preventing crime. One is to give boys a chance to live. If the state is going to undertake to school them it should equip them for life. That means, not schooling that will enable them to bound Nebraska, but training that will give them some means of living. The other is to bring about a more equitable distribution of wealth, which you and I know is not distributed as it should be.

What is a sound theory of punishment, and its proper relation to crime? The way most folks look at it, the only thing that is necessary when anything happens is to punish someone, and punish him good and hard. By way of parenthesis, before we discuss theories of punishment at all, I want to say what I think about parole laws. I am not familiar with the Nebraska statutes, but I think I know what such statutes usually provide. Beginning about forty years ago, every state in the Union began to adopt them. The idea originally underlying them was to provide for indeterminate sentences. Before that time our judges or juries, as the case might be, fixed sentences.

The result might have been expected. Persons accused of crime get off easier if the jury fixes sentence, than if put at the mercy of a parole board, who never heard the trial or had any information about the crime. The parole, as it acts in this country, is not shortening sentences, but lengthening them. Let me show you how. In our state, and I presume it is a general law, for the crime of manslaughter, a person is sentenced to the penitentiary. Generally the statute now reads that he shall serve a term between one year and life. He is now really sentenced for life for running over a man with an automobile—mere sport—and if he had no friends he would stay there for life unless paroled. The result is that large numbers of prisoners are held under indeterminate sentences, who would have received shorter sentences had they been fixed by courts and juries. None the less, the parole act is right in theory. The parole board, however, ought to be composed of intelligent and scientific men, instead of politicians, as it generally is. It ought to be composed of humane men, who observe every prisoner and find out just what he is, what the causes are for his being there, what his crime is, and whether he is going to come right back in again if turned out. And, of course, he ought to be confined until he can be safely turned out into the world and the world can exist in safety with him out. If that doesn't happen, he ought never to be released. The ordinary parole board acts as if it thought all prisoners would act just alike if let out. Under the system as it exists it is hard to find well-trained men to administer such a law, but separating it from politics would certainly be a step in the right direction.

The sole purpose of punishment should be to protect society, by keeping the man who has violated its code away from it. Punishment, as such, does not prevent crime. Do you suppose that a burglar who would get five years in the penitentiary, if he is caught in a strange house and somebody shows fight, takes his five-year sentence, and submits, or does he risk the gallows rather than be arrested for burglary? The extreme penalty has nothing to do with it. That was all worked out in England years ago. They believed there that the only safe, sure and effective punishment was hanging, and that only general fear would prevent crime. So, up to one or two hundred years ago, they hanged them for some two hundred offenses, but juries refused to convict, and the cruelty of the penal code was relaxed and crime lessened.

The general theory is that it awes everybody else into virtue to see someone locked up. When Tom Jones sees what has happened to Tom Smith, the theory is that Jones is going to be good. Let's see if it would work that way. We are all the time locking people up so that other people won't kill or burglarize. But it doesn't stop them. There isn't a man living who can show me the relationship between punishment and the fact that someone has not committed a crime. It is purely theoretical. Let's get some simple barnyard psychology. What is the effect of fear on crime? Take the case, for instance, of little Johnny, who likes raspberry-jam. He is told by his mother that he mustn't get into the jam because she is saving it for the preacher. Johnny says to himself: "Well, I like raspberry-jam just as well as that old preacher, and I am not going to wait until he comes." So he waits until his mother goes out to gossip with the neighbors and then eats the jam. His mother comes home and sees that the jam is gone and finds Johnny's face covered with jam. Woman-like, she takes it as circumstantial evidence that he got the jam. Then she tells Johnny that if he ever does it again she will break his neck. What effect has this on Johnny? It doesn't make him hate raspberry-jam or love his mother. If it has any effect, it is like the effect prohibition has on the man who likes to drink. Johnny probably says to himself, "Old woman, we will just see who is smarter, you or me." The next time his mother goes out to visit with the neighbors he gets into the jam; then after he eats what he wants he washes his face and hands. Then he takes a little of the jam and spreads it on his little baby sister's face, or the cat's. Fear keeps no one from being cruel, but makes men cautious. Is that a reckless statement? I think people know enough about burglars and robbers to know that they don't wish to kill anybody. They never intend to. But the man who risks a five-year sentence for burglary will kill if he is in any danger of getting caught, the severer penalty nothwithstanding. The fear of punishment, which is relied on to deter criminals, accomplishes nothing.

Most of our so-called ideas about crime, like those concerning punishment, are based on sentiment and not on fact. Most of the crime statistics currently published are pure nonsense. Reports of crime are sent from Chicago, and the newspapers have played up crime until people are afraid to come down there and give us their money; when Nebraskans don't come to Chicago and give us their cash, things are pretty tough for us.

I am much more interested in this subject than in any other. I am interested in it because I am interested in all the people who live. I know there isn't any man in the world wise enough to tell his fellow men just what they should do. The principal thing to remember is that we are all the products of heredity and environment; that we have little or no control, as individuals, over ourselves, and that criminals are like the rest of us in that regard. Life is not an unmixed good. For many, perhaps for most, it is hard—terribly and tragically hard, and there is pain enough in it without our trying to add to the total. Punishment in itself never will help us or the world in general. The way to make this world better is to make it kinder. The only way to cure its evils is to bury hatred. That is an old philosophy, which many repeat on the ends of their tongues, but which few follow. When we learn to understand each other and put some faith in each other, the relationships of men with each other will be more humane. If we are ever to solve the problem of crime and its punishment, we shall have to discard the idea of vengeance, and adopt the scientific method of following effects back to their causes. The individual criminal is only a by-product. The causes of his being a criminal are social and economic, and go to the foundations of our whole way of living. Until they are found and removed, the effort to prevent crime will remain just as useless in the future as it has been in the past.

Capital Punishment

THE REAL REASON WHY so many people tenaciously cling to the idea of capital punishment is because they take pleasure in inflicting pain on those they hate. Of course, they would not admit that this is the reason; at the same time the proof is very plain. All early punishments were mainly vindictive, but then, primitive people are more honest than civilized ones and are not so anxious to hide their motives. Civilized people think more of themselves.

Primitive people used the death penalty for all sorts of offenses and the general practice continued even until within the last 200 years. At that time some 200 crimes were capital offenses in England, including poaching and petit larceny. Not long ago good folks not only used the death sentence for most offenses, but inflicted it in the most terrible ways—by hanging, flaying, dismemberment, throwing down from a high wall, crucifixion, drowning, stoning, starving and so forth.

No matter what the method of killing, death was preceded by torture; not the torture of notifying the condemned of the exact time and way of his death, but physical torture which to these simple minds was

---

This essay, first published in the *New York Herald Tribune Magazine* (January 1, 1928): 4–5, is perhaps Darrow's most forceful and concise statement of his opposition to the death penalty. He had addressed the issue on numerous previous occasions; see, e.g., *Debate, Resolved: That Capital Punishment Is a Wise Public Policy* (1924), a debate with Judge Alfred J. Talley, and "Futility of the Death Penalty," *Forum* 80 (September 1928): 327–32 (rpt. in *Verdicts out of Court*, pp. 225–32).

much more obvious than mental torture. As distinctions were made in punishments, those offenses which caused the most hatred, like religious and political crimes, were visited with the severest penalties.

At no time in the history of the world, not even now, were the offenses which are the most serious punished in the most brutal way. From every standpoint, except the loss of life, murder is not one of the most serious offenses and not one which marks the culprit as being the most dangerous and abandoned. A large portion of the trusties in prison are those who are confined for murder and are under life sentences. This is because they can be relied on better than those who are in prison for many other offenses. The terrible crimes of the world which have always demanded the most horrible penalties are crimes like witchcraft, heresy, blaspheming, Sabbath breaking and treason, real or constructive; in other words, religious or political offenses.

Most persons are familiar with the case recorded in the Book of Numbers, where the children of Israel, whole journeying in the desert, found a man gathering sticks on the Sabbath Day. They brought him to Moses and Aaron, who were not fully satisfied what to do with a man who was so wicked that he gathered sticks on the Sabbath, so they put him in jail and sent for the Lord. The Lord told them that he must surely be put to death by stoning, and so all the congregation took him outside the camp and stoned him "until he died."[1] Many more persons have been put to death for witchcraft and heresy than for any, if not all other crimes, and yet few people believe in such an offense as witchcraft now, and only a small number believe in capital punishment for heresy.

Next to death the most popular punishment in olden times was banishment. This sentence at an early date really meant death. It meant death at the hands of wild beasts or from starvation, or thirst. In some ways these were more terrible than sudden death. Anyhow, the dissolution lasts longer than lightning.

The early Anglo-Saxons of England made their statutes clear as to the purpose of punishment. They provided as follows for habitual criminals:

"At the second time let there be no other bot if he be foul than that his hands be cut off, or his feet, or both, according as the deed may be, and if then he have wrought yet greater wrong then let his eyes be put out or his nose and his ears and the upper lip be cut off; or let him be scalped, . . . so that punishment be inflicted and also the soul be preserved."

Those who believed in the most cruel vengeance were still worried about the victim's soul. In the pronouncement of the death penalty now the judge adds: "May God have mercy on your soul." Probably this is true, because the judge does not know how to destroy the victim's soul himself and the lawmakers, as a rule, consider this beyond their jurisdiction. However, with most punishments lawmakers and executioners do the best they can even to accomplish this end. When judges blithely and sonorously add to the sentence: "And may God have mercy on your soul," they have their fingers crossed.

The people of to-day deny that they punish from vengeance. They admit that they have indignation against the criminal, but their indignation is "righteous" indignation. The word "righteous" only confesses hypocrisy. Hatred is hatred. Prefixing the word "righteous" makes it in no way different. People punish those whom they hate. No one can inflict pain or torture upon an individual without hating him. In the preparation for war, when nations begin to mobilize, the first unit in the field is the liar. These are called into this pleasant service to make soldiers hate the enemy, so that they will kill them. In punishment every effort is made all down the line to magnify the ferocity of the act and the moral delinquency of the condemned, so that the punishment will be fixed in hatred and anger and carried out in the same spirit. This carefully created emotion is called "righteous" indignation.

Every one nowadays has given up defending capital punishment on any theory except that hanging or otherwise killing one man keeps others from committing a capital offense. No one who considers this question believes it, but it is repeated over and over again by those who either do not know or do not care.

Are men kept from killing their fellows because they are afraid to die? Every one who kills, excepting those who kill in the heat of passion, prepare a way of escape. The killer never intends to be caught, and often he is not. In the crimes of profound feeling and passion consequences are thrown to the wind and the certainty of the punishment of death does not prevent the act. If people are really kept from killing through fear of punishment, then the more terrible the punishment provided the greater the fear. The old forms of torture should be brought back. For instance, boiling in oil, which was once a favorite means of putting to death, should once more be established. The old rack, which tore victims limb from limb, should again be called into service. These measures would have a tendency to scatter fear all over the place. The public has grown so soft that present methods no longer terrify. They forget the injunction of Nietzsche, "Be hard!"[2] Our degenerate and effeminate lawmakers even seek to make death by the state as painless as possible, and thus take away most of the fear that is supposed to prevent the weak from committing crime.

If one should take the pains to ask a dozen men and women which they would prefer, life imprisonment or death, almost all of them would say that they preferred death. True, when the time came to die they might wish to live under almost any circumstances. But as a theoretical proposition, without the imminence of death, most all men and women prefer death to long imprisonment. There is certainly much less fear of death than of long imprisonment in the mind of one who is about to kill.

This can practically be proven. A large number of people make burglary a profession. The cause of this is not in our province to discuss at this time, but the fact is plain that their profession is burglary. The last thing they wish to do is to kill. The burglar takes every possible precaution against killing. He uses all care in turning the knob of the door. He takes off his shoes when he goes inside the house. He uses every precaution not to awaken any one in the room but, if perchance a sleeper is awakened and shows resistance, then the burglar shoots and shoots to kill. While he never wishes to destroy life, he almost always carries a gun, that he may be prepared to prevent arrest.

The burglar knows that if he is convicted of burglary he will probably spend five years in the penitentiary. If he is convicted of murder he will likely be killed by hanging or otherwise, or at least be imprisoned for life. Yet to prevent an arrest, which would result in a short term, all burglars deliberately place themselves in the position where they incur danger of life imprisonment or death. This of itself shows the absurdity of the glib statement that "death is all that the lawless fear." Death is about the last thing they fear. What is true of burglary is true of robbery and many other offenses. A large majority of the executions in the North are executions of men who took life as a means of saving themselves from arrest while in the act of burglary or robbery.

If hanging John Smith is to keep other people from murder, how is it to be accomplished? Plainly it must be necessary that the public should know that John Smith is hanged. Both in England and America this was once made clear by hangings on a high hill in broad daylight, which were attended by thousands of people. These were abolished mainly because it was found that the spectacle, instead of preventing crime, caused it, through suggestion. No country, however fierce and barbarous, would provide for public hangings to-day. This method of killing is not even contained in the Baumes law.[3] As a rule, the state kills people in the dark, with no one present except a few officials, a physician who is not there to save his life and a minister who is supposed to inform God to watch out for the victim's soul.

He is killed in silence and darkness so that the people will not witness the brutality of the State. If this terrible act is to prevent killings, then it should certainly be open and, instead of keeping people away from the scene, they should be compelled to go. But we are even more inconsistent and foolish than this. No motion picture is allowed to reproduce the crime of the State. Men, women and children cannot see the hapless victim, strapped and slaughtered, even in the movies. It would be a wise thing to do if this transparent pretension of the advocate of capital punishment was anything but a pretension.

If men are to be kept from killing by fear, then all human beings of all ages, especially the young, should see what it means to die at the hands of the State. In this way the wicked impulse to go out and kill would visualize something of the wages of crime. These pictures are not shown because, in spite of the hatred and vengeance of the public, even the very common man still has some vague feeling that the young, especially, act from suggestion. All observers know that many cases are re-peated over and over almost in every detail, due to suggestion. Intelligent people are perfectly aware that to show such pictures on the screen would not prevent murders, but would induce them.

If the full details of executions could be vividly told; if men and women could visualize the horror coming from the fear and dread of this shameful and cruel death; if people could feel the agony of the days of waiting; if they could grasp every detail—all normal human beings would be so shocked to think of their part in the horrible deed as to get rid of the barbarism that inspires the desire to have some unfortunate killed by the State. The newspapers do much to bring this home to the average citizen. The trouble is that most men and women will not read them or permit the young to read the ghastly details. The weak or erotic who enjoy the story are sometimes induced by suggestion to repeat the crime.

No facts can be produced by anyone to show that the death penalty ever lessened murders. From the nature of things it could not be shown. It does not follow that one refrains from killing because he is afraid of death. Very few people ever desire to kill. If anything could be shown from results, then the figures in America are plain; that there are less murders in States where there is no capital punmishment than in States which still cling to the barbarous practice.

This does not necessarily mean that the abolition of capital punish-ment is responsible for it. It may only mean that the States where the people are so humane as not to go into the killing business in an orga-nized way would naturally have fewer citizens who, under any circum-stances, would kill. Because two facts exist together does not warrant the inference that one is the cause of the other. This may or may not be the case.

There is nothing so unequal and unfair as capital punishment. Only the poor are put to death. Those who have the means and opportunity to have their cases so presented that a jury and even a court may under-stand and realize the terrible responsibility of taking a life are not in much danger of death. Few people ever consent to commit such a deed if they have the victim before them and realize what it means.

The question of human responsibility has always been a subject of debate. It is at least certain that no two organisms have the same power of resistance to motives. Most men who kill are of a very unstable nature and are easily moved by outside pressure. No two organisms are affected to the same extent by the same sort of inducement. A very large proportion of those who commit crime are really psychopathic. It is safe to say that with all of them the cause was sufficient to affect and overcome their special structure. No one can put himself in another's place. To do this he must have not only the same outside surroundings, but the same structure. For this reason no one can fairly judge another.

Crime and poverty and ignorance go together, as a part of the inheritance of the defective and the victims of circumstances. When the world understands this and knows that every act is preceded by a cause or causes, it will seek to remove the causes of crime and poverty and ignorance, and then, and only then, will the great mass of these human maladjustments disappear from the world.

THREE

On Politics and Society

Woman Suffrage

PERHAPS NO NEW ARGUMENTS have been advanced for or against "Woman Suffrage" for a hundred years.

More than a century ago the advocates of equal rights, with unanswerable logic, proved that to disfranchise one-half the race for the accident of sex was an outrage to the sense of humanity and justice too. Still, against reason and logic and in the face of fairness and equality, man has arrogated to himself the right to determine his own sphere and that of woman too.

It is for him who denies the right of equal suffrage to show why sex, and sex alone, should determine the right and duty of citizenship; to show that the right to vote should not depend upon intelligence, learning, property, strength, health, courage, morality, nativity, or any other qualification, excepting that of sex. To fix any other limitation whatsoever upon the right of franchise would give some women at least the right to vote and take from some men that ancient prerogative, which has so long been given for the sole virtue of not having been born a member of the so-called "weaker sex."

"Woman Suffrage" is the transcript of a debate by Darrow and others held at the Sunset Club, Chicago, on November 5, 1891. It was published in the *Sunset Club Yearbook 1891–1892* (Chicago: Sunset Club, 1893), pp. 25–37. Darrow's chief antagonist was Stephen A. Douglas (1850–1908), a lawyer and master in chancery in the County Court in Chicago (1880–91) and prosecuting attorney (1891–1908).

Let us determine the principle on which suffrage rests.

The ballot has not always been an institution in the world. Before men made states the strongest chiefs, with club and knife and other instruments of war, enforced their power on all the other members of the tribe. The laws enacted in this rude beginning of a state sprang from the cruel, savage brain of those whom strengh and cunning gave the right to rule. No monarch of these early states was called to place and power by the other members of the tribe, but he called himself instead.

The kings and monarchs of the ancient world, like the barbarous chiefs who went before, thought that their rights descended from the gods, and allowed no worm of earth to raise a question of their right to rule. And through the long and cruel ages of the past, the favored few, with sword and rope and rack, enforced obedience from a world of cringing slaves.

The human race had lived for countless centuries on the earth before the faintest thought had ever come to ruler or to ruled of the common origin and destiny of man.

In the minds of the most favored retainers of monarchs and of kings the spirit of liberty first commenced to grow; and these lords and nobles, by the force of arms and on the field of battle, wrung from their reluctant rulers some fragment of political power in return for loyalty and support. These privileges were guaranteed in constitutions and charters, that rulers might not forget that there were limits to their power.

More and more as the spirit of liberty has penetrated the darkness of the world, have rulers of high degree and low, surrendered power and place and privilege at the demand of the common people of the earth, until to-day, in the constitutions of states and nations, full political privileges are guaranteed to those who once were chattel slaves.

The days when unorganized men, with club and knife, battled for supremacy with their fellow-men are gone, let us hope to return no more. The power of the individual in the state cannot, to-day, be expressed by the strength of his arm, but it rests in his vote instead. Every individual, who has the right of suffrage, has a weapon in his hand as potent as was the club of the savage in the ancient world. True, it may be wrongly used; it may be nullified by others; it may at times do neither him nor the community any great amount of good, but disarm him of this power and he is helpless then indeed.

The commonest observation shows the great power that comes to the individual from the ballot. In a land of politicians, like our own, rulers are influenced only by what they believe the majority will do. Our public officers are obliging. The same fellows will give us either protection or free trade, silver money or gold, prohibition, high license or free whisky. They are always obedient to petitions when these are signed by voters. But a petition signed by every woman in Chicago would have less weight with a legislative body than a resolution of a labor organization, which perhaps existed on paper alone.

The day after one of our late local conventions had adjourned it was discovered that the party had made a great mistake, one that must be remedied to avoid certain defeat. It was a mistake so grave that all marveled to think a convention of politicians could have made it. No Bohemian was on board the ticket. The mischief was afterward rectified. Some one was "pulled off" and a Bohemian placed there in his stead. It did not matter who was taken off, or who was put on, so long as the nationality was right. All the Chinamen in the United States have not as much influence as one German-American, Irish-American, Swedish-American, or even American, club.

Every human being is a portion of the state, subject to its laws and regulations, his life, interests and destiny linked with all his fellow men. And each one of these human beings, because they are human beings, should have the same privileges and rights as all the rest. It is unjust and cowardly in the rulers of any state to place a weapon or a tool in the hands of a portion of its members and deprive the rest of this defense and aid.

Unless the state is an institution that conduces to the highest good of those who make it up, unless the state is an organization that adds to the happiness of man, unless in some way it aids the weary pilgrirn on the thorny path of life, and makes the burden lighter, which all of us must bear, unless this is true the state has not the right to be, but, if from the political organizations of the world any good can come to man, then the weakest and the humblest voice should have the right to speak.

The ideal voter should be intelligent and just; should have a broad and tolerant mind; should study carefully his country's needs and forget all selfish interests in the higher and the broader good. These qualifications are not masculine alone. These, and all other qualifications, may be possessed by women and by men alike. The power to vote does not depend upon the power to fight, but the enlightened conscience of a later world chose this peaceful way to accomplish that which in early times was done by bloody strife. In theory at least the weak and helpless cripple, with the ballot in his hand, is as strong as the most brutal man, who, by reason of his sex, has inherited the right to vote.

Men, and men alone, have made the laws. They have assumed this right because they could, and have left one half the race as dependent on their will as were the early serfs upon their king's caprice. With that grace which the strong have ever shown the weak they insist that women can rely upon the generosity and justice of the stronger sex to grant them all the rights they ought to have, and more. The unequal laws that men have made for women for a thousand years show what justice means to those who have undisputed power, and the generosity of man is shown by his willingness to grant to woman all she wants, except the right to make her own demands in the way that men make theirs, at the ballot box. To further justify the arbitrary use of power by man it is said that women do not wish to vote.

For a hundred years and more many of the best and brightest women of the world have appealed to man for equal rights, and here, within our midst, within the week our sense of justice has been shocked by the sight of women of refinement and of brains, yes, and courage too, who in vain have pleaded before the courts for the smallest vestige of that right which the meanest and the vilest man may sell for whisky or for cash. If all the women in the world but one should say they did not wish to vote, they still would have no right to limit or confine that woman's life. Not all the laws that man can make could place a ballot in unwilling hands. They can give the opportunity to vote and nothing more. In all the ages of the world since man has ruled his fellow man, the weak and poor of earth have struggled, not for help, but for the liberty to help themselves.

The manifest absurdity of saying that sex is any natural bar to suffrage, drives all who seek to uphold the injustice of the present into a wider discussion of woman's sphere, and the consequences that might follow to woman should she be allowed to vote.

The rulers of the world have been ever busy in defining spheres, and making laws to keep others in these artificial spheres. The world of yesterday, with caste and custom, with chain and dungeon, divided humanity into spheres and classes, and made barbarous laws to keep them there; the world of to-morrow, grown wiser and holier, will respect and reverence every atom of the great surging sea of human life, and leave each one unfettered by custom or by law, to find its individual sphere.

The careless observer, looking over the history of the world, and seeing the position woman has ever occupied, may be excused for believing that she has been assigned a certain sphere and that it is his duty to help to keep her in it; but the student of sociology sees the reason for the present and the hope for the future.

Evolution teaches us that the man of the present had his origin, countless centuries since, in the lowest form of life that blindly grew and struggled in the sea; that during vast periods of time he developed through all the grades below, until he reached his present stage.

"A state of nature is a state of war;" the stronger animals, including man, have ever grown and flourished by devouring and trampling on the weak. Through all the ages of the past, and even in the present time, the vast majority of men and beasts have ever waged a hard and cruel fight for the barest opportunity to live. By wit and strength they have fiercely sought to obtain a spot of ground on which to stand, and the scanty food that sufficed to save their lives; those least able to maintain their place have been distanced in the long and cruel race, and left by the roadside to faint or die.

In nearly every land and age the lot of woman has been cast with that of the lowly and the weak; man has always trampled on her rights, and made her little but a slave.

Yet woman did not always occupy a position inferior to the stronger sex. The time once was, long ages since, when man and woman lived on equal terms. The first age of man upon the earth we might call the "period of brute force." At that time each struggled fiercely with the rest to gain by physical means, as now in other ways, an advantage over those with whom he dwelt. The chief pursuits of that barbarous age were those of hunting and of war.

The maternal functions and instincts of woman, which were necessary to keep the race alive, rendered her unable in this brute struggle to compete with man. In the language of Olive Schreiner, "Ages ago, the age of the 'Dominion of Muscular Force,' found her, and when she stooped low to nurse her young her back was broad, and man put his burden of subjugation upon it, and bound it with the broad band of 'inevitable necessity.'"[1]

All the oppression, injustice, and outrage woman has suffered in the past has been due to one fact, her inability to physically contend with man. This has made her life dependent on the will of the stronger sex. Her present condition, the wrongs she suffers, the legal outrages she endures, are due to her economic dependence on man.

No man or woman ever was or can be free while they must look to others for their daily bread. Chains and whips, dungeons and racks, are but the first rude instruments that man has ever used to enslave his fellow-man. The real opportunity of the tyrant can never come until the poor and weak, upon their bended knees, must look upward to their master's face and beg him for the crust that keeps the wolf outside the door. Through the countless centuries of the past, woman, weak and poor and suffering, has knelt before her brother, man, and, with shivering form and outstretched hand, has begged him for the right to live.

For a woman to have any other ambition than marriage is to be at once considered different from the rest of her sex; to be regarded with doubt; to be called "strong-minded" and "unwomanly." "She has no right to be a man," says society. "A woman's place is at her home, in the kitchen, in the sewing-room, in the laundry. A man's place is in the senate, the pulpit, at the bar, in the office, and the store." Why? I do not know that nature ever meant it thus. If nature had made any laws upon the subject, man would long since have repealed them with his statutes. But there is abundant reason for the difference that exists to-day between the spheres of man and woman. If we go out on the plains and ask the wild savage, he can tell the reason why.

The Indian warrior shoots the game, smears his face with paint, and does the fighting for the tribe; the squaw cooks the buffalo, carries the tent and pappoose on her back, and minds the house. This division of labor was made long ages since; it was not made by the squaw, but by the noble warrior, and he enforces it, if need be, by the tomahawk and knife. Civilized, or rather semi-civilized, man learned the sphere of woman, together with many other things, from the Indian on the plain; he learned it ages since, when he was a savage too. He has forgotten much as the centuries have rolled away, but the knowledge of woman's sphere, and the way to keep her in it, is green in his memory still.

I am quite sure that the division of labor, as now observed, was not made by nature. Men can cook, and do, when the employer is willing to pay the wages they demand. Men can wash and scrub and sew, and whether nature fitted them for this or not, they always receive better wages for doing woman's work than she can get herself.

But there are occupations, commonly supposed to be beyond a woman's sphere, to which man has invited her to come. He has opened the store, the factory, and the mill, and asked her to come inside the doors; aye, he has even called her down into the mines, into the bowels of the earth, to work for him. But he has invariably invited her on one condition, that she should labor cheaper than her brother. No matter how hard or disagreeable the task, man has never yet seen any reason why woman should not perform it, if she did not charge too much.

And what has followed from all this? Let us contrast the position man and woman occupies to-day.

"Man rules the world." He sits on almost every throne. His voice, and his alone, is heard in the councils of almost every political organization on the earth. He alone makes the laws and enforces them; he makes them for himself and woman too, and enforces them on both. He moves the commerce of the earth. He owns the world and all the property therein. Nearly all the business of the world is done by men, and of course all the wealth it represents is theirs. The farms, mines, factories, and in short, almost all the industrial institutions of the world are controlled and owned by men. Here and there are found a wealthy widow, whose childless husband has left her stock or lands, or a daughter, whose father had no son to confer his goods upon, with something that they call their own, although given them by some-one else. Woman has been banished from the active field of business life. If she knows aught of the industrial institutions of to-day, it is as one of the cheapest hirelings who serve for pay.

Social customs and institutions, and even the selfishness of man, could not keep all women from the field of literature and art, for genius knows no sex and when it kindles the brain of an Eliot or a Hosmer,[2] it illumines the earth with its radiant light. But however much woman has contributed to literature and art the world can never know the fires of genius that have been quenched, the hopes and desires that have been blighted, and the bright intellects that have been circumscribed and stunted because of the false and cruel social customs that have defined woman's sphere.

Every human being needs first of all freedom, the right to be an individual, the right to live and breathe and move and act, the right to live their lives, and make the most of their sojourn on the earth.

Life is a toilsome journey that we travel step by step. Sometimes the road is smooth and straight, and we feel the morning air upon our brow and scent the perfume sweet of lands and flowers, that are thickly strewn along our path. Again the road is steep and hard, and as we slowly journey on our way the rocks and thorns make us cry out with anguish and with pain. Sometimes a sunny sky hangs over our heads and the world seems filled with gladness and with hope; again the clouds obscure the day, the lightnings flash, the thunder rolls, and we are blinded with the fury of the storm; we know not where the road will end, it may be in a garden bright as the clouds when tinctured with the sunset's rosy hue; it may be a precipice from which we step into the dark and silent sea, but this we know, in spite of hopes and fears, of desires and doubts, we must ever travel on. All true men and women desire to make this journey for themselves. It matters not how steep the way, how hard the road, how furious the storm, they had rather perish in the effort to climb the mountain height than be confined to the level plain below. They had rather journey step by step, though every foot-print that they leave behind is stained with blood, than travel in a chariot though fitted up with luxury and ease.

All laws or customs or institutions that deprive any fellow-mortal of making this journey for himself, or that take away one hope or aspiration from any traveler, man or woman; that confines or fetters or hinders in the race, must go down before the march of progress and the enlightened conscience of the world.

The prizes of this life, for which we strive, fame, money, office, honor, position, or whatever else we may consider worth the seeking, these may be hollow bubbles which will break and fade, as we reach out to clasp them in our arms. It may be that like the boy who runs to dig the golden pot on which the rainbow rests, we will find, for all our pains, only the cold damp earth at last. But these same painted bubbles that we sought have cheered us on the cold and rugged path of life, have carried us through woods and tangled ways, and over dark, miasmatic swamps, where friends and comrades fainted by our side and passed forever from our sight. What if we never reach the higher ground, we had a vision while we toiled of the mountain top above the clouds, bathed in the golden sunlight of eternal peace, and we worked and toiled and lived and died buoyed by the inspiring hope that the day would come when we should realize our heart's desires.

In the era of conscience, which all of us hope is the era of the future, man will not say to woman that she must be a lawyer, a physician, a merchant, or that she must vote, he will simply say she *may*.

Man may lose some of his gallantry and chivalry, but he will replace these with justice and common sense. He will regard woman as an individual and leave her to work out her destiny for herself. No longer will he prescribe her sphere but leave her free and untrammeled to find out for herself where she belongs.

It may be that justice will never reign on earth; it may be that the human race, unfit for a higher life, will go back from whence it sprung, but if there ever comes a time when intellect and conscience rule the world, that day will know neither rich nor poor, neither high nor low, neither man nor woman, neither bondman nor free.

[*Printed below are Darrow's comments in a discussion following his lecture.*]

THIS IS A QUESTION that ought to be settled on general principles. We have been told this evening by the opponents of woman suffrage what is the best kind of a woman, what they think is woman's proper business, a woman's duties, and what makes a woman lovely and all that. One gallant gentleman says that he does not know any women who want to vote, although he is familiar with their sex, and would not want to know any woman who desired to vote. I don't know what kind of women the gentleman is acquainted with, but if they are women who have no ideas above such as are usually found in drawing-room or kitchen talk, then perhaps he is acquainted with just such women as he ought to be, and would not appreciate a broad-minded woman, with sense and intellect, if he happened to meet her. Very likely in that society man chooses those who with the countless wiles that men have allowed women to use, have told him he was good looking when he was not; have told him he was smart when he was foolish; have told him he was great when he was small.

There are other gentlemen who say the women should stay at home instead of voting. Is it for you or any other man to say to a woman that she shall stay at home and rock the cradle; that is her business. We may say that we do not choose to do it but who has the right to say that a woman's whole life, her whole energy and spirit, shall be circumscribed by the four walls of her home? No woman can be great, or grand, or a fit companion for even the gallant General,[3] who had no ideas beyond the four walls of her home.

All the arguments or alleged arguments that have been advanced tonight and that are always advanced against woman occupying these positions grow from the desire of men for flattery. They come from men who like to say pleasant things, largely lies, to women, and like to have women tell them pleasant lies in return. And both know they are lies. They do not reach the true basis of this question, and all other sociological questions, that no human being should be his brother's keeper; that in this world of doubt and trouble, of toil and strife, it is enough for any one man or any one woman to take care of themselves, and choose their own spheres without setting limits to the life of any other.

We are told that if the good women vote so will the bad ones. I hope so. Why not? All men vote. Why not all women? Sometimes bad men vote more intelligently than good ones, and very likely sometimes bad women will vote more intelligently than good ones.

I am not one of those who desire to see the women vote that they may vote in prohibition, for I don't believe in it. I don't believe in the saloon, but I believe in something better than prohibition, and that is human liberty. You can only make great men and great women by giving free scope to their individuality, and with fear and suffering let them work out their own destiny.

This is an abominable doctrine that a woman cannot be a little bad and still very good. There is not a human being, man or woman, who may not be a little bad and still very good.

And it is just possible too that the bad women ought to be protected. I submit to the gentleman, the police prosecutor of this city, that, if the bad women of this city had a hand in the making of the laws, sometimes the men who frequent those houses of ill repute might be fined as heavily as the inmates.

We are told that women crowd into the different walks of life and lower the wages of their sisters. Why? Because from the earliest ages women have been taught that their only fate was to tie themselves to some man, and if they could not do that to sell their life perhaps as the only alternative. And therefore when woman has desired to avoid either of these things she has been forced to overcrowd those occupations, to bid against her sister, and in turn to bid against her brother. Leave the world open, give her an equal opportunity with man; and do not fear that the laws of nature will not be strong enough to determine what woman's sphere properly is. The law of natural selection and of sexual selection is stronger than any human law.

It is said here that the women of Germany raise corn to support their brothers on the field of battle; perhaps if the women of Germany had the right to vote they would call their brothers back from the field of battle, and inaugurate an era of peace and good will among the nations of the earth.

The inventions of the past fifty years have made it possible for the weakest woman or child to perform labors that were once impossible to the strongest man. The work of to-day is not done by bone and muscle; it is done by machines. All over the world work in all departments of industry is done by women and children and can be done by them as well as by the men.

It is not for us to say that women must do this or that; we must recognize that they are human beings like ourselves. There was a time in the history of this world when it was generally believed that woman had no soul. Of course it was assumed that men had, as the only way to prove it. We have passed that period and let us hope the time will soon come when we shall say to women "You may find your own proper mission for yourselves. We will not fear you in the race of life. We will give you equal opportunity and in the great struggle for existence will trust that the strongest may come out ahead."

Patriotism

"THERE IS NO SUCH thing as patriotic art or patriotic science. Both art and science belong, like all else that is great and good, to the whole world, and can only be promoted by a free and universal interchange of ideas among contemporaries with constant reference to that which we have inherited and learned from the past."[1]

This sentiment of Goethe has been expressed over and over again by the great and wise of every age and land, still, after long years of so called civilization, the shoddy sentiment of patriotism is almost as strong for mischief in the human heart as in the days of the savage who knew only the members of his own tribe, and knew no trade but war.

From the time of the primitive man, rulers and robbers have used the sentiment of patriotism as their chief asset in their selfish schemes. Whether the strong Nation wished to conquer and despoil a weaker land or plunder the people of their own, they have ever appealed to patriotism, to blind the ignorant to the real motives behind their schemes.

With a primitive people knowing little and seeing little, there was some reason for the belief that their own tribe held all the greatness,

"Patriotism" was first published in the *International Socialist Review* 11 (1910–11): 159–60. It argues for a renunciation of narrow nationalism in light of the broader artistic, scientific, and moral ties that bind all humanity.

intelligence and virtue of the world, but in modern life it is only the narrow and ignorant who can really think that their own land is better, wiser or more advanced than many others on the globe. Even as to governments, no one can tell which is best or which is worst, and in fact, the real governments of every land are much the same amongst people of a like grade of intelligence.

Forms of government, like forms of religion are matters of growth and development and, all things considered, fit the particular time and place where they hold sway.

The history of the world shows the ruin and bloodshed and destruction that the spirit of patriotism has caused. Ambitious rulers have always appealed to this blind, senseless passion to move their dupes to give their lives and their fortunes to help the ignorable schemes of a few. In the great wars of the world, waged for no real cause, the rulers and they alone have reaped fame and fortune, while the people have given their labor and their lives.

The common people, the ones who toil have done the fighting, have shed the blood, have borne the burden. And these common men have had no cause to fight and no land to serve.

The real work of the world to-day is not for destruction. True, the vainglorious, those who like applause or offices or honor, are as ready as ever to shed the blood of the innocent and helpless. It matters not who may suffer or die, if they be made generals or colonels, or even majors. These schemers want notoriety; they must be talked about in newspapers; must hold offices; must acquire money. Neither life nor liberty can be permitted to stand in their way. Still it is true that the work of the world is along peaceful lines. The builders of to-day are subduing the wilderness; they are tunnelling the earth; they are sailing the seas, not with men of war, but with ships laden with the food and clothing and comforts that conduce to modern life.

The real men are studying the laws of the universe and the laws that make for the happiness of man. One almost nameless biologist, working patiently and obscurely to coax from nature the secrets of life and learn the mystery of death is worth more to the world than all the generals of antiquity. The man who discovered and applied anesthetics is of more value than all the armies of Europe. And the man who can find a way to pull one tooth without giving pain, is of more consequence than all the vain strutting colonels who were anxious to assassinate Spaniards and Filipinos, so they might run for office when they came back from the "front."

Truly no country has any monopoly of the geniuses of the world. If you study the heavens, you can find no American or English astronomy. This learning reaches back to the nomadic tribes who tended their flocks and herds on the lonely plains and looked up at the trembling stars at night to learn some of the infinite mysteries that the heavens hold.

Wise men and great, in all lands, have builded on these small foundations to perfect the marvelous science of astronomy we have to-day. So too, not the patriot, but the student, has read the history of the world during the long silent ages before man was born; has read it in the rocks and soil and constructed a tangible theory of the earth and life. Science, not patriotisin, has ministered to the afflicted, has vanquished pain, lengthened life and destroyed diseases that once scourged the world. Science and Industry have utilized the blind forces of nature and made it possible for man to produce amply, to satisfy his needs and desires.

Art and Music and Literature owe nothing to Patriotism, although this blind and narrow prejudice has wrecked and destroyed them with the new ambitions of almost every lunatic who strove to conquer the world and wished to make his own name so great that he might furnish the topic of conversation for all time to come.

Art and Literature and Music were not born in any one land, nor nurtured under one flag. They were born of the sky and sea and earth and of human souls that could be inspired and moved by feelings universal to the race. Their devotees and patrons have lived and worked through all time and have made all nations great. Their thoughts and feelings have been as universal as humanity itself. The great artist and poet have never known the narrow lines which bind the feelings of the patriot.

To him, injustice and oppression is no less sordid and mean when practiced in his native land. The claims of the poor, the weak and the oppressed appear no different to his heart, whether the victim live far or near.

The scientist, the student, the artist that knew nothing of the work or literature of any but his own land, would be poor indeed. In fact, this could not be, for the knowledge and achievements of all the world are so woven into a complex mass that no chemist could be clever enough to separate the particles that form the whole.

As the world grows older and more complex, the lines of states and nations become fainter. Commerce and Industry, like Science and Art, make all lands one in intent, thought and feeling. The good that comes to one land is reflected to the rest and the calamities of one leave the whole world poorer for the suffering of a part.

Modern life and common interests must leave the feeling of patriotism to the politician, the vainglorious and the cunning. When a man waves the flag with his right hand, it is well to see what he is doing with his left.

In the aspiration and work for social justice there can be no state lines. The workers of the world have always had a common interest and should always have a common Cause. Under any ideal social system, every man who produces something in any land helps all the rest and every man who is idle in any land lays a burden on every worker of the world. The social cost of armies and navies and other paraphernalia of patriotism is a heavy burden on the poor and the social cost in the narrow, brutal sentiments of the race cannot be told!

Salesmanship

A FEW DAYS AGO I picked up a popular magazine and read the advertisements. I was surprised to see the number of schools and universities offering courses in salesmanship. These advertisements all featured in large type such expressions as: DON'T ENVY SUCCESSFUL SALESMEN—BE ONE! and BECOME A SALESMAN—BIG JOBS OPEN! The headings were followed by seductive reading matter about men "who make from $5,000 to $30,000 a year, who travel first class, stop at the best hotels, and are in daily contact with Prosperous Business Men." Often there were pictures. Two boys were represented, starting out with equal chances and equal ability. In the next picture they had both grown old, but one was associating with Prosperous Business Men and the other was still a laborer. One had studied Scientific Salesmanship. The other had stuck to hard work.

It was not with the idea of getting a job, but mainly through simple curiosity that I sought to find out what all this was about. All my life I had been interested in books, but somehow I had overlooked books on salesmanship. Literally hundreds of them, it appears, are now on the market, and used by our colleges, universities and Y. M. C. A. night

---

"Salesmanship" first appeared in the *American Mercury* 5 (August 1925): 385–92. A pungently satirical examination of manuals for assisting salesmen in their work, the essay indirectly conveys Darrow's opposition to capitalism in its implicit scorn of money-grubbing. Because Darrow does not specify which manuals have come under his examination, it is not possible to identify them.

schools in the laudable business of giving hope and cheer to the overworked and underpaid. The topics they deal with range from those which might properly be placed under the heads of calisthenics, physical culture, hypnotism, phrenology, psychology, dress, and deportment, to specific directions for the treatment of hard customers and tricks for getting the unwary to buy.

Here I shall let these books speak for themselves, with only such comment as will be necessary for clarity. There is a matter of terminology which we must get straight before the show begins. Among the first things which attract attention in this literature is the fact that a prospective purchaser is not regarded simply as a human being, or even referred to in terms of his occupation or social position. For the salesman all men are Prospects. It seems to me only fair, then, that we look upon every one who attempts to sell anything as a Prospector.

Obviously, if a Prospector is to be successful, he must prepare himself for his arduous life of gold-digging. All the books thus start out with chapters on the general subject: "How to Get Ready and Why." The first thing the aspiring salesman must do, it appears, is to develop the physical basis for the combative spirit necessary in forcing a Prospect to buy:

> Many young men are not highly developed in the faculty of combativeness and in order to become good salesmen they require this faculty brought into positive function, that they may not give up or become undecided and discouraged. Combativeness functions through the shoulder and arm muscles as shown by the soldier, prize fighter, athlete, etc., and, well developed, it imparts a feeling of enthusiasm, physical vigor and power of decision that no other faculty can give; the best way, then, of bringing it into proper function is to take up some form of exercise that will call into use the shoulder and arm muscles, each morning immediately upon arising, devoting ten or fifteen minutes to this. The same amount of time may be devoted with profit in the evening if one feels the extra need.

But this is not enough. No ambitious salesman will be content with the development merely of his physical powers. He will also cultivate his spiritual gifts for the contest. Thus he is instructed to say to himself: "I *will* succeed. I will *awaken* tomorrow feeling good. I will go through the day doing work better than I have done it before. I will meet every one with a feeling of good will!"

It is a good idea, we are informed, to keep on repeating this formula until one falls asleep; then the subconscious can carry on while one is sleeping. By morning, one will thus have made as much progress as if one had stayed awake repeating the formula all night!

> Bed time suggestion is especially helpful in preparation for an ordeal next day, such as interviewing a formidable customer.

An example of one of these bedtime incantations reads as follows:

> At 2 P. M. tomorrow, precisely, I will walk into Hornyhand's office. I am not afraid of him. I am as good as he is. I will be absolutely confident of my ability to face him in an interview. I *will* be confident.

An illustration of the remarkable results which can be achieved by this method is given by a salesman from San Francisco, engaged in selling paint. His testimony, with the author's approving remarks, is as follows:

> "Today I am learning the secret of doing my work scientifically. Before going out on any deal involving a considerable amount, I spend an hour or two in concentration. I sincerely believe that it helps me. I believe I influence my prospect's mind before meeting him."
>
> Of this we can be certain: that this paint salesman, through concentration, is making himself stronger mentally, and that his prospects will find it more difficult to *resist* him.

In other words, under this treatment a Prospect will buy paint whether he has anything to be painted or not.

II

All this mental discipline, of course, is possible only if the salesman has some training in and understanding of psychology. Accordingly, each one of the books I have examined devotes a few pages to explaining the fundamentals of that recondite science. One book gives an elaborate diagram of the human head divided into thirty-seven compartments, and labeled "amativeness," "parental love," "combativeness" and so on, down to "inductive reasoning." I had seen such charts forty years ago in Fowler and Wells' famous treatise on phrenology,[1] but I had thought that they were extinct. It appears, however, that they have been carried down to a book on salesmanship published in 1922 and used in one of the best schools. Of course, the new books do not lay quite as much stress on phrenology as would have been the case forty years ago, but they are very strong on the use of what they call psychology. One of them sagely advises the student to "spend a few evenings studying psychology." Out of that study, brief as it is, he is supposed to attain to complete control of the Prospect:

> To master conviction it is essential that you have knowledge of the human mind and how it works. You must know what takes place when a customer deliberates. What change takes place in his mental consciousness, what is his mental attitude, and what is his state of mind while being convinced.

One would think that with all this subtle knowledge the scientific salesman would be ready for the fray. But no. He must next carefully prepare a Selling Talk. All the books lay great stress on this. It is never even suggested that people buy goods because they want them. They must be told that they want them. The only exception I have been able to find in the literature is in a few sentences distinguishing between the business of a salesman and that of a mail-order house. We are told that "some goods are sold without salesmen. Mail-order houses use a catalogue in selling their merchandise. *The individual who orders from a catalogue usually* WANTS *the goods and utilizes the catalogue to ascertain the price.*" But the scientific salesman is above selling merchandise to those who actually want it. What he must do is put in a simple way by one of the most popular books on the subject:

> You get an order from a prospect because of what he *thinks.* Signing an order or handing over money must be a *voluntary* operation. The prospect must be *willing;* he must think certain thoughts. *You* must lead him *to think those thoughts.*

Another author calls this process "uncovering a need for the goods." We are informed, however, that merely uncovering the need is not sufficient, for it might result in the customer buying some other person's goods and fail to convince him that he should buy *now.* The Selling Talk, therefore, must induce the prospect to make a favorable decision at once. In fact,

> The one and only purpose of a Selling Talk is to get the order. . . . All that a salesman says to a Prospect can be printed in a circular or typed in a letter and mailed to the Prospect, but the salesman can bring to bear in the personal interview every power of language and every bit of force that is in words, and focus them on the mind of the customer while he demonstrates his goods. The whole purpose of the Selling Talk, then, can be summed up in: 1. It must uncover in the Prospect's mind a need for the goods. 2. It must convince him that your goods are the goods he needs. 3. It must bring him to the point of *deciding* that he needs your goods more than he needs the money they cost. 4. That he must have the goods as quick as he can get them—so he orders. Any Selling Talk that does not accomplish this purpose has missed the mark.

In many of the text-books, the salesman is carefully instructed as to the use of particular words and as to their proper pronunciation and warned against errors in grammar. However, he must understand, too, that it will not do to be over-particular about grammar. He must be democratic and despise the snob. One of the best books gives this suggestion:

> I know a man who found it helpful with his general methods to deliberately cultivate a few incorrect habits of speech, such as dropping the *g*'s in words ending in *ing*—saying *goin'* for *going* and *advertisin'* for *advertising;* and saying "there *ain't* any" for "there is none" (*sic*). By *unaffected* use of these expressions and careful use of otherwise *good* grammar and pronunciation, they secure an added impression of *earnestness* in what they are saying.

The text-books give a large number of opening sentences that are certified to be effective. As, for example, "All that you say is true, but . . . ; A little reflection will convince any one that . . . ; Fortunately, that can be taken care of . . . ; I assert without fear of successful contradiction . . . ; There can be no two opinions about . . . ; You are right in your judgment, but . . . ," and so on down to this gem: *"Your desire to think it over is commendable, but . . ."*

The student is further instructed that "four salesmen out of five have got to be *actors.* In fact, *all* salesmen ought to be more or less actors. Follow the good actor's lead and learn your lines and then throw your feelings into them. Learn the places to get enthusiastic, the places to get calm, the places to bang your fists on the prospect's desk and the places to shut your mouth and keep quiet."

Having mastered all these principles, the student is ready for his first Prospect. But before he can make Selling Talks, he must manage to run his quarry down. If the Prospect is a business man in a down-town office, a careful plan of attack must be formulated. If the Prospect is a housewife or a farmer, a different and perhaps more subtle method must be used.

In discussing the stalking of a business man, many of the books give full instructions for getting past what they refer to as the Outer Guards.

These guards are generally office boys and stenographers. Some none too astute salesmen hand the office boy a card reading:

Mr. B. Clyde Edgeworth,
Boston, Mass.

with the inscription in the corner, "Representing the United Bond Co." But this is bad practice, for

> The office boy takes this to the inner office and returns a few moments later with the answer that the president is too busy today to see you. You have committed an error in your approach. There is nothing for you to do but leave and try at some future time when you have worked out a more unique method of getting the interview.

Here it is perfectly plain that the Prospect was warned that he was expected to part with money. He should not have been told in this abrupt way. The next time you call, if you are a good salesman, your card will read simply:

Mr. B. Clyde Edgeworth,
Boston, Mass.

The Prospect will be glad to see Mr. B. Clyde Edgeworth from Boston, Mass. If he is a lawyer, for example, he will probably surmise, or at least hope, that Mr. Edgeworth has come from Boston, Mass., to give him money. So Mr. Edgeworth is at once ushered in, and once he gets in he can take his choice of any number of approaches. One book suggests that he may even forget his card and explain to the office boy that he has none. This may induce the Prospect to think he has a client waiting outside. It is even suggested that "many will insist on using a name so difficult that the office boy will forget it. Something like this is used by a clever salesman with a national reputation who enters the outer office and gives the name of Mr. Eishenhimmel." No office boy can remember this name, so the manager hears only that some gentleman from Boston wants to see him. This arouses his curiosity and the interview is granted.

Sometimes the Prospector finds an office unprotected. The proper method of procedure in this case is to stroll carelessly in, "indicating by this attitude that he is familiar with the surroundings." When the Prospect appears, the salesman informs him that he has been waiting for some time. This immediately puts the Prospect on the defensive. Still another way is for the salesman to walk up to the girl in charge and ask for the Prospect and then walk right in to his private office. This will lead to the belief that the girl has sent him in. "While the Prospect is wondering what is wrong with his office system, the salesman is getting warmed up on his talk."

The methods which are suggested for getting into the home and talking to the housewife are even more interesting. We are assured that the following plan is used with great success by the talented representative of a large canned soup company. He carries a thermos bottle filled with hot soup. He rings the bell and the door opens.

> "Good morning, Madam."
> He pours a small portion of the hot soup into a paper cup which he has handed her.
> "I just want you to try this soup."
> While she is tasting the soup, he gives a brief explanation and then endeavors to book her order for three or four cans. He explains that the order will be given to her grocer and delivered the same day. She need not pay until the end of the month.

The farmer, it appears, must not be approached too abruptly. If you are to get his money you must break the news to him gently. You should first talk about horses, soil and market conditions. This conversation will show that you are interested in things close to him and likewise give you a chance to study his temperament and "to learn his likes and dislikes and *discover his weaknesses.*"

When the Prospector gets well in touch with his Prospect then all his learning in psychology is called into play. To persuade or hypnotize the Prospect, it is of first importance to get his attention. This does not mean that he merely listen politely, but that he give Real Attention to the salesman. Giving him a mental shock is sometimes valuable.

> This you can do by dropping your pencil or striking the table. The effect of this is very good providing that the instant you have his attention you drive home some selling point.

But all Prospects, of course, cannot be treated in the same manner. One canvasser was selling a household appliance. He always took note of everything that was to be seen both before he rang the bell and after the lady of the house appeared.

> If the woman came to the door in an apron or working dress he said: "Have I interrupted you in your work? I am sorry." The average woman, overcome by his solicitous tone, protested that it was no trouble and the foxy salesman had a few sensible remarks to make on housekeeping, which brought him naturally to the appliance he had to sell.

Occasionally a sharp woman would come back, "Yes, I am busy and have no time today!" Thereupon, the salesman would agree quickly: "I'll *bet* that's true. When I was first married, my poor little wife just worked herself sick keeping up a house. And I made up my mind then that every little thing that I could get for her to save a little bit of work or time I would if it would take my last dollar." The woman is softened. "And I accidentally ran across the cleverest thing you ever saw for saving her back—here it is right here—I've helped, oh, I guess 2,000 women, to get one like it." And he is on with his canvass.

Some methods are a little more drastic. One book tells of excellent success following making the Prospect angry.

It was up to me to get their attention. What did I do? I tramped on their corns. I reached over and plunked down on their corns. I really did this; I am not stuffing you. When they got red and mad all over, I knew that I had their attention. Then I would say: "I was clumsy, wasn't I? But profits, profits for you today and profits you haven't dreamed of. . . ."

After the salesman gets the attention of the Prospect, he is ready to unlimber all of his psychological artillery. Of course, he understands that no sale can be made unless he first induces a Desire to Buy. This is a fundamental axiom in all the text-books:

> There must be enough desire in any particular instance to over-balance all obstacles and make the man desire to do the thing more than for some reason—either concealed or expressed—he desires not to do it. The whole question is, can the salesman produce this much desire? If he can, he can sell. There is the whole problem of salesmanship in a sentence.

Nothing could be clearer than this. Contrary to the political economists, sales are not made because the purchaser needs the article and wants to get it, but because the Prospector creates a Desire to Buy in him—a desire which the Prospect never had before, or which at least lay dormant in his unconscious. We are instructed that for creating this desire suggestion is much more important than argument. The Prospect should be in a passive and receptive mood to get the best results. For example, it is easier to make a sale if you are sitting in a semi-dark room than if you are in one brightly lighted. Impressionability and sensitiveness are apt to be overcome by bright lights.

When one really understands this principle, the rest is very simple. So simple that one can't help wondering how a Prospect ever keeps his money. To quote again:

> Another stratagem successfully used by a great many salesmen, especially in so-called "high pressure" selling, is to get the Pros-

pect into an agreeable frame of mind just as soon as possible, and then lead him on from one agreement to another until he has the habit. Then, when you ask him to agree to give you an order, he is just that much more apt to do so. This is called the "yes" method of closing.

A life insurance salesman, for example, starts in by getting the Prospect to agree that it is a nice day, or that his offices are very bright and cheerful. Then he leads him on, tactfully and adroitly, from that small beginning to agree that life insurance is a good thing. The next step is to get him to agree that every man should invest a percentage of his income in insurance, and so on up the ladder until finally the salesman gets him to agree to be examined.

In working such sorceries, considerations of age and sex are important.

The young are more readily influenced than the mature, because their fund of knowledge on a given subject is smaller. Women are more liable to succumb to suggestion than men because they are impatient of deliberate process and like to reach conclusions quickly. In business transactions the common citizen is more easily swayed than the professional buyer. Fatigue increases susceptibility, as shown by laboratory experiments. Intoxicants also increase it.

I know that the last sentence was not written for the purpose of giving advice. I am sure of it, for it appears in a book on Salesmanship published by the Y. M. C. A. Still, I have quoted the sentence literally and I have heard that, in the good old days, certain wicked salesmen did use this means of getting the Prospect into a receptive mood.

Now we have our Prospect in a passive state of mind and ready for suggestions. To the untutored the simplest and most direct way to awaken the Desire to Buy in him might seem to be by telling him something about the excellence of your wares and his crying need for them. But there are subtler ways, and the books are nothing if not subtle. Let us go back to their theoretical training in psychology.

Salesmanship is the science and the art of influencing the mind through the five senses. The number of senses that can be played upon depends on the line or the article to be sold.

A wine merchant or salesman can play upon all five senses. The sense of sight is played upon by the merchant's or salesman's manner, expression, gestures and the color of the wine. The sense of smell by the bouquet and the flavor of the wine. The sense of feeling by the generous warmth imparted by the wine to the feelings. The sense of hearing by the salesman's voice and argument.

Operating upon the sense of hearing is by far the most important, for through hearing the salesman can persuade the mind that the other senses are mistaken in their perceptions, or that the consensus of opinion favors the direct opposite of what his mind conceives.

The voice can be trained to become so strong and forceful that its very force carries conviction to the mind of the hearer. It can be trained to become so even and matter of fact that its very tone suggests truth, and the mind of the hearer unconsciously adopts the suggestion that the proposition is entirely as represented. The voice can be trained to become so subtly soft and low that it deadens the resistance of the brain like a soothing narcotic.

It is only fair to add that the book in which all this appears was published before the Eighteenth Amendment and not by the Y. M. C. A. But singers, speakers and actors have long observed these effects of the human voice. Many a man has been charmed by an oration and after going away from a meeting has been unable to remember a single idea that the speaker suggested. Nature creates such magical voices, but art should not be neglected. People, it appears, are taken quite unawares when the great gifts of the rhetorician are suddenly launched against them by one selling mouse-traps or cockroach powders.

Meanwhile, the scientific salesman must not overlook the power of the magnetic eye. This power was first used by snakes in charming birds, and it has been long used in taming lions and other wild animals. Here is its modern application:

> Can you look a prospect straight in the eye? Can you keep him looking at you while driving home a point? If you can't, learn how. If you want to be master of the situation, if you want to cast an influence over his mind that will be hard to resist, do it with the eye. If you can hold your gaze on a man without wavering, you can practically persuade him in every instance, unless your proposition is too unreasonable.
>
> While looking a prospect straight in the eye, *it gives him no chance to reason or reflect.* An idea is planted on the subjective mind. It is not analyzed. It is not compared with some past experience. *It is taken as a truth.*

The Prospector is given plenty of illustrations of the way to awaken the Prospect's imagination and create a Desire to Buy. A story is told of how a very talented expert was called in to increase the business of a shoe-store. He soon discovered that it would be impossible to give its customers any better shoes or any more shoes for their money. Then he asked himself the question: "What more *can* we give?"

> By clearly understanding that it was the customer's *thoughts* he had to influence more than their *feet,* the sales-organizer built up a canvass which did not actually *require* a single word to be spoken by the salesman. Of course, the salesman talked more or less, but no words were laid down for him.
>
> The salesman was required to take off the customer's shoe, get the size and an idea of the style desired.
>
> Ordinarily, the next step would have been to bring out a few pairs of shoes and perhaps try them on.
>
> Not so, now.
>
> The salesman must examine the foot carefully. He must span the width with his fingers. Lift the foot up and put one hand on the sole and one on top as though getting its contour

well in mind. Then he lays it on the floor and asks the customer to put his weight on it. Feels of each joint, squeezes the balls of the toes, and presses upward on the arch.

All this before he has made a single move towards actually fitting it.

The salesman then straightens up and looks at the foot critically—then examines the other foot.

The customer is watching and begins to feel that an *expert* is fitting him—and that he never had such careful attention before.

The salesman then goes to the shelves for shoes. He brings back only one. Does not put it on the customer's foot, but just compares the foot and shoe with his eye. Then returns it to the shelf and brings back another. This one he tries on, but with the same excess of carefulness as he used in his examination.

When the salesman pronounces the customer's foot fitted, it generally goes.

And the customer goes out with the shoes feeling that he has indeed received big value for his money.

I defy anyone to resist this method. Somewhere in my unconscious mind there lurks a suspicion that a Prospector has somewhere worked this game on me.

To thoroughly influence a Prospect, it is important to have an eye for details. As a rule, the salesman cannot get too close to the customer. The magnetic effect of personal proximity is immense.

It is much better in talking with a Prospect not to sit at too great a distance from him. It has been demonstrated that if you sit or stand close you can make a better impression and will have more influence than if at a distance. This may be accounted for by your personal magnetism, or the radiating of energy which at close range cannot help but prove more effective than at a distance.

The real purpose of all the foregoing is "to make *your* will the Prospect's will." He must not be allowed to make his own decision, nor even think about it. He may not need your goods or want them, but *you* want him to buy them. You must be the complete master in the whole transaction. Now and then, it would seem, a Prospect shows fight. He has a foolish idea that he ought to have something to say himself about how he spends his money. A good salesman is alert to catch the first sign of this untoward resistance. The Prospector is carefully enjoined, to quote the words of one of the books, that

> If you keep a tight rein on a skittish horse, you can handle him, but the minute you let him grab the bit and feel he is boss, then you have a dangerous chance of a runaway.

This admonition is followed by a touching story of a clever salesman whose Prospect began to take the lead in the conversation. Disregarding all the rules, this Prospect forced the salesman to follow in *his* lead. Promptly the salesman shut him off.

> At the first sign of unruliness in the Prospect, he began to lick at his thumb nail. As the Prospect got further out of control he would examine the supposedly afflicted thumb anxiously. Then in the middle of the Prospect's remarks he would say, "Pardon me, but have you a sharp knife?" The Prospect produces a knife and generally apologizes for its not being very sharp. The salesman says that it will do and begins to cut at an imaginary hang-nail and complains of what a nuisance hang-nails are. The Prospect generally sympathizes and as he draws up to look at the operation, the salesman says, "There, I guess that's fixed," shuts the knife and with a sigh of relief looks up at the Prospect again. "Let's see, what were we talking about? Oh yes, about so and so . . ."

One's mind wanders to the question of the fairness of this subtle method. What chance has an ordinary man when a Prospector so deeply learned in psychology has at him? However, this point is covered in a perfectly logical manner by the textbooks.

> When a Prospect has granted you an interview; when he has given you his attention at its best or comes into your store, or when a woman has opened her house door to you, that interview is *yours* and you have a right to manage it and direct it according to your own particular plan.

Fair enough! The impudence of a Prospect having anything to say about spending his own money! Especially in his own home!

The whole procedure may be summed up in one sentence, taken from a leading text-book: *Do not permit the Prospect to reason and reflect.* A scientific salesman must always bear in mind that it is his first duty to get control.

> The salesman must not be entirely confined to one method of approach, or a single talking point, or to any particular and exact program. He must be versatile. If he can't get his customer one way, he must get him another. A thoroughly trained psychologist, by observing the facial expression of his Prospect, his feeble remarks, his wariness, and his show of fight, ought to be prepared at any moment to change his tactics. The expert fisherman tries out the fish—if one kind of *bait* doesn't get the strike, he changes. And if one kind of hook doesn't *land* them he changes hooks. If he is alert, aggressive, masterful, persistent and a thorough psychologist he perseveres. He carefully lays his snares, places his bait and then the unsuspecting Prospect falls into the trap.

No matter how good an approach you have made, regardless of how clever or how perfect your Selling Talk may be, it is all of no avail unless you close the sale. Therefore, you should have a Reserve Talk in readiness if the need should arise. In large letters the salesman is told that "many Prospects must be led; others driven. The closing argument must be directed at the Prospect's *weakness*. Tie your Prospect up so that he must act. The majority of salesmen make it too easy for their Prospect to slip away. Tie him up so that he cannot *possibly* back down."

V

Many a Prospect, after he has taken the fatal step, has glimmering thoughts, it appears, of pay day or of the needs of his customers. This sometimes brings him cold feet and a sinking sensation at the pit of the stomach. He wishes that he hadn't. Here the well equipped, thoroughly trained master of psychology is prepared.

> No matter how great the advantage won in a purchase, there nearly always comes an instant after the decision when the purchaser grows cold and "sorter wishes he hadn't done it," and that is the time when the good salesman puts one final long, strong tooth into his talk. He must keep the customer's interest going until he gets into some other subject. The salesman in a large cut-price tailoring establishment had suffered much from cancelled orders and has now been trained in this knack of speeding the customer's interest up after a purchase. As the customer's measurements are finished, the salesman again picks up the selected goods and pats them affectionately.
>
> "I wanted a suit off this piece myself," he says regretfully, "but the buyer wouldn't let any of us boys have it. It's an unusual piece of goods and they don't waste such a piece on any of us fellows in the shop. Yes, you'll never regret *this* suit," and then he goes on to make out the sales ticket.
>
> In all that you say or do after the sale, be brief, remind the purchaser of the excellence of his bargain, make some complimentary remark about his business, his home or whatever

concerns him most, and as he leaves, shake his hand. In a word, be courteous, calm and confident.

It is obvious that these astounding books on salesmanship are symptomatic of the age. In literary quality, they are crude to the last degree. The motive back of all of them is not even veiled. The reader is simply urged to get the money and get it quickly. Alluring advertisements are sent broadcast to the struggling and the dull-witted, asking them to part with their cash to buy books and take courses that they may get money from others even more dull-witted than themselves. They are told that they need only learn a few tricks, and they can at once overmatch the credulous Prospect. I am informed that less than fifty per cent of those who buy the books and make their first payments ever finish the course of instruction, and that of those who get through only a few ever ride in Pullman cars, "live at the best hotels, and enjoy the companionship of Prosperous Business Men." They simply have a dream, and then go back to work.

Of course, no one could make money out of a school to educate Prospects in resisting the wiles of the Prospector. Still, some philanthropist might endow such a school. Better yet, our existing institutions of learning might lay out courses to teach the public what to buy, where to buy, and how to buy, including instruction in what not to buy, and where not to buy it. Every one knows how many hard-working men and women, in the hope of getting relief from toil for themselves and their families, have invested their money in fake oil stocks, mining stocks, patent rights, real-estate subdivisions, and all sorts of similar frauds. Many of these are now toiling in their old age, many are receiving alms from their relatives and friends, many others are in poorhouses and in jails. Something might be done for this ever-growing army of Prospects. These are the victims of the new High-Power Salesmanship.

The Eugenics Cult

IN THE LAST TEN years the reading public has been bombarded by books and articles on eugenics. In the main these articles have set forth a single thesis: that doom hangs over the human race. Of course, we have all known for a long time that each individual of the human race is doomed. Though we seldom speak of it and try not to think about it, every man inevitably comes to the realization that in time his own life must pass. The eugenists' concern, however, is not over the fact that we die one by one. What alarms them is that the race is apparently bent upon committing a wholesale biological *harikari*. So there has been much beating of drums, blowing of trumpets and hubbub on the street-corners; there have been cries in the night of "race suicide," "the rising tide of color,"[1] "the race is dying out at the top," and "torrents of degenerate and defective protoplasm." . . . It is vain to ask the question, What of it? That does not stop the clamor. Neither will the remarks that I am about to make on the subject.

The evidence with which the eugenists support their contentions is simple and overwhelming. Are not the weak and unfit breeding much

First published in the *American Mercury* 8 (June 1926): 129–37, this essay vigorously opposes eugenics both as bad science and as an infringement of civil liberties. Darrow had previously warned of the dangers of the eugenicists in the essay "The Edwardses and the Jukeses," *American Mercury* 6 (October 1925): 147–57, a discussion of an upper-class family and a lower-class family, the latter of whom were taken to be hereditarily inclined toward pauperism and crime.

faster than the strong and the fit? College professors, lawyers, doctors, and the like average not more than two children to the family. On the other hand, carpenters, bricklayers, bootblacks and the other unfit average at least twice as many. Everybody knows that dagos, hunkies, wops, bolsheviks and all the other undesirables are begetting children at an indecent rate. These children are surely bound to overrun the earth, along with the morons, the insane and the criminal. Inevitably the superior stocks will be submerged. The only wonder is that with the persistent and senseless breeding of the unfit this hasn't happened long ago. Right here in our own country, which was settled by the Nordics after the Indians were driven out, the superior race is fast going down before the misfits of inferior races. In the face of the promiscuous breeding of these latter such noble strains as the Edwardses and the Adamses will be swamped by mere force of numbers. The good old *Mayflower* stock is suffering the same unhappy fate as the good old pre-Prohibition liquor. It is being mixed with all sorts of alien and debilitating substances.

Semi-cultured citizens read the eugenist books, and, sitting on hard Chautauqua benches, listen to the speakers. Then they shudder with horror at the thought of the rising tide of undesirables. They believe it all, of course, for they assume that they themselves are the intelligent and the well-born. The professors, the preachers, the lawyers, the bankers, all the good solid citizens, are worried. Something, obviously, must be done to save the world, and the eugenists are ready and even importunate with their remedy. *Organized society*, they say, *must in some way control mating and birth.* True, most of them seem to pause purposely just before they draw the logical conclusion that the state should interfere with the production of humans, as man already does with the production of hogs. When they come to this point they falter and quibble, raise doubts and get cold feet. They take refuge in vague generalizations and leave the intelligent reader and the more intelligent politician to do the rest. But that rest will evidently be a plenty.

However, some of the eugenists are not so shy. Mr. Albert Wiggam, for instance, speaking with his wonted clearness, force and sureness, tells us that society must take stern measures to prevent the unfit from producing their kind. He pleads with us to take heed of the laws of science. If we only knew it, says Mr. Wiggam, "we already have enough science at hand to bring the world into an earthly paradise! It remains only for all men to apply it."[2] Again, there is Mr. Herbert W. Walter, who joins a Mr. Davenport in sounding a call for race improvement. In his book, "Genetics," he quite definitely sets forth the necessity for the control of the production of human beings by state agencies. "A negative way," writes Mr. Walter, "to bring out the better blood in the world is to follow the clarion call of Davenport and 'dry up the streams of defective and degenerate protoplasm.' This may be partially accomplished, at least in America, by employing the following agencies: control of immigration, more discriminating marriage laws, a quickened eugenic sentiment, sexual segregation of defectives, and, finally, drastic measures of sterilization when necessary."[3]

Mr. Walter later informs us that already our face is turned toward the light. Eight States have sterilization laws, and if such laws could be enforced in the whole United States "less than four generations would eliminate nine-tenths of the crime, insanity, and sickness of the present generation in our land. Asylums, prisons, and hospitals would decrease and the problems of the unemployed, the indigent old, and the hopelessly degenerate would cease to trouble civilization." Mr. Wiggam is right: paradise is just around the corner. Amazingly simple, isn't it? Just a law providing for a "minor operation on the male which occupies but a few moments" and in the case of the female "the removal of a portion of each Fallopian tube" and presto! in four generations we are rid of nine-tenths of our criminals, paupers, insane, etc. No wonder the man in the street marvels at the wonders of science!

II

But except for his proposal of the sovereign remedy of sterilization, Mr. Walter lacks any very specific administrative programme for "drying up the streams of degenerate protoplasm." Luckily, however, we have with us Dr. William McDougall, who has evolved a plan for carrying out the ideals of the eugenists which has the virtue of being at once both definite and simple. It is so simple as to be almost fool-proof, even in a democracy. Dr. McDougall is certainly an eminent authority; he is the head of the psychology department of Harvard and was lured to this position from Oxford, the well-known headquarters of the Nordics. He has been recognized for these many years as one of the leading psychologists of the world and his writings are eagerly devoured by the classes who believe in the essential aristocracy of the Nordic germ-plasm.

Dr. McDougall, in his book, "Ethics and Some Modern World Problems," begins by saying that two classes of undesirables in the population can be immediately determined: the mentally deficient and the convicted criminals. The first class can be selected "through our highly organized medical science and institutions," and our legal "institutions can select the latter."[4] (This must mean doctors, lawyers and judges.) For Dr. McDougall it is a "simple and indisputable truth" that both of these classes should be disenfranchised. The third category, which we are informed can be just as easily recognized, is that of the illiterates. These, too, should be disenfranchised.

So far, so good. Now we come to the eugenic high-point in Dr. McDougall's plan. On the basis of literacy tests the population is to be divided into two classes, which we may call the A and C classes. *Intermarriage between these two classes is to be strictly prohibited.* Those who cannot read will not be allowed to marry those who can. In this manner, Dr. McDougall tells us, the A class will be constantly purified by shedding into the C class those who do not fit into the higher order. But there should be an opportunity for the best progeny of the C class to be elevated to the A class. This could be accomplished by creating another class with a probationary status, which we may designate the B class. Every candidate "for admission to the A class would have to spend at least twenty or twenty-five years of his life as a probationer in the B class."[5] But children whose parents were both of the A class would have the status of the B class as their birthright, and these favored ones, upon attaining adult life, would be admitted to the A class if otherwise qualified, *i.e.,* if they had learned to read intelligently. On the other hand, children born of parents *either one of whom* was in the C class would have the status of that class, and when they had passed the qualifying education test they would enter the B class only as probationers. Only after twenty years there and the discharge of the recognized obligations would they go into the A class.

The state system of education, says Dr. McDougall, should be free to all, but compulsory to none. To pass from a lower status to a higher one, there should be, beside the time requirements, educational tests and examinations. It might be wise also, he tells us, to provide that any citizen of the A class who married a member of the C class should automatically lose his status and revert to the C class. "In this way the nation would achieve the benefits of a simple caste organization, namely: the preservation of the qualities of the superior strains." The scheme would likewise "avoid those features which condemn to stagnation every society founded upon a rigid caste system."[6] In time, the three-class system would bring three great advantages: first, political power would rest in the hands of a select body of citizens; second, the nation would be fortified against the fatal tendency of civilization to die away at the top; third, the class of full citizens would be protected against the lowering of its average by the inmixture of blood of inferior quality.

Here then, we have a "neat but not gaudy"[7] little plan for saving civilization: a simple caste system in which the literate sheep are carefully separated from the illiterate goats. What may be called literary miscegenation by members of the A class is forbidden on pain of the offender being reduced automatically to the illiterate group from which neither he nor his descendants can escape, save by going through the purgatory of twenty years in the B class. The inference to be drawn from all this is as clear as it is inevitable. Dr. McDougall is of the opinion that there is a definite and direct correlation between the ability to "read intelligently" and desirable germ-plasm. All those whose parents are members of the A class are forthwith members of the A class (provided that they can pass the necessary examination); the presumption is that they have good germ-plasm. But those whose parents (or either of them) are members of the C class carry a bad germ-plasm, and it must be aged in the wood, as it were, for twenty years before it reaches the A class standard.

What could be simpler than all this? Nothing, perhaps, except Dr. McDougall's biological innocence. On the basis of what biological principles, and by what psychological hocus-pocus he reaches the conclusion that the ability to read intelligently denotes a good germ-plasm and desirable citizens I cannot say. Here I merely rehearse his plan. I present it as Exhibit A of the scheme of the eugenists to save civilization.

III

Quotations from other eminent authorities might be multiplied to show just how far the biological uplifters are willing to go. Their romancing would not be worth discussing were it not for the fact that the public apparently takes it at its face value. "Aren't these eugenists scientists? And you can't get around scientific law, you know." The politicians stand ready with their usual willingness to deliver what the people want. So-called eugenic laws are already on the statute books of various States. When one stops to consider what a radical departure in the conduct of human beings in the most important concerns of life is called for by the movement, the measure of success that it has already obtained is enough to inspire the most substantial hopes or fears—depending upon one's point of view.

The question which naturally arises at this point is, What evidence do the eugenists have at hand to support their demand for the organized control of human breeding? Everyone who has any knowledge of the matter knows that the biologists have experimented for years in the production of sweet peas, pigeons, white rats, guinea pigs, fruit flies and domestic animals of various kinds. Such deductions as have been drawn from this controlled breeding of animals and plants are formulated in the so-called Mendelian laws, the theory of unit characters, and that of the continuity of the germ-plasm. But what has all this to do with the production of human beings? What, if anything, can be learned about the proper and desirable breeding of men from experiments with fruit flies? The biologists have discovered that by regulating the breeding of various species and taking notice of what are called unit characters (such as eye color, tallness and shortness, fatness and leanness, long hair, etc.) they can within certain limits produce strains that will breed true to almost any type desired. In this fashion, for example, we are able to get the draft horse, the race horse, the milch cow, different kinds of flowers, and fruit flies with various and sundry characteristics. How natural to suppose, then, that man, also an animal, must have his unit characters, which can be manipulated and bred, out or in, as desired!

The eugenist would have us believe that on the basis of these experiments on plants and the lower animals, together with some alleged observations on the so-called degenerate germ-plasms of human beings, plus certain reflections on the haphazard character of human mating, we are justified in the conclusion that all that is needed is to use the same skill and force with humans that has already been used with hogs, and the miracle will be wrought. A new humanity will arise full grown in place of the ignoramuses and misfits that now cumber the earth.

But can we actually draw any such conclusion? Let us turn for an answer to Dr. H. S. Jennings, an eminent biologist at Johns Hopkins University. Dr. Jennings is an experimental biologist and not a eugenist. In his little book, "Prometheus," he warns us against this very fallacy of placing too great reliance on experiments with animals as a basis for the breeding of the human race. To those eager colleagues who are too ready to make assumptions about human heredity he says:

> When the biologist, from his knowledge of other organisms, is tempted to dogmatize concerning the possibilities of human development, let him first ask himself: How correctly could I predict the behavior and social organization of ants from a knowledge of the natural history of the oyster? Man differs from other organisms used in these experiments as much as the ant does from the oyster; for these distinctive aspects of his biology, only the study of man himself is relevant.[8]

And then, to the further edification of Messrs. McDougall, Wiggam, Walter *et al*, he tells us that so far as our present experimental knowledge goes we know little or nothing about unit characters in human heredity and that what we do know leads us to the general conclusion that the very nature of human bi-parental reproduction effectively prevents the continued reproduction of what the eugenists would regard as a desirable type. In this matter, Nature not only seems to have something to say, but is all powerful. Says Dr. Jennings:

> If an ingenious inventor were set to work to devise a system for the purpose of heading off completely anything of this sort (i. e., the production of specified human types) he could hardly produce one so effective as the one found in Nature. This might rather seem devised to the end of giving the greatest possible variety; of yielding the extremes of diversity at any one time; of inducing most thorough-going and continuous changes as generations pass. Personified Nature might well be held to abhor uniformity and constancy for the higher organisms.[9]

We have made no actual experiments in the breeding of human beings. It is obvious that the biologists have not and cannot experiment by mating men and women, as they mate guinea pigs and rabbits, and then studying the offspring. Even if our folkways and mores would permit such experiments, the generations of men are so long that no conclusive results, comparable to those in animal experimentation, could be obtained except over a period of several hundred years. Thus all observations on human heredity up to this time have involved starting with a specific individual and then seeking to trace his heredity backward as far as possible. But no authentic record of specific human beings goes back very far, and even if such records were available it would remain a fact that with each new mating the germ-plasm would be changed. In the course of a few generations many different lines are crossed. But the investigators start with a human organism which they consider either good or bad and then arbitrarily assume the direction of the "stream of the germ-plasm" at each cross-roads in order to confirm their preconceived theory. In this way they frequently find what they are looking for. In any possible number of ancestors, no matter what the line, you can go but a little way without finding both strength and weakness. So this method, by and large, has meant only seeking evidence for what someone wanted to prove.

IV

But let us assume that man can, by breeding, change the human race. Do we really know that we can make it what is called "better"? Do we even know what we mean by the word? The eugenist, who is always lamenting that man has taken no such pains in breeding humans as he has in producing desirable plants and animals, assumes, of course, that he has done a good job with plants and animals. By carefully mating fat hogs and discarding lean ones, he has produced the Berkshire from the razorback, and after persistent selection the Berkshire now breeds fairly true. But is the Berkshire a better hog than the razorback? For my part, I am convinced that it is nowhere near as good.

Of course, I am here considering the change from the standpoint of the hog. He has not been able to speak for himself, and men have not spoken for him. Turn the Berkshire and the razorback out to shift for themselves. Which would fare the better and live the longer? The Berkshire, in fact, would probably soon smother in its own fat. And even if it should survive to reproduce, the hog race would slowly return to the razorback type. Take another case: that of our thoroughbred cows. They must be carefully tended, fed and milked. They are not healthy animals. In fact, they are not cows at all; they are simply milk machines. Again, there is the thoroughbred running horse. It is valuable to man for betting purposes—but the draft horse can pull loads. The race horse, if turned out without a blanket and left to get its own living, would probably die of pneumonia before it got very far from the paddock. And if it should survive turning out, then, in the course of time, its descendants would be like the scrub animals on the plains. I am inclined to think, indeed, that man never bred a plant or animal without weakening it or injuring it.

Thus it cannot be seriously argued that any "thoroughbred" animal or plant is better than one in a natural state. If so, better for what? Nature knows but one meaning of the word "better" and that is "fitted for survival." There is no evidence that even the "mind" of the thoroughbred hog or horse or cow is better than that of the scrub. The evidence seems to be the other way. When we speak of improving animals, we mean only that they have been improved for man's purposes, not for the purposes of living in competition with other organisms.

But to return to the point I have assumed for the sake of the argument: that man can be changed by controlled breeding: If we should eliminate the lean, and breed only the stout, we might get a race of mostly fat men. By eliminating the short and breeding only the tall, it is conceivable that the race would increase in stature. We might breed men who were lean or fat, or tall or short, but this could only be done within limits. Probably nature would rebel at any considerable variance from the present type. It has taken too long a time to produce the species in its present state to make possible a wide divergence of type.

But on what grounds would anyone be rash enough to want to change the physical type of man? Have we any assurance that a different type would be more desirable? If so, what kind of type? Furthermore, haven't the eugenists, in their zeal for "bringing the world into an earthly paradise," forgotten that man, as he stands, is created in the image of God? Is it possible that they are also ambitious to meddle with the perfection of the very Cosmic Plan itself?

But perhaps they do not desire to breed a different physical being. Perhaps, with Dr. McDougall, they will say that their real aim is to breed for better intellects. The world, unfortunately, is largely ruled by phrases, and there a convenient and fetching slogan for those who think the race may be improved by breeding has been supplied. "A healthy mind in a healthy body"[10] is the new slogan. But are good minds necessarily domiciled in healthy bodies? The history of the race does not prove it. There is something about a healthy body, apparently, that does not lure a good mind. It is probably too healthy. No; you cannot sort out intelligence by physical symmetry. The workings of heredity are obscure enough in the body; they are hopelessly indefinite in the mind. No eugenist knows anything about breeding for intellect. That the manifestations which we call mind are in some way a product of bodily functioning seems to be fairly well established. But what appears to be the healthiest and most symmetrical body may not produce the best mind. A slight and utterly obscure variance in some part of the structure may make a wide difference in mental strength. It is not unusual to find imbecility in the same family with first-rate intellects. To talk about breeding for intellect, in the present state of scientific knowledge and data, is nothing short of absurd. No scientist has ever pretended to advance any theories for breeding intellect; we do not know what intelligence is, much less how to breed it. Are we even convinced that better minds are desirable? The question of human welfare is not so much a question of more strength as of a better use of such strength as we have. About all that we can say about a good mind is that it adds to the effectiveness of the individual. What will be accomplished with the mind, good or bad, is not a matter of breeding; it is a matter of education.

V

It is, in fact, in no sense a foregone conclusion that the general welfare of man would be improved by increasing his intellect. It cannot be shown that the intelligent are happier than the ignorant; still less can it be shown that they contribute more to the happiness of their fellows. The great mass who are born and die are not "intellectual"; yet they survive and their tribe increases. Real intelligence is as rare, and perhaps as unnatural, as idiocy. One can imagine a human being so imaginative and sympathetic that he would pity the genius as much as the simple. No idiot knows that he is an idiot. As a rule, those of small intellectual equipment are so sure of themselves that they are eager to make the race over in their own image. This is a controlling reason why they should not be encouraged to exercise their power.

Is there any way to tell what class is the happiest? It cannot be shown that riches or learning or power or intellect have anything to do with happiness. Those who in a measure possess these gifts seem not to be sure of the happiness that they bring. It is not unreasonable to suppose that the cocksureness of ignorance, the lack of imagination that goes with conceit, and the crude hopes and dreams born of stupidity give more contentment and pleasure, and less pain, than the vision and imagination that are born of intelligence.

Assuming, for the sake of argument, that science could furnish us with such exact data on the method of breeding as would permit the elimination of morons, idiots and imbeciles, and at the same time vastly increase the numbers of the intelligent, scholarly and well disposed, I repeat that it is not at all certain that it would be desirable to accomplish that result. The large mass of men and women, the world over, must do manual work, and one of the first indications of intelligence and training is that an individual separates himself from such work. What would happen to the operation of factories, railroads, buildings, and all the various activities of men if everyone became a genius or a scholar? Are not the morons, so-called, also important in the scheme? In the processes of living, are they not even more important than the geniuses? Would not a well-developed system of birth-control leave out the vast number of people who do the manual work of the world? And if so, what would become of the intellectuals who were compelled to take their places? All men must live in houses, wear clothes and consume food. No society would be possible that did not take into account the vast army who must supply these primitive wants, and be more or less directed by the intelligent who do not perform manual work. Where is the assurance that any organized society, such as the state, through the regulations of breeding could produce the proper proportion of laborers and *intelligentsia* to improve the general standard of comfort and welfare of the whole people?

Even if human breeding could be so controlled as to produce a race such as the eugenists desire, we might still lose much that is worth while. It is hardly possible to breed certain qualities in without breeding others out. I, for one, am alarmed at the conceit and sureness of the advocates of this new dream. I shudder at their ruthlessness in meddling with life. I resent their egoistic and stern righteousness. I shrink from their judgment of their fellows. Every one who passes judgment necessarily assumes that he is right. It seems to me that man can bring comfort and happiness out of life only by tolerance, kindness and sympathy, all of which seem to find no place in the eugenists' creed. The whole programme means the absolute violation of what men instinctively feel to be inherent rights. Organized society shall say who must and must not breed, and establish stern rules for picking out mates.

But of the various ways that the individual has found for attaining to pleasure, one of the greatest is the business of selecting mates. A large and important part of life is made up of the gestures that precede and go with mating. Every Jack pursues his Jill, and every Jill lures her Jack. In this prime occupation of life they want to be free to do their own choosing. The boy and girl resent the proffered advice of even parents. It is safe to say that few fathers or mothers at fifty would approve of their own conquests in early life. It is still safer to say that in such a primitive affair as mating, the young would not give a fig for the opinions and wisdom of the old and seasoned. The youth does not even know why he is specially attracted to some special mate. The urge of life calls him, and he feels that he knows whom he wants. No one can imagine a boy or girl going to a committee and asking its members to pick out a mate. Nature does not work that way, and it is not easy to understand how it ever could work that way.

The normal boy and girl, indeed, do not go a-wooing in order to find mates to improve the race. They are thinking of themselves and their happiness, which is far more vital to them, and probably to the race, than the character of the human beings who will inhabit the earth in the distant future. It is the immediate feeling that preserves life. True, much mating is improvident, and many unions do not bring the anticipated joys, but still their emotions and hopes perpetuate the species, and so the race survives. If the scheme of the eugenist could be carried out, it is easy to conceive of a thoroughly mechanical human being, preserved for a time by his disappearing emotions, but eventually going down to annihilation. Is there any certainty that the intellectual control of life would bring more pleasure and satisfaction and variety than the seeming haphazard and instinctive mating that has at least produced most of the zeal and interest of living?

The bigoted and the ignorant are very sure of themselves. No business seems to be too important or too personal for them to undertake.

One of their chief pastimes is the regulation of other people. They are willing to do anything to others that to them seems important. To compel all others to adopt their own views and ways of living is their aim. In fact, one of their chief sources of comfort and pleasure is making others unhappy. How safe would it be for the human race and the comfort of the individual units if the production of human beings were left in their hands?

VI

It is well enough to rhapsodize over what should be done when there are no facts to sustain the theories. Mr. Wiggam may wax eloquent over the wonderful potentialities of man, to be realized by manipulating the germ-plasm. It is well enough to say that eugenics means that the enhancement of "man's inborn capacities for happiness, health, sanity and achievement shall become the one living purpose of the state" and that eugenics is "simply the projection of the Golden Rule down the stream of protoplasm" (whatever that might mean if it were translated into prose). To one who likes such things it sounds well to declare that "had Jesus been among us he would have been president of the first Eugenics Congress."[11] (A great deal of time has been wasted in discussing what Jesus would have done and been had He lived to-day. Not long ago, a preacher declared that Jesus was the first great Rotarian and another enthusiast declared that He was the first great advertiser. And of course He is claimed both by the wets and the drys. Whether man was made in the image of God may still be a subject of debate, but there is no question that Jesus has been made over and over again in the image of every fanatic who has a crude and undigested idea about what should be done.) It is well enough for Dr. McDougall to say that intelligent physicians operating through their societies could sort out the morons and the unfit, and that the courts could sort out the convicted criminals, and that some other organization could sort out something else. But it requires unlimited faith, unbounded hope, and a complete absence of charity to believe that the human race, which has been slowly developing for half a million years, would actually profit by placing the control of breeding in the hands of the state. Even assuming that we know what kind of man we should breed, and how it could be accomplished, is there any reason to believe that it could be done through any existing agency?

If the state is to regulate the production of human beings, it is important to know what we mean by the word "state." It can mean nothing else save the individual members who make up the political unit. And in the last analysis, those who manage to get power are its real rulers. It is hardly necessary to ask: Are these men the scientists? Are they the idealists? Are they the tolerant, the humane, and the well-disposed? It is doubtful if anyone would even contend that they are. Of course, all the classes I have named, working in their own way, and quite independent of government, do have some influence upon the actions of men, but that influence has no direct relation to forcible control. Every informed man knows what the state is and who it is. Imagine cities like New York, Chicago or Boston picking out boards of control to organize, in the eloquent language of Mr. Wiggam, "a method ordained by God and seated in natural law for securing better parents for our children."[12] It is not necessary to take New York, Chicago or Boston; every part of the country and every other country is controlled in the same way. Those in power would inevitably direct human breeding in their own interests. At the present time it would mean that big business would create a race in its own image. At any time it would mean with men, as it now does with animals, that breeding would be controlled for the use and purpose of the powerful and the unintelligent. Every social organization, every religious creed, every fad and fancy would set this power above every other function of the state. If any such scheme should be seriously considered, it would bring in an era of universal sexual bootlegging.

I am not a blind worshipper of Nature. I can not say whether she is good or bad. Man has no means of knowing. We can say only that, like all life, he is her product, that she is strong, if not invincible, and that she seems to delight in undoing the puny work of those who seek to meddle with her laws. I don't believe we could escape from her power, no matter what we sought to do. Neither do I believe that we could improve her job if we did escape. The history of the race shows endless examples of the pain and suffering that men have inflicted upon each other by their cocksureness and their meddling.

We know something about biology. We know a little about eugenics. We have no knowledge of what kind of man would be better than the one that Nature is evolving to fit into the environment which he cannot escape. We have neither facts nor theories to give us any evidence based on biology or any other branch of science as to how we could breed intelligence, happiness or anything else that would improve the race. We have no idea of the meaning of the word "improvement." We can imagine no human organization that we could trust with the job, even if eugenists knew what should be done, and the proper way to do it. Yet in the face of all this we have already started on the course, and the up-lifters are urging us to go ahead, with no conception of where we are going, or what route we shall take!

In an age of meddling, presumption, and gross denial of all the individual feelings and emotions, the world is urged, not only to forcibly control all conduct, but to remake man himself! Amongst the schemes for remolding society this is the most senseless and impudent that has ever been put forward by irresponsible fanatics to plague a long-suffering race.

FOUR

On Clarence Darrow

Farmington

CHAPTER XIII. ILLUSIONS

As I look back upon my childhood, it seems as if the world were an illusion and everything was magic that passed before my eyes. True, we children learned our lessons in our arithmetics and geographies and readers, but we only learned by rote and said them from our lips; they had no application to our lives,—they were only tasks which we must get through before our foolish parents and unkind teachers would leave us free to live. We seem to have breathed an enchanted air, and to see nothing as it really was. And still, can I be sure of this? Are the heartbeats of the young less natural and spontaneous than those of later life? Are the vision and hearing and emotions of youth less trustworthy than the dulled faculties and feelings of maturer years? Certain it is we children lived in a world that was all our own,—a world into which grown-up people could not come, from which in fact they had long since passed out never to return.

But we had our illusions and our dreams. Time and distance and proportion did not exist for us. Time is ever illusive to young and old alike;

Farmington (Chicago: A. C. McClurg, 1904) is, as its subtitle states, "An Idyl of Boyhood." One of the most frequently reprinted of Darrow's books, it conveys a haunting sense of nostalgia at the lost joys of childhood and adolescence. Darrow writes the book as a fictionalized autobiography, referring to himself as John Smith and setting the work in a fictitious Pennsylvania town.

it is no sooner come than it is gone. The past is regretted, the present disappointing; the future alone is trusted, and thought to be worth our pains. Childhood is the happiest time of life, because the past is so wholly forgotten, the present so fleeting, and the future so endlessly long. But how little I really knew of time, of youth and of age, when I was young! We children thought that old age lay just beyond the time when childish sports would not amuse. We could see nothing in life beyond thirty that would make it worth living, excepting for a very few who were the conquerors of the world. True, we dreamed of our future great achievements, but these were still far off, and to be reached in strange fantastic ways. The present and the near future were only for our childish joys. We looked at older people half in pity, half in fear. I distinctly remember that when a child at the district school I thought the boys and girls at the Academy were getting old.

As to my parents, they always seemed old; and when I was not vexed about things they would not let me do, I felt sad to think their days of sport were past and gone. I well remember the terrible day when they laid my mother in her grave, and the one consolation I felt was that she had lived a long life and that her natural time had come. Even now, as I look back on the vague remembrances of my mother, I have no thought of any time when she was not old. Yet last year I went to see the little headstone that marks her modest grave. I read her name, and the commonplace lines that said she had been a good wife and a loving mother; and this I have no doubt was true, even though I found it on a church-yard stone. Poor soul! she never had a chance to be anything else or more. But when I looked to see her age, I felt a shock as of one waking from a dream; for there, chiselled in the marble stone and already growing green with moss, I read that she had died at forty-eight. And here I stood looking at my old mother's grave, and my last birthday was my forty-sixth. Was my mother then so young when she lay down to sleep?— and all my life I had thought that she was old! I felt and knew, as I sadly looked upon the stone, that my career was all before me still, and that I had only been wandering and blundering in a zigzag path through childhood and youth, to begin the career I was about to run. True, as I drew close to the marble slab to read the smaller letters that told of the virtues of the dead, I put on a pair of gold-rimmed glasses to spell the chiselled words. And these glasses were my second pair! Only a few days before, I had visited an oculist and told him that my old ones somehow did not focus as they should, but warned him not to give me a new pair that magnified the letters any more than the ones I had. After several trials he found a pair through which I could see much clearer than before, and he assured me on his honor that they were no stronger than the ones I was about to lay aside,—only they were ground in a different way. And although I had lived on the earth for six and forty years, I believed he told the truth. I remembered, too, that only a few days before an impudent college football hero gave me a seat in the street-car while he stood up. But then college boys were always thoughtless and ill-mannered, and boastful of their strength. I recovered from the shock that came upon me as I realized that my mother had died while she was really young; and then my mind recalled a day that had been buried in oblivion for many, many years,—a day when I rested upon the same spot where I was sitting now, and when the tremendous thought of eternal sleep dawned upon my mind. No doubt it was my mother's stone that so long ago awakened me to conscious life. I remember that on that far-off day I was fifteen years of age, and that I consoled myself by thinking that at any rate I should live until I was sixty, which was so far away that I could not even dream that it would ever come. And now I was here again, and forty-six. Well, my health was good, my ancestors were long-lived,—all except my mother, who came to an untimely grave,—and I should live to be ninety at the very least. And then—there might be another world. No one can prove that there is not.

But I am lingering too long around the old graveyard of my childhood home, and if I do not go out into the living, moving world, no one will ever read my book. And still I fancy that I am like all the other men and women who were ever born; we eat and drink, and laugh and dance, and go our way along the path of life, and join the universal conspiracy to keep silent on the momentous event that year by year draws closer to our lives.

Distance was as vague and illusive and as hard to realize as time. A trip to the next town, four miles away, awoke in my mind all the feeling of change and travel and adventure that a voyage across the sea can bring to-day. I recall one great event that stands out clearly in my childhood days. For months and months I had been promised a long trip with my older sister to visit my Aunt Jane. She lived miles and miles away, and we must take a railroad train to reach her home. For weeks I revelled in the expectation of that long-promised trip. I wondered if the train would really stop at our station long enough for me to get on board; if there would be danger of falling out if I should raise the window of the car; and what would happen if we should be carried past the town, or the train should run off the track. I am always sure of a fresh emotion when I think of the moment that we were safely seated in the car and the train began to move away. How I watched and wondered as the houses and telegraph poles flew past in our mad flight! And how I stored my mind with facts and fancies to tell the wondering boys when I returned! if indeed I ever should. I remember particularly how I pleaded with the train conductor to let me keep the pasteboard ticket that had been handed to me through the hole in the little window at the station when I took the train. I felt that this would be a souvenir of priceless worth, but the conductor regretfully told me that he must deny my wish. It seems even now as if I journeyed across a continent, there were so many things to see that were wholly new and strange. And yet my Aunt Jane lived only twenty miles away, and the trip must have been made in one short hour or less. Many times since then I have boarded a train to cross half the continent. I have even stood on the platform of the Oriental Express in Paris, and waited for the signal to start on the long journey across Europe to Constantinople;[1] but I have never felt such emotions as stirred my soul when the train actually moved away to take me to see Aunt Jane.

Men and their works are indeed inconsistent. The primitive savage who dwelt at home went to a foreign land when he moved his tent or paddled his log canoe across the stream; but civilized man, with his machines, inventions, and contrivances, has brought the world into such close connection that we must journey around the earth to find something new and strange.

Not time and space alone, but also men and women, were illusive to our young minds. My Sunday-school teacher, a fat asthmatic woman, who always held her lesson-paper between her stiff thumb and finger, covered with a black glove, seemed a wonderful personage to me. How was it possible she could know so much about Palestine and Jerusalem and Judæa and the Dead Sea? Surely she had never visited these mythical realms, for there was no way to go. As easily might she have gone to the moon, or to some of the fixed stars; and still she talked of these things with the familiarity with which she would have spoken of a neighboring town. I never had any idea that she was like a common woman, until one day when I went to her house and found her with her sleeves rolled up and a great apron reaching around her dress, and she was washing clothes. After that, the spell was broken. How could anyone wash clothes if she really knew about Paul and John the Baptist and the river Jordan?

All the grown-up men seemed strange and unreal to my mind, and to have nothing in common with the boys. No matter what we did, we thought that if any man should come around he had a right promptly to make us stop. Most of the men never seemed to notice us, unless to forbid our doing certain things, or to ask us to turn a grindstone while they sharpened an axe or a scythe; and there were only a few who even knew our names. Once in a long while some man would call me "that Smith boy," but even then he seemed a little doubtful who I really was. If now and then a grown-up man took a friendly interest in our sports, or called us by our first names, we liked him, and would have voted for him for President of the United States if we could have had the chance.

I well remember Deacon Cole. I used always to see him in one of the front pews at church. Every Sunday morning he drove by our home, and he was usually the very first to pass. He wore a ruffled shirt, a long black coat, and a collar that almost hid his chin. His face was long and sad, and he never looked to the right or left during the services at the church. I had no doubt he was a very holy man. He always took up the collection just before the benediction had been said, and his boots would creak as he tiptoed from pew to pew. I did not know just what a deacon was, or how anyone ever came to be a deacon. I remember I once asked my father; and although he could tell me all about Cæsar and Plato and Herodotus, he could never make it clear how Mr. Cole ever became "Deacon Cole." But one day when I was down at the mill, a farmer drove up to the door with a load of corn. He wore overalls, an old patched coat, and a big straw hat. I looked at him closely before I could believe that he was Deacon Cole, and then slowly another illusion was dissolved. I found that a deacon was a man just like my father and other men that I had known.

CHAPTER XVI. RULES OF CONDUCT

I was very young when I first began to wonder why the world was so unreasonable; and now I am growing old, and it is not a whit more sensible than it used to be. Still, as a child I was in full accord with the other boys and girls about the stupidity of the world. Of course most of this perversity on the part of older people came from their constant interference with our desires and plans. None of them seemed to remember that they once were young and had looked out at the great wide world through the wondering eyes of the little child.

It seemed to us as if our elders were in a universal conspiracy against us children; and we in turn combined to defeat their plans. I wonder where my little playmates have strayed on the great round world, and if they have grown as unreasonable as our fathers and mothers used to be! Reasonable or unreasonable, it is certain that our parents never knew what was best for us to do. Any how, I thought so then; and although the wisdom, or at least the experience, of many years has been added to my childish stock, I am bound to say that I think so still. Even a boy might sometimes be trusted to know what he ought to do; and the instinct and teachings of Nature, as they speak directly to the child, should have some weight.

But with our parents and teachers all this counted not the least. The very fact that we wanted to do things seemed ample reason why we should not. I venture to say that nine-tenths of our requests were denied; and when consent was granted, it was given in the most grudging way.

The one great word that always stood straight across our path was "No," and I am sure that the first instinct of our elders on hearing of our desires was to refuse. I wondered then, and I wonder still, what would happen if our elders and the world at large should take the other tack and persuade themselves to say "Yes" as often as they could!

Every child was told exactly what he ought to do. If I could only get a printed list of the rules given for my conduct day by day, I am sure they would fill this book. In arithmetic and grammar I always skipped the rules, and no scholar was ever yet found who liked to learn a rule or could tell anything about it after it was learned.

I well remember what a fearful task it was to learn the rule for partial payments in the old arithmetic. I could figure interest long before I learned the rule; and although I now have no trouble in figuring interest,—and if I have, some creditor does it for me,—still, to save my life, I could not now repeat the rule for partial payments. When was there ever a boy who knew how to do a sum, or parse a sentence, or pronounce a word, because he knew the rules? We knew how because we knew how, and that was all there was of the matter. Yet every detail of conduct was taught in the same way as the rules in school.

I could not eat a single meal without the use of rules, and most of these were violated when I had the chance. I distinctly remember that we generally had pie for supper in our youthful days. Now we have dessert for dinner, but then it was only pie for supper. Of course we never had all the pie we wanted, and we used to nibble it slowly around the edges and carefully eat toward the middle of the piece to make it last as long as possible and still keep the pie-taste in our mouths.

I never could see why we should not have all the pie that we could eat. It was not because of its cost, for my mother made it herself, just the same as bread. The only reason we could see was that we liked pie so well. Of course we were told that pie was not good for us; but I have always been told this about everything I liked to eat or do. Then, too, my mother insisted that I should eat the pie after the rest of the meal was done. Now, as a boy, I liked pie better than anything else that I could get to eat; and I have not yet grown so old but that I still like pie. I could see no reason why I should not eat my pie when I was hungry for it and when it looked so good. My mother said I must first eat potatoes and meat, and bread and butter; and when I had enough of these, I could eat the pie. Now, of course, after eating all these things even pie did not seem quite the same; my real appetite was gone before the pie was reached. Then, too, if a boy ate everything else first, he might never get to pie; he might be taken ill, or drop dead, or be sent from the table, or one of the other boys might come along and he be forced to choose between going swimming and eating pie,—whereas, if he began the meal according to his taste and made sure of the pie, if anything else should be missed it would not matter much.

Our whole lives were fashioned on the rules for eating pie. We were told that youth was the time for work and study, so that we might rest when we got old. Now, no boy ever cared to rest,—it is the very thing a boy does not want to do; but still, by all the rules we ever heard, this was the right way. Since I was a child I have never changed my mind. I do not think the pie should be put off to the end of the meal. I always think of my poor Aunt Mary, who saved her pie all through her life, and died without eating it at last. And, besides all this, it is quite possible that as we grow old our appetites will change, and we may not care for pie at all; at least, the coarser fare that the hard and cruel world is soon to serve up generously to us all is likely to make us lose our taste for pie. For my part, I am sure that when my last hours come I shall be glad that I ate all the pie that I could get, and if any part of the meal is left untasted it shall be the bread and butter and potatoes, and not the pie.

Of course we were told we should say "Yes, ma'am," and "No, ma'am." I observe that this rule has been changed since I was young,— or possibly it was the rule only in Farmington and such provincial towns. At any rate, when I hear it now I look the second time to see if one of my old schoolmates has come back to me. But I cannot see why it was necessary for us to say "Yes, ma'am," and "No, ma'am," in Farmington, and so necessary not to say them in the outside world.

But while the rule made us say "Yes, ma'am," and "No, ma'am," it did not allow us to say much more. We were told that "Children should be seen and not heard." It was assumed that what we had to say was of no account. As I was not very handsome when I was young, there was no occasion for me to be either seen or heard. True, we were industriously taught how to talk, yet we had no sooner learned than we were told that we "must not speak unless spoken to." It is true the conversation of children may not be so very edifying,—but, for that matter, neither is that of grown-up folk. It is quite possible that if children were allowed to talk freely, they might have a part of their nonsense talked out by the time they had matured; and then, too, they might learn much that would improve the conversation of their later life. At any rate, if a child was not meant to talk, his faculties of speech might properly be withheld until a riper age.

To take off our hats in the house, to say "Thank you" and "Please" and all such little things, were of course most strictly enjoined. It did not occur to our elders that children were born imitators, or that they could possibly be taught in any other way than by fixed rules.

The common moral precepts were always taught by rule. We must obey our parents, and speak the truth. Just why we should do either was not made clear, although the penalty of neglect was ever there. The longer I live, the more I am convinced that children need not be taught to tell the truth. The fact is, parents do not teach them to tell the truth, but to lie. Children tell the truth as naturally as they breathe, and it is only the stupidity and brutality of parents and teachers that drive them to tell lies. In high society and low, parents lie to children much oftener than children lie to parents; it would not occur to a child to lie unless someone made him feel the need of doing so.

I remember that when I was a child two things used to cause me the greatest trouble. One was the fact that I had to go to bed so early at night, and the other that I had to get up so early in the morning. I have never known a natural child who was ready to go to bed at night or to get up in the morning. I suppose this was because work came first, and pie was put off to the end of the day; and we did not want to miss any of the pie. Of course there were exceptions to the rule. We were ready to get up in the gray dawn of the morning, to go a-fishing or blackberrying, or to celebrate the Fourth of July, or on Christmas, or to see a circus come to town, or on any such occasion. And likewise we were ready to go to bed early the night before, so that we might be ready to get up. I remember one of my lies in connection with getting up in the morning. It was my father's custom to call us some time before breakfast, to help do the chores; and as this was work and the bed was warm, we were never ready to get up. On this particular morning I was called twice, but seemed to be sound asleep, and did not move. Thereupon at the next call my father came up the stairs, saying, "You know what you are going to get," and asking why I had not come before. There was nothing else to do, and so I promptly answered that I did not hear him the first two times. Somehow I learned that he surmised or found out that I had lied, and after this I regarded him as a sort of Sherlock Holmes. I did not know then, any more than my father did, that the reason I lied was that I was afraid of being whipped. Neither did my parents, or any of the others, understand that to whip us for lying only served to make us take more pains to conceal the truth.

We were given certain rules as to our treatment of animals. We were told to be kind to them, but no effort was made to awaken the imagination of the child so that in a way he might put himself in the place of the helpless beings with whom he lived. I am sure that had this been done the rule would not have been required.

In our association with each other, we were more simple and direct. When we lied, we soon found that our tales were disbelieved, and thus the punishment was made to fit the crime. But among ourselves we were generally truthful, no matter how long or persistently our teachers and parents had made it seem best for us to lie. We knew that the other boys cared very little for the things that parents and teachers thought important; and, besides, we had no jurisdiction over each other, except as the strongest and most quarrelsome might take for himself, and against him we always had the right to combine for self-defence.

I seem to be living again in the world of the little child, and so hard is it to recross to that forgotten bourne that I cannot help wishing to linger there. I remember that as I grew beyond the time to play base-ball and to join in other still more youthful games, I now and then had the rare privilege of revisiting these early scenes in sleep; and often and often in my waking moments, when I realized that I dreamed and yet half thought that all was real, I tried to keep my eyes tight shut that I might still dream on. And if I can now and then forget my years and feel again the life of the little child, why should I not cling to the fond remembrance and tell the story which he is all too young to make us understand?

It is rarely indeed that the child is able to prevent the sorrows of the man or woman; and when he can prevent them, and really knows he can, no man or woman ever looks in vain to him for sympathy or help. But the happiness of the child is almost wholly in the keeping of men and women of maturer years, and this charge is of the most sacred kind. If schools for the education of children were closed, and those for the instruction of parents were kept open, surely the world and the children would profit by the change. No doubt men and women owe duties to themselves that even their children have no right to take away; but these duties are seldom inconsistent with the highest welfare of the child.

As I look back at the father and mother who nourished me, I know that they were both wise and kind beyond others of my time and place; and yet I know that many of my deepest sorrows would have been spared had they been able to look across the span of years that divided them from me, and in thought and feeling become as little children once again.

The joys of childhood are keen, and the sorrows of childhood are deep. Years alone bring the knowledge that in thought and in feeling, as in the heavens above, sunshine and clouds follow each other in quick succession. In childhood the shadows are wholly forgotten in the brilliant radiance of the sun, and the clouds are so deep as to obscure for a time all the heavens above.

Over childhood, as over all the world, hangs the black pall of punishment,—which is only another name for vengeance and hate. In my day, and I fancy too often even now, parents believed that to "spare the rod" was to "spoil the child." It was not the refinement of cruelty that made parents promise the child a whipping the next day or the next week, it was only their ignorance and thoughtlessness; but many times I went to bed to toss and dream of the promised punishment, and in the morning, however bright the sunshine, the world was wrapped in gloom. Of course it was seldom that the whipping was as severe as the fear that haunted the mind of the child; but the punishment was really there from the time it was promised until after it was given.

Few boys were mean enough to threaten to tell our parents or teacher of our misdeeds, yet there were children who for days or even weeks would hold this threat over their playmates and drag it forth on the slightest provocation. But among children this species of cruelty was generally condemned. We knew of no circumstances that could justify the threat to tell, much less the telling. A "tattle-tale" was the most contemptible of boys,—even more contemptible than a "cry-baby." A "cry-baby" did not rank much below a girl. Still, we would suffer a great deal without flinching, to avoid this name.

In my time boys were not always so democratic as children are supposed to be. Somehow children do pick up a great deal from their elders, especially things they ought not to learn. I know that in our school there was always the same aristocracy as in our town. The children of the first families of the village were the first in the school. In games and sports these would usually get the foremost places, and each one soon knew where he belonged in the boys' social scale. Certain boys were carefully avoided,—sometimes for sanitary reasons, more often, I fancy, for no reason at all. I am sure that all this discrimination caused the child sorrow and suffering that he could in no way defend himself against. So far from our teachers doing anything to show the cruelty and absurdity of this caste spirit, it was generally believed that they were kinder and more considerate and what we called "partial" to the children of influential parents than to the rest. And we were perfectly sure that this consideration had an important bearing on our marks.

As a general rule, we children did not care much to read; and, for that matter, I am inclined to think that few healthy children do. A child would rather do things, or see them done, than read about how someone else has done them. So far as we did read, we always chose the things we were told that we should not. No doubt this came from the general belief that the imagination of children should be developed; and with the ordinary teacher and parent this meant telling about fairies, giants, and goblins, and sometimes even ghosts. These stories were always told as if they were really true; and it was commonly believed that cultivating the imagination of a child meant teaching him to see giants instead of men, and fairies and goblins instead of beasts and birds. We children soon came to doubt the whole brood of fairies, and we never believed in ghosts except at night when there was no candle in the room, and when we came near the graveyard. After these visions were swept away, our minds turned to strong men, to kings and Indians and warriors, and we read of them.

My parents often despaired about the rules that I would not learn or keep, and the books I would not read. They did not seem to know that all the rules ever made could cover only the very smallest fraction of the conduct of a child or man, and that the one way to teach conduct was by an appeal direct to the heart, an effort to place the child in harmony with the life in which he lived. To teach children their duty by rule, or develop their imaginations by stories of fairies and angels and goblins, always was and always will be a hopeless task. But imagination is more easily developed in the little child than in later years, because the blood flows faster and the feelings are deeper and warmer in our youth. The imagination of the child is aroused when it really feels itself a part of all the living things with which its life is cast; feels that it is of kin to the parents and teachers, the men and women, the boys and girls, the beasts and birds, with whom it lives and breathes and moves. If this thought and this feeling take possession of the heart of the child, he will need no rules or lessons for his conduct. It will become a portion of his life; and his associations with his fellows, both human and animal, will be marked by consideration, gentleness, and love.

George Bissett

SOME TIME IN 1910 a woman came to me in Chicago to consult me about a case. She was old and poorly clad and had the look of grim despair that haunts so many faces of the unfortunate. She told me that her son was in the Chicago jail and had just been convicted of murder, and the jury had given him a life term in the penitentiary. She told me that her son had no money, and that the court had appointed a lawyer to defend him; later the judge had denied a new trial, and in the meantime the lawyer had died.

I said I did not see how I could possibly undertake the case, as the chances were that nothing could be done in the Supreme Court, no matter who handled it. I explained that if the Supreme Court should grant a new trial I would be obliged to try it in the lower court, that there was no chance to get any pay for my work, and some money would be needed for costs; much as I would like to help her, I could not afford to go into it, and I told her so.

She went on to say that she had a little home that could be sold and would bring me something and I could have that for the costs and my fee. I answered that I did not see how I could go into the matter under any circumstances, but that if I did I would not let her sell her home. It

---

This extract is chapter 23 of Darrow's autobiography, *The Story of My Life* (New York: Charles Scribner's Sons, 1932), recounting his dealings with a troubled man who made an unusual offer at one of the low points of Darrow's life.

was really out of the question. She made no complaint, but went away with the look of despair that comes into the eyes of so many who have learned that for them life offers no hope. The face of this woman haunted me the rest of the day, and would hardly let me sleep that night. I began to regret that I had not taken the case.

But the next morning she was in my office again. I looked at her and knew that I could not resist. I asked if she had the testimony, written out by the court reporter. She had it at home. I told her to bring it to me, and if I could see any chance of getting a new trial I would go into the case. I assured her that I would not take her little home, either for myself or costs. Anyhow, the amount would not have been enough to do me any good, and would only have prevented my feeling of pride in taking the case without a fee. When I examined the record I was satisfied that there should have been no conviction, and that I probably could get the case reversed.

The next day I went to the Chicago jail to take a look at my client. He was a large man, about thirty years old. His countenance was not prepossessing, but I had lived long enough not to take countenances too seriously, especially if I met them inside a prison. He was a man without education. He had spent his life as a common laborer, but he had some ideals and a good deal of ambition. With all the rest, he was an intense Socialist, and was constantly talking about it and trying to make converts. I had learned from reading the testimony that he had once served a short term in the penitentiary, for an attempted burglary. One conviction is generally all the evidence that is needed to justify a second one, and I felt sure that this was really the cause of this conviction. I asked him why he tried to burglarize the house. He replied that he had wanted to start a Socialist paper, and as he had no education he could never get the necessary money by working.

The case for which he was now in jail grew out of a quarrel with two policemen in a saloon; none of them were drunk, but all had been drinking. The policemen were "plain clothes" men wearing no uniform, and were in the saloon when Bissett entered. Both officers knew of his former conviction which, according to their view, justified addressing him in any way they wished. They all drew revolvers and began to shoot. Bissett was hit by two or three bullets, all taking effect in the abdomen, puncturing the large intestine. He was taken to a hospital to die. Unfortunately, as I then thought, he recovered from the wounds. One of the policemen was killed by a bullet through the heart, and the other, though shot, had recovered.

Bissett's revolver was found on the floor with the requisite number of empty shells to match the policemen's wounds. Bissett denied shooting, when he took the stand in the first trial, but the empty holster of the revolver, and the empty shells, made it clear that his statement was not true. Two other eyewitnesses were unable to say who shot first, but testified that both policemen and the defendant used their guns.

It was plain that the case should have been tried as one of self-defense, but his lawyer had seen fit to believe his client's first story, and Bissett had sworn that he did not shoot. I asked him why he denied it, and he answered that he was afraid to admit that he had shot, fearing that an admission, taken with his first conviction, would be fatal. I pointed out that his only chance was in telling the story as it really happened—that he did shoot, and was afraid to admit it in the first trial. It was evident that he had no motive for killing the policemen excepting fear of being killed himself. The policemen made no attempt to arrest him; and no charge was pending against him.

In due time the case was argued in the Supreme Court and was reversed and sent back for a new trial. Then, of course, there was nothing left for me to do but defend it.

George Bissett is not brought into this book on account of that case. It is enough to say that on the second trial he was promptly acquitted, as he should have been at first. I had seen George from time to time in the jail, and learned to understand him quite well. It was not easy to talk to him on any subject but Socialism. All the other prisoners had put him down as a "bug" on account of his interest in Socialism. Socialists are not often in jail except for believing in and practising free speech, and then generally for only a short time. And although George strongly insisted that if we had Socialism there would be no need for jails, he found few converts, especially amongst those who owned the jails.

When the trial was ended I took George over to my office to talk with him about what he should do in the future. I did not lecture him. I never believed that this did any good. I mentioned that he had evidently become almost a professional burglar, and asked him if he thought that it paid. I tried to make him see that no one ever really made much at any such trade, and I hoped he would find something else to work at.

He assured me that he did not expect to try anything of that sort again, but he was as anxious as ever to have a Socialist paper, and that he couldn't get a paper by working; that no one ever did. He thanked me most earnestly for what I had done for him, said he wanted to pay me, and would do it. I told him not to bother about me; that I did not want him to think about getting money to give to me, that the satisfaction of having freed him would be enough. I had learned to rather like him, just as we all learn to like most people when we really know them. And so he went away, and I did not hear of him again for three or four years.

But George and his troubles, and his ambition, sometimes came to my mind, and still he was only one more being in a sordid world. He had professed great appreciation and gratitude for what I had done to help him, and had promised to see me occasionally, to report how he was getting along. That he had not returned caused me no surprise. Very few take so much pains, and then, he might be dead, or in jail, or even managing his Socialist paper at last. He drifted out of my thoughts, which were filled with other events.

But it was written that I was to see George Bissett again. He came to me in Los Angeles in 1912. I was waiting for the trial of the indictment that had been brought against me charging me with a conspiracy to bribe a juror, as told in the last chapter.[1] It was one of a long series of days when I was very sad and when my friends looked good. I was sitting in my private office; the clerk came and told me that a man was outside who wanted to see me; he said the man looked dirty, like a tramp. I asked him to show the man in, which he promptly did. I saw before me my old client, George Bissett. I arose, shook his hand and said, "George, you are a long way from home; what are you doing here?" He said he had heard that I was in trouble and thought that he might help me. I asked how he got there. He said he had come from Chicago, riding on freight-cars and on the bumpers. I asked where he was staying, and he gave me the address of a cheap lodging house. I said, "George, it was fine of you to come all this distance to help me, and I appreciate it more than I know how to tell you, but what did you think you could possibly do?"

"Well," he answered, "I have been here about a week and have been getting a line on Franklin"—the Los Angeles detective previously spoken of.[2] I asked George what he had found out about Franklin. He said he had found out where he lived, had watched what time he went away in the mornings, had some dynamite, and was going to kill Franklin the next day when leaving his home. All along through my life I have had many warm demonstrations of friendship, but this was the first time any man had offered to kill some one for me. I looked at George, and thought of this rough, unlettered man riding two thousand miles on car tops and bumpers and in seriousness offering to risk his life out of gratitude for what I had done for him.

I did my best to show my appreciation of this most astounding proffer. I said, "But, George, you have no idea what you are about to do. For two years this city has been deeply stirred. The cases and events have been published in the newspapers all over the world; the State's attorney's office has every means at hand for running down every clue that might have any bearing on any of the cases, directly or indirectly connected with the destruction of the Los Angeles *Times* Building. Here you propose to kill the chief witness for the State against me—in broad daylight. You must be crazy to think that you could do it without being hanged."

"Yes, I've thought of all that," he responded, "but I owe my life to you, and I'm here to take the chance. I want to do it for you."

I did not answer immediately. I pondered, wondering how to save him from almost certain death, and at the same time have him know how thoroughly I understood his motives, and how deeply I estimated his loyalty and devotion. Both of us sat in silence for a few moments, and when I turned to him I could hardly talk, but I managed to say, "George, I presume other men have run great risks for those they have wanted to help, but no such thing has ever before come to me. You have a deep affection for me on account of what I once did to save you; but let us look at this question as it is. Suppose you could kill Franklin, and suppose that by that means I could be acquitted, and suppose that your life was taken for my sake, should I ever again have a moment's peace or happiness? Could I accept your life to save myself? I think I have never consciously done a cruel act in my life; I hate killing in any way; could I let another man be killed—even Franklin—without trying to save him? I fancy few men have made such an offer of self-sacrifice, George; nothing like it has ever happened to me. But it must not be done!"

It flashed into my mind that I must somehow make sure of it. I added, "But—I will give this a little more thought. I believe that I am in no danger here, really. I have reason to think that I shall have positive evidence within an hour that will make my acquittal a certainty. Let me have the name of the place where you are staying, and, if I am not assured very soon of the evidence that I expect, I will come and tell you. If I do not come, promise me that you will go back home. And, George— let me give you some money to pay your fare."

"No, no!" he insisted. "I will do what you say, and if I don't hear from you by to-night I'll go back, but I won't take any money of yours; I never pay railroad fare." There were tears in his eyes as I bade him good-by. My own feelings cannot be described.

For a time I sat motionless in my chair. I had known all sorts of men. I had so often found the good and the bad hopelessly mixed in almost all the people that I knew; I wondered if any human being really could pass judgment on another. I thought, too, of that verse I had so often used: "Greater love hath no man than this, that a man lay down his life for his friends."[3]

Well, I did not need poor George's help, but it seemed to have been ordained that I should see him again, and this happened about five years later. This time I was sitting in my office in Chicago, as of old. The telephone rang; I picked up the receiver, and a harsh voice that had a familiar vibration asked if the caller was speaking to me. I said he was. He asked, "Do you know me?" I said I thought I knew, but was not sure. He said, "This is George." I knew, and asked, "Where are you?" He answered,

"In the marshal's office in the Post Office Building." I said that I would be right over. It was my old friend, George Bissett. I shook his hand through the bars and asked the marshal to let him come outside for a talk with me, which he did. I said I was sorry to see him there, and asked him to tell me all about it. He informed me that he, with another fellow, who had turned state's evidence, was indicted for stealing some five hundred thousand dollars from a building that he broke into; it was formerly the post office, but was now used by the government as a storehouse. The building was in Minneapolis, and the marshal was holding him, waiting for requisition papers to take him back. I said, "I suppose they have a good case against you." He answered that they wouldn't have a case only they found the money in a trunk. I asked where they found the trunk. He said, "In my house." I asked, "Where were you?" He answered, drily, "Oh—I was there asleep."

I reflected, and said, "Well—it looks suspicious, at the best. I don't see anything ahead but a plea of 'Guilty.' Don't bother them to get a requisition, George; just go back quietly, and I will be there in a week or so and see what can be done." I expressed regret that he had gotten into this trouble. He answered, dolefully, "So'm I; I made a clean getaway, and was going to start that paper."

In about a week I was able to go and see George, and found him safe and sound in the jail. Before going to him I had dropped in to see the district attorney who had charge of the case. He was a high-minded, humane man whom I had known for many years—Mr. Janquish, an able lawyer, who lives in Duluth, who was appointed United States district attorney by Woodrow Wilson. I told him the whole story, omitting nothing, not forgetting to tell that George had served a term in the penitentiary. I explained that he had come back there through my advice, and I wanted to make the best terms possible, within reason, and enter a plea of "Guilty." He asked if the man had ever been in the penitentiary more than that one time, and I replied that so far as I knew he never had, and if there had been anything else it would have been brought to light in Chicago; but he could take his time to look into it if he wished. I inquired what was the lowest penalty the government allowed for burglary. He said, "Two years." Which he felt would be pretty low for this case. I agreed that perhaps it was, but that I never could judge how much or how little punishment any one deserved, or if they deserved any. He finally said, that if I wanted to plead my client "Guilty" we would go over and see the judge and I could tell him the story; so we went right then.

The judge thought it a strange and interesting tale and asked the district attorney what was the lowest penalty he could give him; the district attorney replied, "Two years." The judge reasoned that on account of George not making trouble about extradition, and the money all having been recovered, he would consent to giving him two years. As I wanted to go back home that night, I asked the judge to have it disposed of that day at two o'clock, which he arranged. I went to the jail with this news. It was midsummer; the weather was hot; George was sweltering. He was a large man with an enormous jaw, that was none too good to look at. He was dressed like all the other prisoners in that weather, without coat, vest or collar. His shirt had done service for a long time, and the bosom was mottled with tobacco juice. I explained our good luck and hurried away, saying I would see him later. He was delighted, as might be expected.

At two o'clock I was in the courtroom. The judge and the district attorney were there, and George was brought in. I turned to speak to him. I was shocked. How could I have neglected to instruct him to shave and put on his "Sunday clothes"! He may not have had another suit, but I might have bought him a clean shirt and collar. How could I have been so stupid? A lawyer just out of school should have thought of that. Would the sight of my client affect the judge as it affected me?

The case was called and I arose, and with very few words pleaded my client "Guilty." I could see that the judge was inspecting George, looking at his great size, at his heavy jaw, at the stubble on his face, the tobacco juice on his dirty shirt; poor, collarless, loyal, sweaty George! I had muffed it; I knew it, but was helpless. The judge looked him over again, asked him to stand up, voiced a few remarks about the case, then said, very slowly, and haltingly, "I sentence you to the penitentiary for two years—and—" (taking another look at George) "and—six months."

I went out with George and told him that I blamed myself for not telling him to dress properly for the occasion. He said, "Yes, I know; but I had no other shirt, and I couldn't get a razor, or get word to you," and he looked forlorn, but resigned.

Later in the afternoon I went back to see the judge. Neither of us could repress a smile. I assured him that I did not blame him. In one way I was glad, as I had always insisted that the length of time fixed for a prisoner depended as much on his appearance as upon the offense, and on how the judge felt about it, and this proved it. I told him that the only unfair element about it was that he should have given me the extra six months instead of my unfortunate client.

I left George at the courthouse door and took the train back to Chicago. Two or three years later I saw his name in a newspaper, in the nature of an obituary. He had been shot and killed in an early morning hour in the street in Detroit, in a quarrel over a woman. I don't know the details, but he seemed to have loved not wisely but too well.

Often I have thought of George Bissett; of what possibilities there were in his strong nature and his wonderful devotion. I have sighed over the motives and ideals, ambitions and limitations that determined his course, and I have felt that life had not been fair to him. He should have had his Socialist paper. I have felt about him as I have felt about thousands of others, about all of those who tread the dark road to doom—that under decent and helpful environment, and with a fair chance and some education, he would have travelled the regular route, the one called the right path, where the pilgrim looks neither to the right nor left, but travels with the majority, on and on and on to a flower-covered grave in a respectable churchyard instead of under a layer of gravel in a potter's field.

At Seventy-two

As a matter of reason, I know that the chance of adding many years to existence at the age of seventy-two is nowhere near so great as the same chance at twenty-five. And yet, I have no doubt that a large number of the living below the age of twenty-five will reach the end before my time will come. I have no doubt that my faculties and capacities for pleasure will rapidly grow duller as the days go by. But if my joys will be fewer and less intense, so, too, will my sorrows and disappointments be less real as time goes on.

Perhaps in a few years the waning emotions that we name pleasure and pain will balance each other, and the real satisfaction of existence be as great or even greater than when life seemed so serious, grief so hopeless, and joy so unconfined.

If there is any way of knowing what age up to seventy-two brings the most satisfaction, my accumulating years have not disclosed that time of life. Living is not an intellectual process. It is an emotional venture of desires and pleasures and pains; of ambitions realized and shattered; of hopes that bore fruition and schemes that crumbled to dust. All that remains at any age is the instinctive urge to go on; the momentum of a going concern which persists until the power is exhausted and the machine functions no more.

"At Seventy-two" first appeared in the *Saturday Evening Post* 202 (July 6, 1929): 23, 109, 114. It is perhaps Darrow's finest personal essay, a touching and bittersweet reflection on the course of his long and turbulent life.

Life is so full of absorbing events that no one checks off the days as he goes along or estimates how much of the vital force is still in store. The flow of time cannot be measured by dots and dashes, each complete in itself. Weeks, months and years are not separately inventoried as they go by. They are not treated by the living organism as a merchant checks up to find what the bygone period has added to his gains. Life is a continuous stream.

The individual existence is a part of the ongoing power that for a longer or shorter time takes the form and substance of the special ego. When for any reason the structure no longer functions, the life stream passes into other forms and entities that are able to distribute and utilize the force which the old organism could no longer house. The individual lives so long as the organism furnishes a tolerable abiding place for the life force as it moves on. Depending upon age and health, on fineness or coarseness, on sleeping or waking, and doubtless on many things of which we are not aware, each living organism persists until its work is done. If this individual ego is the structure that now pens these lines, is there any way of telling whether life is more or less satisfactory at the age of twenty-five than at the age of seventy-two? I am able to look back at the years that have gone by, but I can measure them only by the feelings, tastes and values of the man of seventy-two, even though I can look forward to an age still more advanced.

I can consider the pains of growing infirmities, the satisfaction of modified and tempered emotions, and the relief of shifting burdens to younger shoulders; but this I can do only with the experiences and feelings of the man of seventy-two. As I review the past I feel sure that many of the activities that in youth I counted as pleasures were not worth the cost. I feel equally certain that my deepest sorrows and regrets were exaggerated and magnified by the immature judgment and false values that moved the child and the youth, and even the maturer man. As I now look back, I feel that every sensation was more or less illusory in those bygone years. From my present vantage point they appear to have been magnified, distorted or veiled by the mists and fantastic images that warped the realities into forms and fancies that could not be real. But I have lived my life and viewed my objects and dreamed my dreams with the emotions and experiences that were incident to the age and the reactions that I was passing through.

At seventy-two I am far from sure that life is less desirable than when I was in my teens. I am not convinced that the urges and emotions upon which my organism persists are in any way changed from the emotions of the early years. I well remember the time when I imagined that no pleasure would be left for me when I should be too old to play baseball. I seemed to live through the week's drudgery in school for the Saturday afternoon when we assembled on the public square to play the longed-for game; the anticipated joy was subdued only by the fear of rain. If perchance the awaited Saturday brought the disastrous storm, my disappointment and sorrow were in no way appeased by the knowledge that other Saturdays were still in store; much less were they modified when our elders pointed out that we needed the rain to help the thirsty crops. For me and my companions there was no other time than this vanishing afternoon.

Likewise, the childish plans for a boisterous time on the Fourth of July filled all the horizon of the youth. To be cheated on that one day admitted of no hope or extenuation. The fact that in only one more year a new Fourth of July would give us another chance in no way lightened our hopeless grief. The child came nearer to the understanding of life than our elders knew. The stream was flowing on; every emotion and sensation belonged to the present, and the joy or grief of the passing moments was all there was to life. Years and experience may give one a longer look forward, and somewhat temper disappointment, but at seventy-two life has the same essential qualities as it had at seventeen. It is the passing stream that brings feelings of pleasure or pain. The water that has gone over the dam has no effect save to tame the expectations with the memory of the experiences of the past.

At seventy-two, the stream still flows placidly on or is disturbed and interrupted in its course. At seventy-two it is the immediate sensation that brings gratification or distress. In youth, satisfaction meant joy, and disappointment meant despair. Slower heartbeats and longer acquaintance with life have measurably moderated both gladness and sorrow, and the softer, duller sensations fit the advancing age. No one can say that on the whole the life stream at seventy-two is any less desirable than it was in youth. With age, as in childhood, it is the immediate occurrence that chiefly creates the interest in living. We all know that at almost any age a toothache is hard to bear, but this consciousness does not seriously affect the enjoyable sensations of living. It is only while the toothache is present that the pain excludes the possibility of joy. All of life is along the same pattern. It is the next month's rent, the need of coal, clothing and food that so often makes life a burden to the poor; when the month's rent is paid there is a period when it no longer interferes with the agreeable emotions incident to living.

The older person finds contentment and happiness in friends who help him enjoy the evening now at hand. Beguiled by fond friends and interesting discussions that would have been stupid in youth, time passes all too quickly, and then follows the feeling of relief at approaching sleep. At an advanced age one does not eat so much as he once did, and the food is not quite the same, but the gratification of the palate is not destroyed by age.

It is true that as we grow older much of our living comes to be almost automatic. We give an hour in the morning to the reading of a newspaper which at one stage of our life would not have been worth the while. We read it carefully, not omitting the obituary notices, now wont to record familiar names. These we scan with scarce a shudder, for the living organism cannot imagine itself as dead; even if it could really vision Nirvana, it would bring only a feeling of rest and peace.

I am inclined to believe that very few who reach mature years are harassed by any thoughts of future punishment. Life has taught the pilgrim the frailty of human judgment, the prevalence of error, the shortness of human foresight, the intricate and impenetrable web of fate that enmeshes all. It has made him tolerant and kindly and understanding. It has taught him not to judge or to condemn. It does not matter what the religious faith may be, he cannot imagine a God with less understanding and charity than he has himself.

I cannot see that either the pains or satisfactions incident to life are greatly changed with the passing years. The tired youth and the weary old man alike turn gladly to their beds at night and welcome the kindly, soothing embrace of sleep; neither in youth nor age is anything quite so satisfying after a day of activity as the consciousness of softly approaching sleep. I cannot avoid the conclusion that, as on-coming drowsiness at night is, after all, the most gratifying of sensations, so the slowly soothing anæsthesia that precedes the inevitable end should be the most welcome sensation following on an active life.

As a child I liked to run and jump in the open field. I liked it for the sheer joy of the outdoors, the fresh air and the coursing blood born of activity and life. I still love the fresh air and the green grass and trees and the great outdoors. True, I walk instead of run. I no longer jump as I was wont to do. A park bench furnishes every opportunity to see the trees and grass, and feel the fresh, invigorating air that blows from the lake, bringing the same sensation that it did long years ago. As a boy at my tasks, or kept indoors by rain, I felt joy when the sky was clearing and I knew that I could soon be back in the outdoor world.

As an old man I look with pleasure at the melting snow, the budding trees and the manifold promises that the spring still holds out to brighten life. At any and all ages I have enjoyed and still enjoy the companionship of friends. Perhaps there is no other emotion quite so gratifying as that which comes through the association of those with whom we blend. In the company of those we love, even conversation is not needful; there are understanding and regard and sympathy which radiate alike in silence and chatter. As the years pile one upon another, this pleasure does not wane. It seems to develop and take the place of others that have fled forever. When one grows old he is lucky if he can understand and sympathize with the young. Old friends may die and leave you forsaken of their companionship, but the children come on eternally. Assume that I may live eight or ten years longer—which is more than many of the young can possibly survive—that eight or ten years will bring a great many pleasant meetings, a great many communions with congenial friends, with pleasures just as real as those in the years gone by. I probably shall have many agreeable realizations of approaching sleep, many wakings in the morning with reinvigorated energies, many breakfasts and dinners, many meetings and rare hours with those that I love.

I still like travel; at least before I go away I have the feeling that I shall enjoy the change; even if my journey proves disappointing and the new prospect does not fulfill anticipation and I pine for the familiar faces of old-time friends, I still can find pleasure in anticipating my return. Gratification is made up not alone of the sensations that we really feel at the fulfillment of an anticipated joy; a part, and doubtless the largest part, comes from the hopes and expectations of wishes that never meet fruition. For all practical purposes the dream is the reality, and whatever the age, no fulfillment entirely completes the dream.

The eyes of the mind look out through magnified lenses. Neither the trouble that we fear nor the joy that we expect is as far removed from the commonplace as time and distance and imagination made it seem to be.

It is the young who marvel over how life can hold any satisfaction to those who, from the nature of things, have almost reached their journey's end. The young can no more view life through the halting emotions of the old than can the aged again realize the pleasures that exhilarate the youth. Neither can the old sympathize with the impatience of youth which comes from the disappointed dreams and desires of the young. Nature is not so unkind as she seems to be. Automatically she brings the individual structure into harmony with failing emotions and changing environment. Nature does not temper the wind to the shorn lamb, but she tempers the shorn lamb to the wind.

Age does not even destroy all dreams and ambitions. Whatever the time or station of life, and whatever the physical structure that seems to be one's home, still from the beginning to the end we really live in air castles built from hopes and fears, from visions and from dreams. The castles of youth are high and wide, the gates are guarded by giants and ogres. There are battlements to scale and drawbridges to cross, and mortal combats that must be waged ere the victory is won. The castles of age are covered with ivy and lichen, the gentle breeze comes through the trees across a peaceful lake, and the grateful sun warms us as we sit in an armchair at the window and alternately read and doze the time away. We do not resign ourselves to idleness; there is much work still to do. Most of our expected achievements are yet unaccomplished, and many of them scarcely begun. We will commence them tomorrow and finish them within the year. What matters it whether our dreams come true or not? They are essentially true while they have the reality to move our consciousness, and when this period goes by, it does not matter whether the work is finished or whether it ever was begun.

The human mind lends itself to ambitions, and every period of life has its fitting desire. The man who has been interested in the show as it passed by, who has tried to keep in touch with the world, has accumulated opinions, beliefs, ideas, or at least habits of thought. All of us are, for some mysterious reason, anxious to have others see the world as the world seems to us. I am satisfied that all men are propagandists. The possession of an idea or opinion somehow generates the emotion to urge it on someone else and make him see the truth as we see the truth. We are like a hen which announces loudly to the universe that she has laid an egg. It is most likely important only to the individual hen, but the nature of the emotion creates the zest for the utterance. All of us are eager that others shall see and feel what we see and feel. This emotion furnishes not only an active interest in life but a sense of duty; no doubt it is a mistaken sense, but it helps us keep our interest in the passing show.

As a propagandist, I see no chance to grow weary of life. I am interested in too many questions that concern the existence and activity of the human race. Not only am I interested in these questions but, for some reason or other, I almost always find myself disagreeing with the crowd. From experience I know how few men ever care to investigate any subject and how few honest opinions are of any value. I also know the strong tendency that most people have to go with the crowd. Social ambitions, ease of mind, business interests and most of the motives that move men induce them to do what others do, believe as others believe, and think the thoughts that others think, if any. Only a few men have ever studied any subject carefully, and in all fields of activity we are obliged to rely upon the experts for dependable information. This fact is one reason why most people align themselves with the majority. It is always the easiest and safest way. The majority have the wealth and power and standing which attract the masses of men to the different opinions, creeds and causes which move men.

I have long stood with the minority on almost every question that divides men. I also know that the truth is many-sided and relative and shifting, and yet it seldom occurs to me that any of my opinions can be wrong. I know by the law of chances that all of them cannot be right, but yet, when any particular view is challenged, I feel sure that my view on that matter is beyond dispute. As a propagandist I realize the work that I shall always find to do. No matter how long I live, I shall still be seeking to convert a blind and credulous people to abandon their idols and join the thin ranks of the minority and help bear its soiled and tattered banner to ultimate victory. Still, I know that I shall fail. I know that, if perchance the majority could be ranged on my side, it would be as intolerant and senseless as majorities have always been.

Of course, age has its discomforts. It brings its manifold aches and miseries to body and mind. It brings loneliness as friends and acquaintances drop out of the field and leave one to march alone. In my weaker moments the power and bigotry of the crowd make me shrink and tremble and grow afraid. They even make me doubt myself. Often and often as I fight to defeat for a hopeless cause, I look at the triumphant majority that, with glee and infinite assurance, marches by, and ask myself why I cannot be with them. After all, would it not be better to hunt with the cruel, barking hounds than to run with the timid, frightened hare? The only reason why I do not join the pack is because my human structure is not adjusted to the easier way of life. To me, the easiest way is the hardest way.

If one has taken his place with the minority, if he has defied the crowd, if he has determined to go alone, he must fearlessly content himself with his way of life. He cannot shrink or ask for quarter. He cannot pity himself. He must take life as it comes, without regret or complaint.

Each age has its special burdens. Often these burdens come from little things scarcely worth noticing. In old age, as in youth, slight affairs are sometimes as trying as serious ones. One of my greatest crosses is my daily mail. It brings its inevitable grist of annoyance and disillusion. It ought to be impossible for an active man who has lived a full life to find new annoyances at seventy-two, but each day brings these at whatever age, and the postman does his share on every round. The old are naturally grateful for kind letters from friends and well-wishers who express appreciation, approval or gratification over things one has done or tried to do; but even these letters should not be long, for at seventy two no one can possibly complete all the tasks that he has set out to do. So, without the encouragement of friends life would be hard and bleak.

But there are letters with requests for money which one cannot give; for employment that is still harder to furnish or find; letters from the poor and unfortunate in sordid homes and in hospitals, asylums and prisons; letters from the families of victims waiting and checking off the days before a loved one shall be led out and put to death by the state. In the eyes of a mother, wife or friend, the victim is not the person that the public hates. Seldom is there any chance to help.

Then there are the letters from those who wish to save my soul. These are generally written by kindly, human men and women who want to do me good. Usually they are written with the utmost care and with the well-meant desire to save me from the wrath of an angry God. Of course, they should save their time, and mine. If I believed in such a God I would go insane.

Not all letters are kindly. Every crank can write. One can read their letters without opening the envelopes.

There are others who write abusive letters for the joy they get in the thought that these cruel messages will give me pain. Of course, they fall short of their mission, for they are never read. Life is harsh enough without seeking hurts.

Books, too, arrive in the mails; most of them sent with the kindliest intentions, and sometimes the request that I may say a word about them that will help their sale, which often I would like to grant, but when can I possibly find time to read them all? All my life I have loved books and have been an industrious reader, and have never been able to peruse more than a small fraction of all the books that I want and still expect to read. Many unpublished manuscripts also clutter my mail. Some of them are well done, I hope; some are from strangers, some from friends; some ask me to read their books and criticize them—by which they mean praise them—and often I am asked to write a preface. What can they be thinking of? Do they not know that I am seventy-two years old?

And yet, age has its advantages too. I lie in bed in the morning as late as I wish or, rather, as long as there is any possible chance of falling into another nap. Why should I dread life, when I never miss a chance to sleep, and am only annoyed because I waken too soon?

After an active existence, it is really a relief to find the regular daily burdens lifted from the tired shoulders. Take it all in all, the Indian summer is very grateful and soothing to a body that really longs for rest. The little child is amused by what his elders believe are senseless toys. These fill the small horizon that his few years have given him to see and understand. In old age, once more the little things stir the feelings that have been so worn by time and sensations that the slightest inducement makes the nerves vibrate like a leaf in the November wind.

No one can reach the age of seventy-two without thinking of the great change which must overtake him in so short a time. As with all others who ever lived, this consciousness has often been active in my life. I am sure that the prospect of death disturbed me more profoundly when I was young than it does today. This was always borne upon me with the passing of someone near to me, and the consciousness that my father or my mother or someone else that I loved might soon meet the same inevitable fate.

I am aware that passing years blunt the sensibilities and prepare the victim for the unavoidable tragedy that is incident to life. It seems to give me only small concern. The living cannot imagine themselves as dead. The belief in an inevitable end can affect only the mind, and this is not vital in the processes of life. Thanks to my father and mother, I never believed in an angry God who would torture me or anyone in an eternal hell. I do not believe in wrath or vengeance. I have more and more come to the firm conviction that each life is simply a short individual expression, and that it soon sinks back into the great reservoir of force, where memory and individual consciousness are at an end. I am not troubled by hopes, and still less by fears. I have taken life as it came, doing the best I could with its manifold phases, and feel sure that I shall meet final dissolution without fear or serious regret.

Notes

INTRODUCTION

1. The best account of the day-to-day events of the Scopes trial remains L. Sprague de Camp's *The Great Monkey Trial* (1968). Edward J. Larson's *Summer of the Gods: The Scopes Trial and America's Continuing Debate over Science and Religion* (1997), though it won the Pulitzer Prize, seems to me unduly sympathetic to Bryan and the Fundamentalists and insufficiently aware of the threat they posed to intellectual advance. See also Ray Giner, *Six Days or Forever: Tennessee vs. John Thomas Scopes* (1958); Jerry T. Tompkins, *D-Days at Dayton: Reflections on the Scopes Trial* (1965); Paul Keith Conklin, *When All the Gods Trembled: Darwinism, Scopes, and American Intellectuals* (1998). A complete transcript of the proceedings of the Scopes trial can be found in the anonymous compilation, *The World's Most Famous Court Trial: Tennessee Evolution Case* (1925).

2. Quoted in Kevin Tierney, *Darrow: A Biography* (New York: Thomas Y. Crowell, 1979), 396.

3. Darrow, *The Story of My Life* (New York: Scribner's, 1932), pp. 381–82.

IS LIFE WORTH LIVING?

1. Oliver Lodge (1851–1940) was a respected British physicist, but he destroyed much of his reputation with several books expressing credulous belief in spiritualism, including *Raymond, or Life and Death: With Examples of the Evidence for Survival of Memory and Affection after Death* (1916), in which

he claimed that he had established contact with his son Raymond's spirit after his death in World War I.

2. The above are not exact quotations from Epictetus but paraphrases of the core of his philosophy. On the general topic of freedom, see Epictetus's *Discourses* 4.1.

IS THE HUMAN RACE GETTING ANYWHERE?

1. John Alexander Dowie (1847–1907) was a Scottish-born American theologian who founded the Christian Catholic Apostolic Church in Zion. He was a predecessor of Billy Sunday in his emotive preaching, faith healing, and promotion of abstention from tobacco and alcohol. Mary Baker Eddy (1821–1910) was the founder of Christian Science and author of the Christian Science Bible, *Science and Health* (1875). Billy Sunday (1862?–1935) was an itinerant evangelist who became immensely popular in the first two decades of the twentieth century for his histrionic outdoor sermons. William Jennings Bryan (1860–1925) was a leading Democratic politician of the later nineteenth and early twentieth centuries. He was Democratic candidate for president in 1896, 1900, and 1908, and secretary of state under Woodrow Wilson (1912–15). His role in the prosecution of the Scopes trial and his encounter with Darrow as defense attorney are legendary.

2. King Herod (ruler of Palestine, 37 B.C.E.–4 B.C.E.) is said to have slain the babies of Bethlehem because wise men told him that the king of the Jews (i.e., Jesus Christ) had been born (Matthew 2:1–19). Fernando Alvarez de Toledo, third Duke of Alva (1507–82) was a Spanish general who, as governor and regent of the Netherlands (1567–73), became notorious for his severity and cruelty.

"THE WAR ON MODERN SCIENCE"

1. The comment was made in the course of Darrow's cross-examination of Bryan in the Scopes trial.

2. Andrew D. White (1832–1918) was the first president of Cornell University (1868–85) and the author of *A History of the Warfare of Science with Theology in Christendom* (1895), one of the two leading nineteenth-century tracts on the subject, the other being John William Draper's *History of the Conflict between Religion and Science* (1874). It appears that Darrow is conflating the titles of the two books.

1. Evidently a translation of Adolf Hägler (1830–1909), *Die Sonntag vom Standpunkt des Gesundheitspflege und der Socialpolitik* (1878).

2. Harmon Hudson McQuilkin (1873–1934), pastor at the First Church of Orange (Presbyterian), Orange, New Jersey (1915–34).

3. Numbers 15:35–36.

4. Darrow may be referring either to John Brown Paton (1830–1911), British Congregational minister and editor of *Christ and Civilization* (1910), or to John Gibson Paton (1824–1907), Scottish Presbyterian missionary who worked mostly in New Hebrides and Australia.

5. Charles Edward Jefferson (1860–1937), Congregational minister and pastor at the Broadway Tabernacle in New York City (1898–1937). He was the author of *The Puritan Sabbath and Ours* (1910) and other sermons.

6. Robert Elliott Speer (1867–1947), Presbyterian missionary secretary who visited Christian missions in India, China, Korea, Japan, and elsewhere. He wrote *Christian Realities* (1935) and other works.

7. There are two Westminster Catechisms, the Larger and the Shorter. Both were completed in 1647 and approved by the Westminster Assembly (a synod appointed by the Long Parliament to reform the English church) on September 15, 1648. They were largely the work of Anthony Tuckney (1599–1670) and came to be widely used in the Presbyterian church; the Shorter Catechism is also used by Congregationalists and Baptists.

8. Galatians 4:10–11.

9. See St. Augustine, *De Civitate Dei* 22.30.

10. Darrow refers to Nicholas Bownde (or Bound) (d. 1613), author of *The Doctrine of the Sabbath* (1595). Bownde was a Puritan divine and pastor of the church at Norton, Suffolk (1585–1611).

11. A succession of acts enforced the Puritan Sabbath in England—in 1644, 1650, and 1655. These laws were somewhat relaxed by an act (1677) under Charles II, but were reimposed by the Lord's Day Observance Act of 1781. Only in the latter part of the nineteenth century were these laws mitigated or repealed.

WHY I HAVE FOUND LIFE WORTH LIVING

1. A misquotation of Robert Browning's "God's in his heaven— / All's right with the world" (*Pippa Passes* [1841], 1.227–28).

2. Possibly a misquotation of the last paragraph of William Makepeace Thackeray's *Vanity Vair* (1847–48): "Let us shut up the box and the puppets, for our play is played out."

IS THERE A PURPOSE IN THE UNIVERSE?

1. Robert Andrews Millikan (1868–1953), the son of a Congregational preacher, became one of the leading physicists of his day, known chiefly for his work on cosmic rays. He won the Nobel Prize in 1923. In the 1920s he devoted his efforts to reconciling science and religion in such works as *Science and Life* (1924) and *Evolution in Science and Religion* (1927).

2. Edwin Grant Conklin (1863–1952) was a professor of biology at Princeton University (1908–33) and a leader in the study of human evolution. He addressed the intersection of religion and science in such works as *The Direction of Human Evolution* (1921) and *Evolution and the Bible* (1922).

3. Charles Darwin (1809–1882), British naturalist and propounder of the theory of evolution by natural selection. Herbert Spencer (1820–1903), British sociologist and philosopher who adapted the theory of evolution to many social and ethical concerns (sometimes in the crude form known as Social Darwinism). Thomas Henry Huxley (1825–95), British naturalist and vigorous defender of science (specifically evolution) against religious obscurantism. John Tyndall (1820–93), Anglo-Irish phycisist who specialized in the study of light. Jacques Loeb (1859–1924), German biologist who emigrated to the United States in 1891 and did pioneering work in artificial parthenogenesis. George Crile (1864–1943), American surgeon specializing in the study of surgical shock.

4. Jean Henri Fabre (1823–1915), French entomologist who also wrote several books of popular science. Darrow's quotation has not been located. Darrow wrote an essay based on Fabre's findings, *Insects and Men; Instinct and Reason* (1921?).

5. Darrow refers to a popular vaudeville duo, Joseph Weber (1867–1942) and Lew Fields (1867–1941), who toured the country as Weber & Fields from 1889

to 1904 and sporadically thereafter. The source of the "too much proud flesh" quotation has not been identified.

6. "And God . . . made the stars also." Genesis 1:16.

7. See Genesis 28:11–22.

DOES MAN LIVE AGAIN?

1. Upton Sinclair (1878–1968) wrote about telepathy and thought transference in *Mental Radio: Does It Work, and How?* (1930).

2. Dr. Albert Abrams (1863–1924), a quack doctor in San Francisco who claimed to be able to cure cancer, tuberculosis, and other diseases. See Miriam Allen de Ford, "Charlatan or Dupe: Albert Abrams," in her *They Were San Franciscans* (Caldwell, ID: Caxton Printers, 1941), pp. 241–61.

3. The quotation appears to be apocryphal. John Quincy Adams (1767–1848) died five months prior to his eighty-first birthday; he was never minister to France, and there is no evidence that his religious convictions wavered at the end of his life. Perhaps Darrow is thinking of Benjamin Franklin, who was minister to France and lived to the age of eighty-six; but the quotation has not been found in his works.

THE ORDEAL OF PROHIBITION

1. The Eighteenth Amendment (ratified on January 29, 1919) prohibited the sale, manufacture, or transportation of intoxicating liquors within the United States. The Volstead Act, named after Andrew J. Volstead (1860–1947), U.S. representative from Minnesota (1903–23), and signed into law (over President Wilson's veto) on October 28, 1919, granted the federal government the power to enforce the Eighteenth Amendment.

2. Later in the essay Darrow attributes this sentence to Ulysses S. Grant. His exact words were: "I know of no method to secure the repeal of bad or obnoxious laws so effective as their stringent execution" (Inaugural Address [March 4, 1869]).

3. Cotton Mather (1663–1728), *The Wonders of the Invisible World* (Boston, 1693), a treatise about the Salem witch trials of the previous year, written at the request of the judges. British theologian Richard Baxter (1615–91), author of *The Saint's Everlasting Rest* (1650), did not write a preface to Mather's book,

as it appeared two years after his death. Baxter had written his own treatise defending belief in witchcraft, *The Certainty of the World of Spirits* (1691). Excerpts from this book and Mather's were published under the former title (London: Smith, Elder, 1834), with a preface by an anonymous editor. Sadducees were a Jewish politico-religious sect who were accused of rejecting the supernatural, specifically belief in the resurrection of the body after death.

4. British theologian Francis Hutchinson (1660–1739) denounced belief in witchcraft in *Historical Essay concerning Witchcraft* (1718).

5. Suspected witches were executed in Scotland in 1722, in Germany in 1793, and in Peru in 1888.

6. John Wesley (1703–91), British religious leader and founder of Methodism, made the quoted remarks in his *Journal* (May 25, 1768).

7. Winfield S. Nevins, *Witchcraft in Salem Village in 1692* (Salem, MA: North Shore Publishing Co.; Boston: Lea & Shepard, 1892), p. 91.

8. The so-called Vagrant Act, 22 Henry VIII, c. 12 (1530–31).

9. 27 Henry VIII, c. 25 (1535–36).

10. The Poor Law Amendment Act of 1834 did not repeal previous poor laws; in fact, in some cases it increased their severity. Further poor laws were enacted in 1844 and 1930. In 1948 the National Assistance Act finally abolished the poor law provisions completely.

11. See Livy, *History of Rome* 39.8–39. The incident occurred in 186 B.C.E.

12. This is the conventional but loose translation of Tertullian's *Plures efficimur, quoties metimur a vobis; semen est sanguis christianorum* ("We multiply whenever we are mown down by you; the blood of Christians is seed") (*Apologeticus* 50).

13. James Coolidge Carter (1827–1905), graduate of Harvard Law School (1853) and a lawyer who practiced mostly in New York. The quotation is from *Law: Its Origin, Growth and Functions* (New York: G. P. Putnam's Sons, 1907), pp. 247, 249.

14. Ibid., pp. 221–22.

15. See Pliny the Younger, *Letters* 10.97. Trajan's exact words were: *Conquirendi non sunt* (Let them not be sought out).

WHAT TO DO ABOUT CRIME

1. William Graham Sumner (1840–1910), *Folkways* (1907), a landmark study of human society based on an interdisciplinary approach fusing the

study of politics, economics, social customs, and religion. Sumner was professor of political and social science at Yale (1872–1910).

2. A *chromo* (more properly, *chromolithograph*) is a picture produced by chromolithography, or lithography using colors. Darrow's comment cynically suggests that wives who murder their husbands tend not to be punished.

CAPITAL PUNISHMENT

1. See "The Lord's Day Alliance" (p. 46).

2. Friedrich Nietzsche (1844–1900), *Also Sprach Zarathustra* (1883–92), part 3, chapter 12 ("Of Old and New Law-Tables"), section 29. The preferred translation of Nietzsche's *"Werdet hart!"* is now "Become hard!"

3. The Baumes laws were a series of criminal statutes enacted in New York State in 1926 upon the recommendation of a crime commission led by State Senator Caleb H. Baumes. Among the stipulations were increasingly lengthy prison terms for repeat offenses for armed robbery. Further enactments were made in 1928.

WOMAN SUFFRAGE

1. Olive Schreiner (1855–1920), South African novelist best known for the novel *The Story of an African Farm* (1883). Darrow quotes somewhat inaccurately from Schreiner's "Three Dreams in a Desert," in *Dreams* (London: T. F. Unwin, 1891), p. 70: "And he said, 'I take it, ages ago the Age-of-dominion-of-muscular-force found her, and when she stooped low to give suck to her young, and her back was broad, he put his burden of subjection on to it, and tied it on with the broad band of Inevitable Necessity.'"

2. Harriet Hosmer (1830–1908), American sculptor who worked mostly in Rome and focused on sculptures of mythological figures.

3. Darrow refers to one of the other participants in the debate, General Milo S. Hascall (1829–1904), who distinguished himself (on the Federal side) at the Battle of Stone River in 1862 and went on to become a brigadier general and later a banker and a realtor in Chicago.

PATRIOTISM

1. From Goethe's "Spruchen in Prosa" (prose aphorisms).

SALESMANSHIP

1. Orson Squire Fowler (1809–87) and Lorenzo Niles Fowler (1811–96), *Phrenology Proved* (New York: W. H. Colyer, 1837), later published by Fowler & Wells (1846f.). Phrenology purported to reveal a person's character based on the bumps and hollows of the skull. O. S. Fowler was a leading American proponent of the pseudo-science.

THE EUGENICS CULT

1. Darrow alludes to a best-selling book by American lawyer Lothrop Stoddard (1883–1950), *The Rising Tide of Color against White World-Supremacy* (1920).

2. Albert Edward Wiggam (1871–1957), *The New Decalogue of Science* (Indianapolis: Bobbs-Merrill, 1923), p. 132. Wiggam was an American lecturer and writer, the author of many books on psychology and eugenics.

3. Herbert E. Walter (1867–1943), *Genetics* (New York: Macmillan, 1913), p. 248. Walter was professor of comparative anatomy at Brown University (1906–37) and instructor of field zoology (1906–17) and assistant director of the eugenics laboratory at Cold Spring Harbor, New York. He is citing Charles B. Davenport (1866–1944), professor of zoology at Harvard (1891–99) and director of the department of genetics at the Carnegie Institution (1904–34).

4. William McDougall (1871–1938), *Ethics and Some Modern World Problems* (New York: G. P. Putnam's Sons, 1924), p. 198. McDougall was a British psychologist who became successively professor of psychology at Harvard (1920–27) and at Duke (1927–38). He wrote numerous treatises on psychology, politics, and ethics.

5. Ibid., pp. 204–5.

6. Ibid., pp. 205–6.

7. The phrase comes from Samuel Wesley (1662–1735), *An Epistle to a Friend concerning Poetry* (1700).

8. Herbert Spencer Jennings (1868–1947), *Prometheus; or, Biology and the Advancement of Man* (New York: E. P. Dutton, 1925), p. 66. Jennings was a naturalist and the Henry Walters Professor of Zoology at Johns Hopkins University (1910–38).

9. Ibid., pp. 82–83.

10. *Mens sana in corpore sano* ("A sound mind in a sound body"): Juvenal, *Satires* 10.356.

11. Wiggam, *The New Decalogue of Science*, p. 110.

12. Ibid., p. 100.

FARMINGTON

1. Darrow rode on the Orient Express in the summer of 1903, on his honeymoon with Ruby Hamerstrom following their wedding on July 16, 1903.

GEORGE BISSETT

1. Darrow's two bribery trials occurred in 1912 and 1913. See Geoffrey Cowan, *The People vs. Clarence Darrow* (1993).

2. The reference is to Bert Franklin, a private detective in Los Angeles whom Darrow had hired to investigate the backgrounds of potential jurors in the McNamara case, and who was the chief prosecution witness in Darrow's jury bribery trials.

3. John 15:13.

Bibliographical Essay

A. PRIMARY

Darrow's work is scattered among a wide array of books, magazines, and newspapers, and has never been fully assembled.

Darrow wrote one novel (unless *Farmington* is regarded as one), *An Eye for an Eye* (New York: Fox, Duffield, 1905), a study of an impoverished man who commits murder. It is an attempt to embody Darrow's beliefs on the influence of heredity and environment upon crime and criminals.

Among Darrow's full-length treatises, *Resist Not Evil* (Chicago: C. H. Kerr, 1902) and *Crime: Its Cause and Treatment* (New York: Thomas Y. Crowell Co., 1922) exhaustively expound his views on crime and punishment. *The Prohibition Mania* (New York: Boni & Liveright, 1927; with Victor S. Yarros) is a searing condemnation of the invasion of civil liberties brought on by Prohibition. Of smaller pamphlets and lectures, *Rights and Wrongs of Ireland* (Chicago: C. H. Kerr, 1895) is a plea for Irish independence; *Crime and Criminals* (Chicago: C. H. Kerr, 1902) is a radical discussion of the nature of crime; *The Open Shop* (Chicago: Hammersmark Publishing Co., 1904) advocates unionization; *Liberty versus Prohibition* (New York: Allied Printing Trades Council, 1910) is an attack on Prohibition; *Industrial Conspiracies* (Portland, OR: Turner, Newman & Knispel, 1912) is an attack on monopolies and trusts; *The War* (New York: National Security League, 1918) and *The War in Europe*

(Chicago: C. H. Kerr, 1918) are commentaries on World War I; *War Prisoners* (Chicago: J. F. Higgins, 1919) is a defense of American entry into the war and a plea to release conscientious objectors; *Pessimism: A Lecture* (Chicago: C. H. Kerr, 1920) is a defense of pessimism as a viable attitude to life. Darrow wrote numerous small tracts for publication by Emanuel Haldeman-Julius (Girard, KS) as part of the Little Blue Books series. These include *How Voltaire Fooled Priest and King* (1921?), a biographical essay on Voltaire; *Insects and Men; Instinct and Reason* (1921?), an essay discussing the theories of entomologist J. H. Fabre; *Absurdities of the Bible* (1928?) and *The Myth of the Soul* (1929?), antireligious tracts; *Facing Life Fearlessly* (1929?), another defense of pessimism.

Darrow's public debates include: *Darrow-Lewis Debate* (Chicago: Worker's University Society, 1910), a debate with Arthur M. Lewis on nonresistance; *Resolved: That the Human Will Is Free* (Chicago: Maclaskey & Maclaskey, 1918), a debate with George Burman Foster; *Is Life Worth Living?* (Chicago: J. F. Higgins, 1917), a debate with George Burman Foster; *Will Socialism Save the World?* (Chicago; J. F. Higgins, 1919), a debate with John C. Kennedy; *Is Civilization a Failure?* (Chicago: J. F. Higgins, 1920), a debate with Frederick Starr; *Darrow-Starr Debate: Is the Human Race Getting Anywhere?* (Chicago: J. F. Higgins, 1920), a debate with Frederick Starr; *Is Life Worth Living?* (Chicago: J. F. Higgins, 1920?), a debate with Frederick Starr; *Has Religion Ceased to Function?* (Chicago: J. F. Higgins, 1921), a debate with Shirley Jackson Case; *Debate, Resolved: That Capital Punishment Is a Wise Public Policy* (New York: League for Public Discussion, 1924), a debate with Judge Alfred J. Talley; *Debate on Prohibition* (New York: League for Public Discussion, 1924), a debate with John Haynes Holmes; *Resolved: That the United States Continue the Policy of Prohibition as Defined in the Eighteenth Amendment* (New York: League for Public Discussion, 1924), a debate with John Haynes Holmes; *Dry-Law Debate* (Girard, KS: Haldeman-Julius, 1927), a debate with Wayne B. Wheeler; *Is Man a Machine?* (New York: League for Public Discussion, 1927), a debate with Will Durant; *Wheeler-Darrow Debate* (Westerville, OH:

American Issue Publishing Co., 1927), a debate on Prohibition with Wayne B. Wheeler; *Do Human Beings Have Free Will?* (Girard, KS: Haldeman-Julius, 1928), a debate with George Burman Foster; *Wishart-Darrow Debate* (Grand Rapids, MI: Extension Club of Grand Rapids, 1928), a debate on "a general purpose in the universe" with Alfred Wesley Wishart; *Is the U.S. Immigration Law Beneficial?* (Girard, KS: Haldeman-Julius, 1929), a debate with Lothrop Stoddard; *Environment vs. Heredity* (Girard, KS: Haldeman-Julius, 1930?), a debate with George G. Whitehead; *Is Religion Necessary?* (Girard, KS: Haldeman-Julius, 1931), a debate with Robert MacGowan; *Does Man Live Again?* (Girard, KS: Haldeman-Julius, 1936), a debate with M. A. Musmanno.

Darrow himself collected his miscellaneous essays only in the early volume *A Persian Pearl and Other Essays* (East Aurora, NY: Roycroft Shop, 1899), which contains five of his literary essays. He edited *Infidels and Heretics: An Agnostic's Anthology* (Boston: Stratford Co., 1929; with Wallace Rice).

Darrow's two autobiographies are *Farmington* (Chicago: A. C. McClurg, 1904) and *The Story of My Life* (New York: Scribner's, 1932).

Many of Darrow's arguments in his court cases were separately published. The most important of these were gathered in *Attorney for the Damned*, edited by Arthur Weinberg (New York: Simon & Schuster, 1957). Richard J. Jensen's *Clarence Darrow: The Creation of an American Myth* (Westport, CT: Greenwood Press, 1992) prints several of the arguments with substantial critical discussion. Arthur and Lila Weinberg assembled some of Darrow's newspaper and magazine essays in *Verdicts out of Court* (Chicago: Quadrangle Books, 1963), although the volume is deficient in contextualizing commentary. *Why I Am an Agnostic and Other Essays* (Amherst, NY: Prometheus Books, 1995) gathers five of Darrow's essays on religion.

B. SECONDARY

Darrow has not been fortunate in his biographers. The first, Charles Yale Harrison, wrote *Clarence Darrow* (New York: Jonathan Cape & Harrison Smith, 1931), which is largely hagiography. Irving Stone's *Clarence*

Darrow for the Defense (Garden City, NY: Doubleday, 1941) is soundly researched but, as might be expected with this author, reads more like a novel than a biography and lacks critical distance. Kevin Tierney's *Darrow: A Biography* (New York: Thomas Y. Crowell Co., 1979) is also thoroughly researched, but the author's lack of sympathy for Darrow's ideals, his unwarrantedly low judgments of Darrow's literary works, his verbosity, and his deficiencies as a philosopher and political analyst are painfully evident. His discussion of the Scopes trial is particularly disappointing. From a very different perspective, Arthur and Lila Weinberg's *Clarence Darrow: A Sentimental Rebel* (New York: Putnam, 1980) is itself sentimental in its attempt to portray Darrow as a man without flaws. Geoffrey Cowan's *The People vs. Clarence Darrow: The Bribery Trial of America's Greatest Lawyer* (New York: Times Books, 1993) is a meticulous treatment of the jury bribery trials of 1912–13, concluding that Darrow was probably guilty of the charge. Two recent books—Phyllis Vine's *One Man's Castle: Clarence Darrow in Defense of the American Dream* (New York: Amistad, 2004) and Kevin Boyle's *Arc of Justice: A Saga of Race, Civil Rights, and Murder in the Jazz Age* (New York: Henry Holt, 2004)—exhaustively chronicle the Sweet trials of 1925–26.

Several meritorious treatises focusing more on Darrow's writings than his life are to be mentioned. John C. Livingston's *Clarence Darrow: The Mind of a Sentimental Rebel* (New York: Garland, 1988) is a slight revision of the author's PhD thesis of 1965 and provides a sound guide to Darrow's philosophical thought. Abe C. Ravitz's *Clarence Darrow and the American Literary Tradition* (Cleveland: Press of Case Western Reserve University, 1962) is a study of Darrow's fiction and its use of realism. James Edward Sayer's *Clarence Darrow: Public Advocate* (Detroit: Wayne State University Press, 1978) is a discussion of Darrow's public debates.

Mention should be made of several works on Darrow for younger readers. Doris Faber's *Clarence Darrow: Defender of the People* (Englewood Cliffs, NJ: Prentice Hall, 1965) is a slim biography for juveniles, while Iris Noble's *Clarence Darrow, Defense Attorney* (New York: Messner, 1958) and Miriam Gurko's *Clarence Darrow* (New York: Thomas Y. Crowell Co., 1965) are aimed at young adults.

The general public's view of Darrow has no doubt been largely shaped by Jerome Lawrence and Robert E. Lee's play *Inherit the Wind* (New York: Random House, 1955), filmed in 1960 with Spencer Tracy playing the role of Darrow. The play simplifies and sentimentalizes the Scopes trial to such a degree that it disqualifies itself as serious historical commentary. Another venture of the same sort, not specifically restricted to Darrow's involvement with the Scopes trial, is David W. Rintels's *Clarence Darrow: A One-Man Play* (Garden City, NY: Doubleday, 1975).

Willard D. Hunsberger's *Clarence Darrow: A Bibliography* (Metuchen, NJ: Scarecrow Press, 1981) is a sound compilation.

Index